WRITING THE SELF IN BEREAVEMENT

In *Writing the Self in Bereavement: A Story of Love, Spousal Loss, and Resilience*, Reinekke Lengelle uses her abilities as a researcher, a poet, and a professor of therapeutic writing to tell a heartfelt and fearless story about her grief after the death of her spouse and the year and a half following his diagnosis, illness, and passing.

This book powerfully demonstrates that writing can be a companion in bereavement. It uses and explains the latest research on coming to terms with spousal loss without being prescriptive. Integrated with this contemporary research are stories, poetry, and reflections on writing as a therapeutic process. The author unflinchingly explores a number of themes that are underrepresented in existing resources: how one deals with anger associated with loss, what a healthy response might be to unfinished business with the deceased, continuing conversations with the beloved (even for agnostics and atheists), ongoing sexual desire, and secondary losses.

As a rare book where an author successfully combines a personal story, heart-rending poetry, up-to-date research on grief, and an evocative exploration of taboo topics in the context of widowhood, *Writing the Self in Bereavement* is uniquely valuable for those grieving a spouse or other loved one, those supporting others in bereavement, and those interested in the healing power of poetry and life writing. Researchers on death and dying, grief counsellors, and autoethnographers will also benefit from reading this resonant resource on love and loss.

Reinekke Lengelle, PhD, is assistant professor of interdisciplinary studies at Athabasca University, Canada and a senior researcher at The Hague University, The Netherlands. She is a poet, a playwright, the co-creator of Career Writing, and a symposium co-editor with the *British Journal of Guidance and Counselling*. www.writingtheself.ca.

Writing Lives
Ethnographic Narratives
Series Editors: Arthur P. Bochner, Carolyn Ellis and Tony E. Adams
University of South Florida and *Northeastern Illinois University*

Writing Lives: Ethnographic Narratives publishes narrative representations of qualitative research projects. The series editors seek manuscripts that blur the boundaries between humanities and social sciences. We encourage novel and evocative forms of expressing concrete lived experience, including autoethnographic, literary, poetic, artistic, visual, performative, critical, multivoiced, conversational, and co-constructed representations. We are interested in ethnographic narratives that depict local stories; employ literary modes of scene-setting, dialogue, character development, and unfolding action; and include the author's critical reflections on the research and writing process, such as research ethics, alternative modes of inquiry and representation, reflexivity, and evocative storytelling. Proposals and manuscripts should be directed to abochner@usf.edu, cellis@usf.edu, or aeadams3@neiu.edu

Other volumes in this series include:

White Folks
Race and Identity in Rural America
Timothy J. Lensmire

Autobiography of a Disease
Patrick Anderson

Searching for an Autoethnographic Ethic
Stephen Andrew

Gender Futurity, Intersectional Autoethnography: Embodied Theorizing from the Margins
Amber L. Johnson and Benny LeMaster

Critical Autoethnography: Intersecting Cultural Identities in Everyday Life
Robin M. Boylorn and Mark P. Orbe

Writing the Self in Bereavement: A Story of Love, Spousal Loss, and Resilience
Reinekke Lengelle

For a full list of titles in this series, please visit:
https://www.routledge.com/Writing-Lives-Ethnographic-Narratives/book-series/WLEN

WRITING THE SELF IN BEREAVEMENT

A Story of Love, Spousal Loss, and Resilience

Reinekke Lengelle

Routledge
Taylor & Francis Group
NEW YORK AND LONDON

First published 2021
by Routledge
52 Vanderbilt Avenue, New York, NY 10017

and by Routledge
2 Park Square, Milton Park, Abingdon, Oxon, OX14 4RN

Routledge is an imprint of the Taylor & Francis Group, an informa business

Library of Congress Cataloging-in-Publication Data
Names: Lengelle, Reinekke, 1970- author.
Title: Writing the self in bereavement : a story of love, spousal loss and resilience / Reinekke Lengelle.
Description: 1 Edition. | New York City : Routledge, 2020. | Includes bibliographical references and index.
Identifiers: LCCN 2020038532 (print) | LCCN 2020038533 (ebook) | ISBN 9780367643331 (hardback) | ISBN 9780367643348 (paperback) | ISBN 9781003124009 (ebook)
Subjects: LCSH: Grief. | Bereavement--Psychological aspects. | Loss (Psychology) | Widowhood--Psychological aspects.
Classification: LCC BF575.G7 L46 2020 (print) | LCC BF575.G7 (ebook) | DDC 155.9/37--dc23
LC record available at https://lccn.loc.gov/2020038532
LC ebook record available at https://lccn.loc.gov/2020038533

ISBN: 978-0-367-64333-1 (hbk)
ISBN: 978-0-367-64334-8 (pbk)
ISBN: 978-1-003-12400-9 (ebk)

Typeset in Bembo
by MPS Limited, Dehradun

Cover: *The Widow Maker*
© 2020 Darrin Hartman

"As human beings, we seek a life story we can make sense of, and that can make sense of us. In this autoethnography of loss, as lucid as it is captivating, Reinekke Lengelle not only reveals but also reflects candidly on her grief over her partner's death, and her reconstruction of their relationship in its wake. More than a mirror of her bereaved soul, her writing is also a magnifying lens that artfully brings into sharper definition the human drama of love and loss, and the power of poetry and prose to foster its transformation."

—Robert A. Neimeyer, PhD, Editor of *Death Studies* and *Techniques of Grief Therapy*

"In this highly original autoethnographic work, Reinekke Lengelle writes not only about her deceased love but continues to dialogue *with* him. As a 'vulnerable researcher' she explores the depths of her own mind where her lost lover is recreated as a living figure in a poetic composition where truth and beauty meet."

—Professor Emeritus Dr. Hubert Hermans, creator of *Dialogical Self Theory*

"Diving into death is both call and response to words and to witness. This book, with its crystal-clarity, bids readers to lean in, to listen. To accept the call to be unafraid. To stand in direct gaze with the tepid, terrifying, and tumultuous days of living with loss, longing, and love's relentless, vivid invitation to survive. And to thrive."

—Margot Van Sluytman, Poet, BA, MA, Executive Director, Theodore's Place Healing Home for Crime Survivors

"Reinekke Lengelle writes: 'I hope in writing this grief journey, awakenings are inspired that ripple out and offer comfort to others.' This was certainly true for me. This book is not only for those bereaved by death, but also for those, like me, who are bereaved of parts of a wider relationship as age or illness takes its toll. An honest and powerful story of a journey towards the end of a life and relationship."

—Kim Etherington, Professor Emerita of Narrative and Life Story Research, University of Bristol, UK. Author of *Becoming a Reflexive Researcher: Using Ourselves in Research; Narrative Approaches to Working with Adult Male Survivors of Childhood Sexual Abuse; Trauma, the Body and Transformation* and other work

"Part tribute, part love story, part memoir, part investigation into our most nascent drive to confront death on its own terms, Reinekke Lengelle's *Writing the Self in Bereavement: A Story of Love, Spousal Loss, and Resilience* is an unflinching account of her husband's determination to die as he lived, with humor and dignity. A frank and moving portrait of one woman's journey through grief and through the power of personal writing that is both poetic and therapeutic, Lengelle's narrative includes the turbulent, sometimes angry, sometimes affectionate emotions tied to grief. This book will appeal to scholars and to laypeople alike; but moreover, it will appeal to any reader who has experienced the death of a loved one, which, one way or another, touches all of us."

—Judith Harris, PhD, author of *Signifying Pain: Constructing the Self Through Writing* and Books of Poetry: *Atonement, The Bad Secret,* and *Night Garden.* Her poems have appeared in *The Atlantic, New Republic, Nation, Slate,* and the *New York Times* blog

"Reinekke's brave honest enquiry will support and inspire the bereaved, those who anticipate loss, and those who work with them. She tells herself 'don't miss it. Use all that fate gives you to deepen your connection with yourself and life.' She demonstrates and illustrates how fate cracked, chipped, or even seemed to break her, but writing illuminated and healed with a seam of gold."

—Dr Gillie Bolton, author of *The Writer's Key: Creative Solutions for Life*

"*Writing the Self in Bereavement* is a deeply useful book: helpful in its honesty, its companionship for those who are bereaved, and leads by being inspirational in the field of grief-writing. It is also a story of real love, to which many people will relate. It is rhythmic, accessible, theoretically, and socially aware, and sensitive to the risks of representing life as it is experienced. We all have something to learn from Reinekke Lengelle's work."

—Claire Williamson, author of *Visiting the Minotaur,* and Programme Leader for Master of Science in Creative writing for Therapeutic Purposes, UK

"In this remarkable description of the first year of widowhood, Reinekke Lengelle displays courage and vulnerability as she uses expressive writing to process her grief. She locates her own experience in the academic literature on bereavement and early on identifies resilience as a key factor in her being able to continue to 'live forward' whilst acknowledging the enormity of her loss.

The early part of the book includes verbatim journal entries, personal poems, dialogues between her and her late husband, and an examination of unfinished business between them. There are unflinching and moving accounts of the pain of grief, the process of watching a loved one die, sexual desire in bereavement, and the delicacy of a developing new relationship.

Later, there is a sense of gaining new perspectives and a need to look more questioningly at sensitive issues and the gains as well as challenges that come with loss. She draws on her own academic work on the Dialogical Self to theorise how writing accompanied and strengthened her resilience during these challenges in a year of profound changes.

Her determination to keep writing through her grief, as well as fulfilling the demands of work, family life, and a wide network of friends, provides the reader with the gift of witnessing the power of expressive writing in action. Her perspective as a theorist and teacher of writing for healing creates a reflective and reflexive space where the raw data of her journal entries and poems are held up to the light and interrogated for meaning.

She also includes many allusions to her correspondence with other writers on grief, including autoethnographer, Carolyn Ellis, with whom she shares a parallel story. In later chapters, she discusses what it means to put sensitive material into the public domain, and the process of deciding what is appropriate to share and what is rightly personal.

Expressive writing can facilitate much-needed sense-making during grief and mourning. In Western culture where mourning is often secular and individual, personal writing can provide solace, wisdom, and resolution as Reinekke demonstrates. This book will be a useful road-map for those interested in using these techniques personally or facilitating their use with others.

Writing the Self in Bereavement is Reinekke's homage to her late husband and their relationship, two academics who were work partners as well as spouses. She shares how he respected her poetic soul but also urged her to write an academic book. Reinekke 'channels' the voice of Frans in her writing and his presence permeates this brave and unusual book. It is a true testimony to their time together."

—Victoria Field, writer, researcher, and poetry therapist

For you
as you grieve
(and for those who sit
with the bereaved)
may your heart be tender
your mind clear and open
and your conversations
compassionate

CONTENTS

BOOK SUMMARY

Writing the Self in Bereavement

To lose loved ones is our common fate. Yet death is something we frequently (and perhaps wisely) ignore until we are faced with the reality of the loss of a beloved, or our own impending death. Our resistance may be prompted, in part, by worries about how we would cope and the assumptions we may make about loss and grieving. For instance, we may believe, contrary to current research, that we will not be resilient, or that grief must unfold in specific stages within an acceptable timeframe, or that we must "stay strong" to cope well. This exploration of the death of the author's spouse is an invitation instead to be vulnerable and open, and to learn to inhabit and surrender to grief's rhythms, while engaging actively and reflexively with the thoughts and feelings that arise.

Reinekke Lengelle tells the story of her partner in life and work, Frans Meijers, who developed a rare cancer and died within 7 months of his diagnosis. She speaks about the way in which they openly faced the news of his illness, how he made end-of-life choices, and how poems she wrote while he was ill and after his death became a way to express feelings, stay close to Frans, and live well without him. The story, as told here, begins on a December morning, 2 weeks after Frans's passing, when Reinekke returns alone from their home in The Netherlands to her home in Canada and writes in detail of her feelings, daily life in Frans's absence, and the history of their relationship. As a professor of "writing the self" (i.e., writing for personal development), she practices what she teaches her students: how to use poetry, narrative, and research findings to reflect, explore, and articulate what a painful experience might have to teach. Writing is a productive and steady companion: it helps her make sense of the myriad and sometimes uncomfortable feelings that accompany the grieving process, allows her to experience continuing bonds with Frans via memories and imagined dialogues, and results in nourishing insights into bereavement in her first year and a half of grief.

A number of specific themes appear throughout the story—threads that Reinekke seeks to untangle and that she notes were underrepresented in existing grief resources. For instance, she found in the early months of bereavement that, along with sorrow and magical thinking (i.e., denial or numbness), she also experienced anger toward Frans about an issue she had hoped to come to peace with. Unfinished business and ambivalence in grief is an area she explores both personally and as an academic, linking her compelling questions to the existing literature on grief. She also found that sexual desire and memories of her attraction to Frans remained alive for many months after his death; arousal was simultaneously and paradoxically a source of comfort and painful yearning. A key insight from the grief literature that corresponded with her own experiential findings was that emotions are not merely symptoms of grief, but have an adaptive function (Bonanno, 2009). She develops the idea that sadness, anger, and even joy all help the griever to become and remain resilient. Emotions rarely last long if surrendered to, unless they are inflamed by unhelpful stories. Other relationships may change in the wake of a spouse's death, and not always positively. Reinekke ascertains that pulling up the bridges instead of burning them in relation to friends and family members can be necessary and wise.

The book tells a story of both Frans's illness and Reinekke's daily experience of grief, with flashbacks to their meeting and falling in love over 25 years ago. In the final chapters, Reinekke analyzes why writing was important, what lessons she learned from loss, and how she decided what to disclose. In the Appendix, she explores identity change and what she means by "the self in bereavement," making use of the Dialogical Self Theory. This theory also helps to explain continuing bonds and healing that can no longer be shared between a griever and the dead beloved.

She concludes that writing is a worthwhile companion in grieving if one can combine the raw, visceral, concrete, taboo, and emotional details of loss and express emotions, while engaging a more detached, observing self. The grieving self is supported, comforted, and transformed by the act of using words to move toward the pain of grief as well as through the creative space that forms around the (often unanswerable) questions that death brings.

Writing the Self in Bereavement is for grievers, those who support the bereaved, those studying and researching grief, autoethnographers, and people working within the therapeutic arts.

AUTHOR BIO

Reinekke Lengelle, PhD, is an assistant professor with Athabasca University in Canada and a senior researcher with The Hague University of Applied Sciences in The Netherlands. She is the author of the book *Jezelf Schrijven* [Writing yourself], published by Gompel & Svacina in 2018, and has written more than 25 scholarly articles and book chapters. Her career began as a poet, playwright, and writing teacher. In the past 15 years, she has worked as a professor and co-developer of the Career Writing method, which uses creative, expressive, and reflective writing to foster career identity development and agency. She is a symposium co-editor with the *British Journal of Guidance and Counselling* and led the development of two issues on the use of Creative Methods in research and professional practice, published in 2018 and 2020, respectively.

Find out more about Reinekke's work here: www.writingtheself.ca.

SERIES FOREWORD

You are about to read a remarkable book about love, loss, and the resilience of the self in bereavement. In this story, Reinekke Lengelle portrays her love for her life- and work-partner Frans Meijers, her grief over losing him, the details of his death by euthanasia, and how she lived through it all. She invites readers to share the experience as she is living, remembering, interpreting, and writing it. She calls on evocative autoethnography and self-writing to understand and convey to readers the process of working through memory and loss, maintaining continuous bonds with Frans, and simultaneously moving on. She leaves few stones unturned as she writes herself deeply into the experience and opens up her vulnerable selves for her own and her readers' examination. For example, she reveals the tight bond she and Frans had, the sexual desire that she felt for him (and continued to feel after he died), the desire sparked by a new love, and what she calls their "unfinished business." In vivid, artful, and imaginative prose, she encourages readers to feel we are there with her in intimate situations, such as her imagined conversations with Frans about their relationship, lying with him as he was dying, or washing his body after his physician-assisted death.

This is real, honest, probing attention to loss, where the warts and blemishes of Reinekke, Frans, and their relationship are shared respectfully in the context of the intense love and care of a soul-touching partnership. Reinekke is mindful of the other people in her and Frans's lives and she writes with compassionate honesty about and for those who love him. Within those boundaries, she takes us on an intimate journey to depths unexplored by most grief memoirs. She reveals her relationship and emotions as lived and remembered in all their complexity and ambivalence, rather than presenting her loved one in the way she might have wished he had been or in the way others might expect her to remember and say he was.

I read this book twice. Both times, I paused on each page to feel and think with Reinekke about the content, what these ideas and insights meant for her, and what they might suggest for me. I was reminded time and again of the emotional intensity of my own story of love and loss and the unfinished business that led me to publish my autoethnography of loss 25 years ago (Ellis, 1995/2018). Even now, more than 35 years after my partner Gene Weinstein's death, Reinekke provides me new insights and ways to think about that relationship, our close and complicated ties, business accomplished and business left undone, and how incredibly important a new love was (and continues to be) for me.

As I read, I often thought (and said to Art Bochner, my new love then, and now my older love of 30 years), "This stands among the most perceptive and intuitive books about grief and loss I have ever read." I recalled the effect that Molly Haskell's (1990) *Love and Other Infectious Diseases: A Memoir* had on me close to the death of my partner. Hiding out in the bedroom and reading Haskell while Gene was cared for in the front room, I found companionship for my anticipatory grief and hope that I would make it through this loss and have a livable life on the other side. As I read Reinekke's story, I again felt this companionship. I also felt in the company again of such great writers as C. S. Lewis (1963), who tells of his grief and longing in visceral and emotional detail after the loss of his wife Joy.

Reinekke moves seamlessly from her experience to a comparison with the insights of C. S. Lewis and other memoir writers, such as Joan Didion (2005), who today would be considered autoethnographers. She draws as well on other literature on grief (such as Berman, 2015) in order to understand her emotions in deeper and broader ways. She integrates poetry, imagined conversations, discussions with friends, storied vignettes, diaries, and creative writing exercises to express and teach through showing. She moves back and forth between observer and experiencer, being "in" and reflecting "about," inviting readers into her head and heart; she moves around in time—when it happened, when she first wrote about it, and now as she reflects back at different points to the experience and to writing about it—modeling in her writing how grief is experienced nonlinearly. She tackles the ethics of writing personally about the self, which always includes others in the author's world who may or may not want or consent to be written about, and with whom the author has to live after the book is published. Then she contextualizes the stories with theoretical and methodological ideas about Dialogical Self Theory and transformation through writing and bringing in—and moving beyond—much of the work she and Frans did together. On multilevels and in multiforms, this aesthetic, emotional, and vulnerable story vividly portrays practices of socialization and culture on every page. This is about the best that autoethnography can offer.

In my classes on autoethnography and writing lives, I often tell my students that one of my goals is for them to become their own therapists. I want them to be attuned to their histories and cultural conditioning while telling their stories and listening deeply to the tales of others who are both similar and different. I want them to realize that they can rewrite their past as well as their present and future to create a life they can live in and with, given the circumstances in which they find themselves. Reinekke's book is an excellent model showing the process of how one goes about writing, reflecting, constructing, and reconstructing a life that confronts head-on the past and present difficulties and yet looks perpetually to the future.

I hope you will use this book in your classes, for example, in autoethnography, self-writing, close relationships, social psychology, counselling psychology, expressive and therapeutic arts, identity, and death, dying, and grief. Your students will be engaged in this book; they will cry and laugh as they read and discuss it, as will you. The conversation will, as my students often say, quickly "get real." Read this for your own benefit as well and pass it on to your friends, especially those who are grieving. Prepare to be changed for the better, as you connect with Reinekke and Frans, one imperfect human being and relationship to another. As it did for me, Reinekke's story may remind you of past and current relationships and loss. You may feel, as I did, that Reinekke's words help you to see, feel, and interpret your grief experiences in new ways, offering you companionship for losses yet to come.

As I finish the last line of this story, I think about the memoir of Viktor Frankl (2006/1946), who wrote about his experiences in a Nazi concentration camp and focused on the human search for meaning and value in the circumstances of life as the primary motivation for living. I think about Primo Levi's *If This Is a Man* (2003) and the power of his diary-like storytelling that invites readers into an unspeakable experience of life in concentration camps. As James Wood (2015, p. 73) says in his review of Levi's work, "He was wounded like everyone else, but with resources that seem, to most of his readers, unfathomable and mysterious, he did not lose the ability to heal and to be healed." These stories, along with Reinekke's "whisperings from her own soul," all call from me again my own deep emotions, a passion to connect the body and emotions to our lived experiences, the yearning to seek out meaning in loss and other difficult circumstances, and the desire to heal and be healed. They call from me to appreciate, as Levi says, that "the business of living is the best defense against death" (cited in Wood, 2015, p. 75).

When you finish the last line of this love story, consider for a moment how your departed loved ones live on in your mind and are never lost. Exhale deeply and then take a walk in the woods or dig in the garden, laugh with your friends and hug your children. Return fully to the "business of living," spent yet fulfilled, resilient, and hopeful, as though (as Reinekke responded in an e-mail) you have "made love to experience."

Carolyn Ellis, Distinguished University Professor EmeritaTampa, Florida and Franklin, North Carolina

References

Berman, J. (2015). *Writing widowhood: The landscapes of the bereaved.* Suny Press.

Didion, J. (2005). *The year of magical thinking.* Vintage International.

Ellis, C. (1995/2018). *Final negotiations: A story of love, loss, and chronic illness.* Temple University Press.

Frankl, V. (2006). *Man's search for meaning. An introduction to logotherapy.* Beacon Press. (Original work published 1946)

Haskell, M. (1990). *Love and other infectious diseases: A memoir.* William Morrow.

Levi, P. (2003). *If this is a man and the truce.* (Stuart Woolf, Translator). Abacus Press.

Lewis, C. S. (1963). *A grief observed.* Seabury Press.

Wood, J. (2015). The art of witness: How Primo Levi survived. *The New Yorker, September 28*, 68–75.

FOREWORD TO *WRITING THE SELF IN BEREAVEMENT*

Whatever doesn't kill me makes me stronger, Nietzsche famously said, but how do we feel when a loved one dies? Are we made stronger? Do we feel like victims of fate? How do we write about our losses without worsening them? Several scholarly studies explore these crucial questions, but none is more insightful or moving than Reinekke Lengelle's *Writing the Self in Bereavement: A Story of Love, Spousal Loss, and Resilience.*

Reinekke Lengelle is a student of grief, among her many other diverse roles: professor, autoethnographer, poet, mother, partner, and lover. The author or coauthor of many scholarly studies about writing for personal development, she is uniquely qualified to combine her academic and personal identities to pen a book about love, loss, and recovery. Reinekke's research for the book is prodigious: she has read all of the noteworthy studies, yet she wears her learning lightly. She presents her own experiences with bereavement but suggests that others may have different experiences. She is never ideological or polemical. She repeatedly raises questions with no clear-cut answers, and she clears a path for others to follow in her footsteps and then head in their own different directions.

Reinekke's study casts light on the complex issues surrounding bereavement, including post-traumatic stress disorder, post-traumatic growth, continuing bonds, grieving styles, cultural perspectives on grief, secondary losses following a romantic partner's death, unfinished business, dialoguing with the dead, and repartnering. She uses a wide variety of established theoretical approaches, including psychoanalytic and cognitive approaches, as well as newer theories such as Dialogical Self Theory, which emerged in 1992. She discusses the great literary accounts of widowhood and bereavement, including C.S. Lewis's *A Grief Observed*, Joan Didion's *The Year of Magical Thinking*, Kay Redfield Jamison's *Nothing Was the Same*, and Joyce Carol Oates's *A Widow's Story*. Her study will thus appeal to literary scholars such as myself as well as clinicians and the educated reading public. The book is elegantly written: her poems contribute to the power of the story, and her academic prose is lucid and graceful. She mercifully avoids psychobabble and its annoying cousin, pharmababble.

Writers have a tendency to idealize their deceased spouses—"speak no ill of the dead"—but Reinekke wisely avoids this temptation. She presents her spouse, Frans Meijers, as a good man with flaws, like everyone else. She brings him to life and *shows* us, rather than merely *tells* us, why she loved him. He remains throughout the story human, all too human. Some of the most riveting sections of the story are those in which she has a conversation with her dead lover, bringing him to life, verbally, as only the best writers can do. Again, like the best writers, she is a paradoxicalist, as when she writes, "without the hope for anything, I was free again," or "I am not unhappy about being sad." Unlike other writers, she never pathologizes feelings.

Reinekke's story is wrenching, disturbing, heartbreaking, and brutally honest. It is also courageous and inspirational. Nothing about the book rings untrue. She shows us the vexing emotions that accompany loss, including relief, which often deepens guilt, but these emotions coexist with love, joy, and gratitude. She writes about taboo subjects that most spousal loss memoirists, including myself, avoid, namely, having sex for the first time with a new partner. Reinekke's book includes other incidents that we seldom see in bereavement stories, including a detailed description of Frans's physician-assisted suicide in the Netherlands. Reinekke is an agnostic and Frans was an atheist, yet when she lovingly washes his body for the last time, readers are struck by the profound spirituality of the moment.

Like Reinekke, I am a student of grief, and I learned much from reading her book. I knew that writing is a "productive and steady companion," as she notes, and that relationships change during the course of bereavement, but I didn't know about the writing-toward-transformation model that she had developed earlier with Frans. *Writing the Self in Bereavement* is not a how-to book, but it offers enduring insights into spousal loss grief, indeed, *any* form of grief, that readers will find valuable. She challenges some of my assumptions about bereavement, as when I cite with approval in my 2015 book *Writing Widowhood* Roger Rosenblatt's statement that "people in grief become more like themselves." On the contrary, Reinekke convincingly argues, they are not more like themselves, but there is more to their selves. Perfectly, and paradoxically, expressed!

Grief is "not a harsh teacher as at first I feared," Reinekke writes in the final poem of her book,

> I have followed her ways and she has opened my life
>
> The best teachers don't tell you
>
> "You can do this … " but "you *are* doing this"

Reinekke herself is one of the best teachers, and her words come alive to the reader. I began with a Nietzsche quotation, and I'll end with another. "Of all that is written, I love only what a person hath written with his blood. Write with blood, and thou wilt find that blood is spirit." *Writing the Self in Bereavement: A Story of Love, Spousal Loss, and Resilience* is written with blood. For that reason, it is a perfect addition to Routledge's *Writing Lives* series.

Jeffrey Berman
Distinguished Teaching Professor of English
University at Albany, SUNY

ACKNOWLEDGMENTS

Friends

There is a room inside me
where my Friends dwell,
the doorways have no doors
and people come and go.
In the middle of the room
there are colored chairs, each piece unique,
large yellow and soft for her,
red and green with black lacquer accents
(Frida Kahlo style) for you.
A mission oak rocker for him,
I always smile when I see it,
and a more serious
medieval wooden stool for the old Celt.
Then there is the blue velvet wing chair for my husband,
but it is now empty and a small pillow with flowers
remains that speaks of the good memories.
Some of the other chairs are empty too,
because someone dear got busy
and forgot to come back.
No matter, I still love them,
and I keep the room warm.
Sometimes a seat is empty because
you quarreled with me
or judged me

but no matter,
I still love you, because I do,
and I didn't choose you.
Life gave me all my friends,
we recognize each other,
and if that recognition becomes music,
eventually, a new chair appears.
Some are often used, closest to the hearth,
you can hear laughter or crying there,
others rest, wait, ready to welcome.
We do not really make friends, it seems,
they come to help make us.

December 4, 2018 (Three weeks after Frans's death)

The list of friends, family members, colleagues, and first readers who have made my life more wonderful in the midst of this difficult time is long. By writing your names down, I see clearly that I have not grieved alone.

I thank Roberta Neault (now Borgen), career colleague and widow. You were one of the first to express faith in this project. You have brought inspiration and joy to my efforts and I appreciate that you read evolving chapters as I composed them. I appreciate hearing of your experiences, your new love, and learning that the vulnerability of sorrow never leaves us, but also does not harm us.

I thank Carolyn Ellis for being a devoted, thorough, generous, kindred, and empathetic editor. Our lives have a remarkable number of similarities! To work with you has been a thrill and a privilege; I have admired you from afar for some years. Fortunately, it is the nature of autoethnography to bring everything closer, including people who belong to this writing community as I feel I now do. Thank you, Art Bochner, for our conversation over lunch in St. Pete's, Florida, during the autoethnography conference, and for saying yes when I suggested I send you, Carolyn, and Tony Adams this manuscript for the *Writing Lives* series. At Routledge, I thank Hannah Shakespeare for accepting the book for publication and for communicating so clearly about every step. I also thank Jeffrey Berman for your high praise and glowing review. Blake Paxton, your book *At Home with Grief*, about grieving your mother, touched and inspired me.

I thank Margot van Sluytman, friend, poet colleague, and witness, for your support and recognition of the work I am doing. I am grateful for the time you spent with me in the early months after Frans's death. You were one of the people who could listen to raw expressions of pain and anger without judgment. We both know grief well and see that it is simultaneously difficult and full of gifts.

Your feisty vitality is a joy and your Sawbonna work a significant contribution to healing.

Thank you, Andrea Hankinson, for your in-depth reading of an earlier version of this manuscript and for proofreading suggestions in the later stages of creation. I saved your feedback until last during the first round of edits as it had so many layers. Your sense of humor tickles my funny bone and makes your critiques entirely palatable.

Thank you, Adrienne Munro, for the final proofread before submission to production and for your enthusiasm right at the start, and at the finish. Your work was meticulous and your comments ever thoughtful. I also thank the copy editor at Routledge.

Bonnie Ryan-Fisher, a fresh widow like me, I appreciate meeting you through sharing this fate. I note our mutual penchant for living-while-reflecting and reflecting-while-living. Thank you, Dorothy Rosen, for sharing the story of losing your husband Steve and for our weekly calls where we witness each other in the present moment and rebuild our lives in the spirit of joy.

Suzanne Wood, faithful reader and companion writer on the road of life—you are continually generous, kind, and insightful. Thank you as well for finding the page numbers to my C. S. Lewis quotes at the last minute! Susanna Suchak, your comments in the margins of an earlier version of this manuscript were like joy bubbles. Thank you, Rachelle Chinnery, for reading with the eyes of a (future) widow in mind and giving me your clear feedback as you considered my audience. Your handmade carved pottery mug sits beside me as I write and has done so now for years.

Victoria Field and Claire Williamson, therapeutic writing colleagues, your presence in my life these many years is treasured. I remember fondly my visits to you both after Frans's death. Vicky, you have been with me every step of the way; Claire, your feedback on the manuscript was deeply meaningful. Cheryl Moskowitz, Gillie Bolton, Kate Thompson, and Jeannie Wright, I have fond memories of our early Lapidus (our spiritual home!) conferences. Agnieszka Konopka, thank you for sharing resources on grieving and artistic methods. Marianne Panneman, it is inspiring to see you work with writing in an inspired and compassionate way. Thank you, Patti McClocklin, for exploring the topic of widowhood and poetry with me 2 years before I knew I would be facing widowhood myself.

Thank you, Katrin Den Elzen, widow, academic, and expressive writing colleague. It is a delight to have met you and found someone with so many common interests. I look forward to our work together. Thank you, Robert ("Bob") Neimeyer, for our conversation over dinner about grief and resilience and the projects that will follow from our meeting in Edmonton. Esther Wafula, I am glad we have met (albeit only virtually) to speak honestly about life, poetry, career counselling, the dialogical self, and what writing might offer those we serve. Kim Etherington, it is good to finally get properly acquainted! Kim

Stafford, your words via e-mail, brief but powerful, were always a blessing. Sheri-D Wilson, our conversations rock with women's wisdom. Sjon Ashby, you often said "hello" right when I needed it. Susan Wieczorek: you immediately got what I am doing—let's meet again! Judith Harris, our conversation has just begun; I look forward to exploring our love for the interdisciplinarity of the poetic and the psychological.

I thank my students over the years as you continually show me the power of writing and remind me of my role as a guide and witness in your personal and scholarly development. Thank you most recently to my student Danielle LaRocque who has written brilliantly about stillbirth in the context of writing and healing.

I thank Tom Luken and Hubert Hermans, for your collegial friendship, personal support, and astute reflections on both my academic and personal writing. Your listening is precious and appreciated. That you both knew Frans well makes you special witnesses. Tom, you listen with care and give back to me what you think you're hearing, which always feels generous. Hubert, you inspire me as you embody the attitude of a true scientist: you listen to learn, not to teach. You make yourself accessible to aspiring scholars. Barbara Schellhammer, we are the next generation of researchers and our work in care for the self, yours in philosophy and mine via poetic creativity, are kindred. I look forward to more.

I thank you, Noel Murasko, for being the only young man to volunteer for reading duties and for telling me how the story of Frans's death impacted you.

Those who supported me during Frans's illness and in my grief in a more personal way have enriched my grief journey and my reflections on it. I think first of my three sisters, Leo Storrier, Elke Haggerty, and Charlene Verweij. Leo, you consistently reached out to me while Frans was ill and brought flowers when the book contract came in! Elke, your listening and empathy have touched my heart. Charlene, your physical and emotional presence in our home when Frans died, you being at my side at the funeral, your gentleness, your belief in this book, as well as your warm welcome in your home in Amstelveen are all deeply appreciated. Thank you, Cheryl Hunt, for the many kindnesses over the years and for helping me to publish my first small book about heartbreak; who knew what was still to come on that score! To my three brothers: none of you speak to me directly about grief and loss, but I know you care.

My gratitude extends to other family members: Madeleine Boerma, Michiel Boerma, Manon Boerma, Siridyal Kaur, and Laura Matthes. I have felt your presence, your love, and your encouragement as I wrote and posted parts of my process on Facebook. Aunt Annemarie van Hunsel, you affirmed my resilience a number of times; thank you. Aunt Bea Binnendijk, you named my giant spruces and your laughter, even remembered, sparks joy. To my two deceased fathers, Theo Gerding and Rudy Andersson: you were the first to teach me about continued bonds after death; your love continues to influence my life.

Thank you, Mama (Hiske): a widow too, you show me that life is worth living, that there is always hope, and that there is so much beauty to appreciate. You are foundational to my resilience simply by how you live and love. Thank you, Mama (and Herman Frank), for showing me that the widowed can love again. Rinia Verweij, mother of my sister Charlene and brother Danyllo, I thank you for your radiance, your resilience, and for greeting me daily with a blessing via text.

Thank you, Keath Lengle, my first husband, for our abiding and significant friendship and your commitment to our daughters. I have never been a single parent because of you. Your willingness to truly accept Frans into my (and subsequently your) life helped make his and my relationship possible. Frans acknowledged this, and whenever he thought of you or spoke to you during his illness, he was moved to tears.

I thank our Dutch friends, first Janus Kolen and Els Berendts, for your willingness to let me be part of your lives, for staying in touch after Frans's death, for coming to see me in Edmonton, for bringing me books and articles on grief, and for affirming the relationship Frans and I had. Thank you, Mamita van Leeuwen, for taking care of Frans when I could not be there. Nico Knook, I thank you as well for acknowledging what Frans and I meant to each other and for visiting me in Canada. Wim Wardekker, I thank you for our great conversation in Amsterdam a year after Frans's death. Gerard Wijers, you were an enormous support for Frans during his illness; we have benefitted from your wisdom. Ellen van Rijssel, Frans confided in you and often benefitted from your insights; thank you for welcoming me right away. Barbara Postma, you were consistently kind and the perfect friend to MC the funeral—heartfelt thanks. Saskia den Broeder, you understood many things about Frans and were willing to speak to me authentically about your experiences.

A number of Frans's colleagues have stayed connected: thank you. Liesbeth Vos, our conversations are wonderful. Beate van der Heijden, your heart always shines through. Nanda Lodders, Heidi Muijen, Nard Kronenberg, Joseph Kessels, Jean Guichard, Fieny Peerboom, Antoinette Sanders, Allison Creed, Carlo Zegers, Rob Poell, Marionette Vogels, Femke Geijsel, and Aniek Draaisma, you have all written or replied over the past year and a half.

Frans's family members have also expressed their compassion and regard, especially during his illness and just after his death. Thank you; you know who you are. I thank Frans's first wife for bringing an abundance of flowers to the funeral; your desire to care for Frans was enduring. I thank Frans's daughters, Sanne and Eva Meijers, and his son-in-law, Jesse Stael, who shared the process of going through Frans's illness and death and created the beautiful funeral. To Jesse's family: I appreciate your ongoing kindness. (Flynn Stael, you often kept the days of illness light. Your Opa loved you so much!)

Frans's doctors and homecare were wonderful and compassionate. You respected his wishes and are part of this story. Annemieke Zwanenburg, funeral director: I knew after one conversation, long before Frans was ill, that you would be the right person for this job, and that was confirmed.

I thank the many writers I have read as they have dared to show their own feelings and experiences. Your contribution to the field has offered me and others relief and sanity. Your names are in the book and in the reference list.

I thank my universities and the many supportive colleagues at both Athabasca University, Canada, and The Hague University, The Netherlands, for supporting my research into writing for personal development, in this and other contexts, and for providing me with an intellectual home base. On both a personal and professional level you have been wonderful. I will name those of you who spoke directly to me about the writing of this book: Angie Abdou, Jolene Armstrong, Adien Dubbelboer, Emma & Joe Pivato, Carolyn Redl, Angela Specht, Jane Arscott, Marc Cels, Lorna Stefanick, Nina Paulovicova, Meenal Shrivastava, Veronica Thompson, Wendell Kisner, Paul Kellogg, Karen Wall, Rhiannon Bury, Ellen Sjoer, Wätte Zijlstra, Laurence Guerin, Mijke Post, Paul Pauw, Simten Goren, Adela Garabal-Gomez, and Mariette Harlaar. Ellen Sjoer, you have been exceptionally articulate about your support of my work; thank you. Angie Abdou, your comments were vital for reflecting on issues of disclosure.

I thank you, Deirdre Hughes (with Robert Hughes) and Anu Bakshi, from the *British Journal of Guidance and Counselling*, for your personal care and professional inspiration. The work we are doing provides meaning and purpose. Frans would have been proud.

Thank you to my other dear friends, colleagues, and neighbors, for writing, calling, coming by, or staying in touch via Facebook. All of you spoke to me about Frans and loss and served me food, real or the soul variety, or both: Eleanor Talbot (your poem is in this book!), Angela Wiens, Judy Walker, Annemie Winters & Diederik Meylemans, Charlotte McLellan & Kelly McLellan, Liz Wall & Peter Binkley, Elise Raat, Nelleke De Noo, Annemarie van Oploo, Maaike van Veen, Dave Redekopp & Cathy Hodgson, Mark Franklin, Ilse Frank, Heather von Stackelberg, Terri Clarke, Debbie Bridge, Sam Bao, Laura Barr, Barbara van Eekeren, Barbara Philips, Janice Robocon, Kat Loutas, Kat McNichol, Leanne Myggland-Carter, Leanne Simpson, Liane Hambly, Sonja Meskanen, Jacquie Paul, Doreen & John Witvoet, Colleen Reichrath-Smith, Deb Sheremeta, Deborah Valentine, Mary Jane Roy, Nathan Deen, Ian Gellatly, Brad Buhr, Gord Moore & Trudy Hart Kurtz, Nick Voorn, Ellen Sjoer, Lori Claerhout & Mike Gismondi, Marliss Weber, Louise Daley, Lorraine Robinson, Carole Stevenson-Roy, Susanna & Jeff Suchak, Pien Bos, Emine Karadag, and Amy Michaud. Thank you for the extra cheer you brought, An Rubens, Anita Martens, and Els Ulenaers from Belgium. An Rubens, your kiss of deep compassion was a spiritual experience. Thank you, Leena Penttinen, Leena Itkonen, and Sanna Vehviläinen from Finland, for heartfelt accompaniment. Namaste to the beloved little group of us studying nonviolent communication and family healing: Elke, Lynn, Violaine, Trishia, Laura, and Naima.

Thank you, neighbor Christine, for the most meaningful hug on the pathway in winter when my grief was rawest. Violet, for being the neighborhood sunray. Sue and Len McNeill, thank you for being loving neighbors for the past 23 years.

Alex Dijt and Kashvi Panday, thank you for your warm hearts and for helping me move just days after Frans's funeral. I smile when I think of you both and look forward to meeting up again. Your hugs are the best, Kashvi, and your embodied wisdom rings original and true.

Darrin Hartman, huge thanks for the cover. It's stunning.

Thank you, Marlene Checknita, for being a witness to my life and allowing me to be a witness to yours; your empathetic listening has healed parts of me over the many years of our friendship. Your *joie de vivre* and resilience are always inspiring.

I thank my daughters, Sophia and Maya Lengle and Sophia's partner, Caleb Witvoet, for our travels, café adventures, and the closeness. And Colleen Imlay, Sheila Mackenzie's daughter, who I call "my third daughter." Colleen, thank you for your loving and thoughtful comments which I mention in this book. There were a few brief moments when I wondered if dying along with Frans might have been okay, but you all didn't let me stay in that mindset for long. The house is lively because young people come and bring fun and laughter. That includes you, Cali Magee.

Thank you, Tim Magee, for witnessing and embracing me in my grief, emotionally, physically, and intellectually. Your useful, sensitive, and thoughtful questions have helped me to complete my thoughts on why I had to write-the-self through widowhood. You spoil me daily with food. Our new love is a surprise and a blessing that deepens my gratitude for life's ability to renew itself.

Last, I thank Frans, because writing, grieving, and remembering you is another harvest of our big love. Today you would have been 70.

Reinekke, May 5, 2020

NOTE

This book naturally reflects my story and perspectives on my relationship with Frans and does not focus on his early life, his first marriage, or his family life. The place to seek those stories, in Frans's own words, is in his short [auto]biography, in Dutch, called *Jongen uit het Dorp* ["Boy from the village"]. Frans and writer Annemieke Van Engelen (2015) collaborated on this [auto]biography when Frans retired from The Hague University in 2015. It was a gift to him from the university for his many years of service. In it, he speaks about his youth, his studies, several of his close colleagues, the mother of his daughters, meeting me, and what he hoped to learn from life. Our career story and parts of our life histories are described in *Poetic Reflexivity and the Birth of Career Writing: An Autoethnographic Love Story* (Lengelle & Meijers, 2019).

INTRODUCTION

Three knocks

Yesterday I sat pensive in a sunny café
the window ahead split into three
past, present, future all in a shot
drawing no conclusions
my old ways loosened
falling to the left and right of me
"You do not need a plan for the future"
the life muse whispered with a little smile
"you are free in the ways the brave ones know how to be
your wheels are slower now
and it's good, very good
wherever you're going is where you need to be."

My snow boots find the ground as comfortable
as bare feet in summer grass
and I walk to dinner with a friend
while another poet's wisdom plays right on cue
and I say aloud
"notice, just when you're fully
moved in and reach up
to hang the last painting,
three angels knock at your door
and you're out"[1]

I look back at the years
the investment of loving
how it has come to this
on a spring afternoon
the first knock—diagnosis
  by fall the second—death
  and the third knock is now
    opening the way
    to my new unknown life.

In the summer before Frans's cancer diagnosis, I read the autoethnography *Final Negotiations* by Carolyn Ellis (1995). In hindsight, this was a poignant and useful coincidence, as it helped to prepare me for losing my spouse and writing about it in this book. In her story, Ellis describes her love and journey with her partner Gene Weinstein. She tells of their falling in love, their complex relationship, Gene's ill health from emphysema, and his eventual death. She does so in honest and ruthless detail, in the name of research and personal healing. In this book, I take inspiration from her willingness to portray her and Gene's life and relationship as it was and not in an idealized form. She writes to make meaning for herself and I hope to do the same here, applying writing-the-self principles and practices.

I am a poet, researcher, and professor of writing for personal development. I spend my professional life guiding people in how words can help them make meaning of the human condition and learn to thrive in the face of experiences that impact them. I adhere to the idea, articulated well by teacher Krishnamurti, that "You must understand the whole of life, not just one little part of it. That is why you must read, that is why you must look at the skies, that is why you must sing, and dance, and write poems, and suffer, and understand, for all that is life." (Chang, 2006, p. 457).

In my academic pursuits, my work in "writing the self" has led to the development of a theoretical model describing the process by which people might transform painful experiences into new narratives (Lengelle & Meijers, 2009). I have used writing throughout my life to draw meaning and wisdom from change and difficulty. When I was in my 20s, I wrote a play about dating. When I got married, I wrote about marriage. When I became a mother, I wrote about childbirth and breastfeeding and how parents might feel when their toddler breaks a tooth. As I became deeply engaged in the world of work, I explored the meaning of career and how creative and expressive writing could contribute to agency and resilience in this context. It is therefore no surprise that now, in the wake of Frans's death, I am compelled to write about grief. Over the span of my life, writing has become both a vital companion and an inspired vocation.

This work has many potential applications and contexts, and various parallels with autoethnographic research. This is a relatively new field that

> shows struggle, passion, embodied life, and the collaborative creation of sense-making in situations in which people have to cope with dire circumstances and loss of meaning. Autoethnography wants the reader to care, to feel, to empathize, and to do something, to act. It needs the researcher to be vulnerable and intimate. Intimacy is a way of being, a mode of caring, and it shouldn't be used as a vehicle to produce distanced theorizing.
>
> (*Ellis & Bochner, 2006, p. 433*)

I intend, by writing both personally and academically, to use an autoethnographic approach to share something meaningful and contribute to the bereavement literature in an integrated and compassionate way.

Writing can offer comfort and insight or, as others have observed about bereaved authors, writing was a "solace and a lifeline" that "helped them re-create their worlds" (Berman, 2015, p. 7). Over many years of writing and teaching, I have concluded that writing is indeed useful in a number of ways when one is faced with (painful) change. Other researchers, authors, and poetry therapists have confirmed this (Anderson & MacCurdy, 2000; Bolton, 2008, 2011; Chavis, 2011; Den Elzen, 2018; DeSalvo, 2000; Lepore & Smyth, 2002; Moran, 2004; Nye, 1997; Pennebaker, 2011; Thompson, 2011; Williamson & Wright, 2018).

Writing allows us to explore and cultivate an intimate conversation with ourselves, in which we might discover that we are more resilient and resourceful than we first thought. We can, for instance, write a conversation between our hurt, grieving self, and our wiser, calmer self in order to offer a moment of reprieve. Writing is a companion for life, and I will illustrate this with my own experience, using poetry, narrative, and reflections that are intended to be both emotionally and academically compelling.

Writing invites us to question our perspectives and try on alternate ones. We need not find ultimate answers, but rather create some space to loosen our insistence on particular beliefs that may limit our connection with others and our sense of well-being. This "unlearning" of what we thought was true is one of the essential ways we eventually grow and write ourselves toward more life-giving stories. Thoughts like "he shouldn't have died so young" or "she should have been more understanding" can be questioned; by doing so on paper, we see the absolute futility of such thinking. As we question what we are believing, our thoughts ease and we become less preoccupied with them (Katie, 2002).

Writing makes it possible to turn our own experience and wisdom into nourishment and wisdom for others. Our pain and struggle may become a source of inspiration and our ability to contribute meaningfully can, in part, ameliorate our sense of loss. As such, I hope the fruits of my labor here represent both shareable personal medicine and a contribution to qualitative research.

In responding to Frans's death and my grief, I was driven to read books and articles on bereavement and find out what others with the same fate had written about it. You might say that the woman, the widow, the lover, the academic, and the poet in me are all alive and at work. Access to and expression of my internal world, combined with the voices and perspectives from my readings and others' experiences, shape the way I am able to tell and transform my story.

This book includes a handful of discoveries I made while going through the first year and a half of grief. For instance, I have found (so far) that there is no closure or end to grief, while I do experience a reduced need to solve or resolve issues that at first seemed urgent and unresolved. Research confirms that sense-making may be an acute or profound need right after a loved-one's death, but that for most people this need dwindles over time, even if no real answers to "why" questions have been found (Coenen, 2018; Hall, 2014).

I also found that my grief included struggles with unfinished business. Research shows that about 43% of people report being preoccupied with issues related to the deceased (Klingspon et al., 2015). In my case, it was an unresolved issue around boundary-setting in the context of Frans's previous partners and his "short fuse" (his term) in discussing anything that he perceived as challenging his autonomy. A deeper exploration of this issue led me to see that we unwittingly aggravated each other's vulnerabilities. It was useful and relieving for me to read that almost everyone who mourns feels emotions that aren't easy to digest (such as guilt and anger), though thus far there is a limited body of research on the topic of unfinished business in the face of bereavement (Klingspon et al., 2015).

Bereavement also brought unexpected shifts in other relationships and circumstances, which meant "secondary losses" (i.e., losses that come forth from the primary loss: for instance, losing touch with members of Frans's family; losing our joint home; a temporary disruption in my connection to two close friends). I experienced these shifts in other relationships as both positive and necessary, as well as negative and unfortunate (but sometimes also necessary). The willingness to examine the reasons for these shifts freed me to acknowledge that I was both an active participant as well as a passive recipient of "secondary losses" (Doka & Martin, 2010).

The narrative that ultimately took shape and became this book affirms that when someone we love dies, our relationship with them continues (Paxton, 2018). While some speak to photographs of the dead, I experienced my ongoing conversations with Frans most powerfully through writing, especially in written dialogues. This may be because we talked a great deal about everything and wrote many articles and book chapters as academic partners. Nonetheless, I believe anyone can use expressive and creative writing to explore an abiding bond with a deceased loved one, and the feelings associated with that bond. It turns out, for instance, that one of the most useful writing exercises for parents faced with the violent death of a child is a dialogue with that child through poetry (Barak & Leichtentritt, 2017). Continuing with such bonds is a "recognition that death ends a life, not necessarily a relationship. Rather than 'saying goodbye' or seeking closure, there exists the possibility of the deceased being both present and absent" (Hall, 2014, p. 9).

I also discovered that the death of a partner does not represent the end of sexual desire for the survivor. At first, this discovery was strange, guilt-producing, and heartbreaking, but it has come to feel natural and self-evident. Life is for the living, and there are forces—despite our preferences—that move us forward. If we let them, that is. There had been surprisingly little written about this aspect of partner loss, even in the most famous widow memoirs where the authors had clearly had passionate and dynamic partnerships (Berman, 2015; Didion, 2005; Price, 2019). It wasn't until 2020, more than a year after Frans's death, that I found a newly published book dedicated to this topic. It was written by a sex expert who had become widowed (Price, 2019).

Loss invites us to stop and touch life in reverent ways. Loss changes us. Loss humbles us. Loss can make us more compassionate; loss can open us so that we might come to know a kind of ecstasy of sorrow. Loss and its accompanying struggles can bring "post-traumatic growth" (Hall, 2014): they can show us places where we might learn about ourselves.

In writing poetry, I have often experienced and expressed this reverence and growth. I am grateful for my poet's soul. I sometimes say to people, "This part of me is not afraid of pain; she moves towards pain to explore it and see what truth or beauty might be found or created." In knowing our pain, we also learn what we value, and we expand our awareness of things we are grateful for.

To those grieving, I want to say, "Don't miss it." Use all that fate gives you to deepen your connection with yourself and life. It helped me, for instance, to allow my feelings to move through me by welcoming them all. I subsequently read that emotions are adaptive and not just symptoms of loss (Bonanno, 2009). It helped me to read about the experiences of others and the newest research; in both places, I often saw myself reflected. Where I felt the readings were missing vital insights or depth, I reflected on my own feelings and articulated things I needed to hear.

As I studied, I also learned to drop assumptions about grieving. For instance, reading Bonanno's (2009) research on adaptive emotions led me to believe that everyone would benefit from emotional expressiveness. However, I also read that some grievers are not expressive and don't wish to share their feelings openly, preferring instead to make plans and take on new projects—and that this too can constitute healthy grieving (Doka & Martin, 2010). In fact, research shows that there is a grieving continuum, and all grievers tend to lean more or less toward one of two ways of grieving: *intuitive* and *instrumental*. Those who grieve by expressing a lot of emotion are referred to as *intuitive grievers*. Others are more action-oriented (e.g., taking up a new hobby, planning projects) and are referred to as *instrumental grievers* (Doka & Martin, 2010). These descriptions from grief studies showed me that I am somewhere in the middle: I am able to cry openly and talk about my feelings, and at the same time, I have made of my loss a full-scale book project, which has required a great deal of work (planning, editing, liaising with editors, etc.).

Readers may be heartened to know that most people, regardless of their approach, are naturally resilient in grief (about 68%, in fact), and only a minority struggles with complicated or prolonged grief (Bonanno, 2009; Neimeyer, 2016).

This book is not prescriptive. Rather, it shows how I have been writing my own medicine. The process of meaning-making through language is not only what I teach, write about, and study in my professional life; it is also my own grounding practice. Recently, in describing what my work entails, I explained that *I facilitate a process where people can return to themselves.* We can be good company for ourselves when we get attuned and can articulate what is unfolding within; when we are honest about the range of feelings, we may have about any given experience.

Author Jeffrey Berman (2015) supports this perspective in his analysis of the lives of five women who wrote about widowhood:

> All affirm the healing nature of writing ... to honor a beloved spouse ... to bear witness to life's greatest tragedy .... No one can deny that writing about spousal loss is wrenching, but the writer invariably felt better. (pp. 202–203)

In the words of psychotherapist and author Esther Dreifuss-Kattan (2016),

> Art-making—with its symbolization and exteriorization at a time of personal loss and trauma—allows for a gradual modulation of affects. It fosters personal reinvention through the reconstruction of the artist's past, allowing her to become her own witness. By expressing one's own story in words or images[,] ... the artist demonstrates a wish to survive these losses and distance herself from the trauma. Looking at one's own creation and sharing it with others, one's internal witness becomes even stronger. Eventually, the newly expressed narrative can be substituted for the actual trauma, helping to regain the coherence and integration of the self. Art-making can thus transcend the past and become linked to the present in an attempt to secure a more balanced future. (p. 3)

One might say that writing is a companion for life because it does exactly the two things that the best companions do: it holds you close enough that you dare to be vulnerable and far enough away that you dare to be honest.

In the end, this book is simply the result of the fact that writers must write, and grievers are compelled to reconstruct their assumptive worlds through story (Berman, 2015; Neimeyer, 2016).

It follows, then, that bereaved writers will create those new landscapes on the page.

Note

1 The words about the three angels are told by David Whyte, inspired by D. H. Lawrence's words, "Who is that knocking on my door? It is someone come to do me harm. No! It is the strange angels, admit them." The angels are events that change our lives and invite us back into fuller living, compassion, and being with the way of it.

1

EARLY GRIEF

When a friend reaches across the table and asks
what do you miss most?
Sorrow rises in me like a lake
for a moment I cannot even speak
water fills the capillary fringe
I do not resist grief's inner surge
I am learning to welcome it all

It is a winter morning: December 1, 2018, to be exact. Despite the snow blanketing the yard, the house sparrows in the giant blue spruce in the front are chirping their wake-up songs. My Aunt Bea calls the five huge conifers around my house *divas* and I have been calling them that for years now too. The birds are company for me as I start this book. They remind me there is cheer in the world.

They seem to say, as Frans did just 2 weeks ago, "Life goes on, my love."

Frans died of cancer on November 16, 2018. He was sick for 7 months, and in that span of time, he went from a healthy, jovial man of 190 pounds to a thin, emaciated man of 140 pounds. He did not lose his vibrant spirit, though, and he spoke about life, work, and politics until the very end. In the last hour, he even spoke about Brexit and then quipped, "Well, that's not my worry anymore!"

He did not want to die, but he knew he would.

***

I have a hunch

That missing someone
is about being known

Having a witness
to what dwells within
beyond the domestic
(but it includes that too).
I imagine how
after a day of writing
or an afternoon talking to the kids
or an evening out with friends
(when I have come home to myself again)
I will sit in bed
take out the pen you gave me
and write as many pages as it takes.
Address: him, general delivery, cosmos
because I will (still) want to tell you
what I think it all means.

I wrote this poem several months before Frans died and shared it with him. We cried together. My poems were sometimes a starting point for our conversations about his illness and impending death. A few lines from this poem were also printed on the invitation to his funeral. Some people have let me know it has touched them and reminded them of their own losses.

I realize I wrote it hoping to bridge the gap between my experience of Frans alive and Frans no longer alive. It was an exercise in throwing an object over a fence into the future so that I could pick it up on the other side and shout back to him, "Yes, remember, I said this would happen, now it has happened and you already knew …. So we can share this too. We can still make memories."

There is no doorway between the yards of past and present, of course, but I reach across this divide through my writing.

Poetry has been a way for me to express feelings, to confront the reality of loss, and to express to Frans how much I loved him and would miss him. This poem comforted me after his death as it reassured me various times that I could reach out to him and also perceive his likely response. This is what author Blake Paxton (2018) explores in his book on continued bonds with the deceased, when he speaks about remembering those who have left us: "These rituals might include telling stories about those who have died, having imagined conversations with the deceased, celebrating their birthdays …" (p. 111).

This visceral reality of having lost my companion and witness visits me often. Even upon revisiting and fine-tuning this manuscript a year and a half after his death, the pain is still palpable and sometimes sits like a watery mass just under the surface. It is the most tender thing to tell anyone, including myself.

When Frans died, a part of my conversational world died off like a favorite room, full of life, that had to be closed before either of us wanted to leave it.

I miss his touch. His voice. Our touch. Our intimate conversation about life, love, and work.

***

Imperfect Us

"Falling in love and losing a partner are exceptionally important and intense psychological conditions within the relational sphere, confined by time." Gerard Wijers[1]

This morning, our friend and colleague Gerard and I spoke about the need for fuller disclosure about a life shared and a love lost. We talked on the phone about what it means to be a poet and to want to tell the truth about one's experience.

He said, "For mere mortals, it might be okay to tell only the good things about a beloved who has died and make them into a kind of saint, but for a poet that is simply wrong."

Yes, I thought, what do you give to the reader if you turn your beloved into a saint? Nothing. And first of all, I give myself nothing.

This conversation helped give me permission to explore everything that called for attention, even the anger that I experienced in the early months of grief.

I read similar sentiments in Carolyn Ellis's (2018) book *Final Negotiations*, where she writes about her terminally ill partner: "The relationship story shows the ambiguous, complex and contradictory aspects of my connection to Gene as we interacted in our day-to-day lives, confronted epiphanies, managed attachment and loss, and struggled to make our life together meaningful" (p. 5).

***

My relationship with Frans had an intensity that I would call at once whole and entangled. He was my partner and lover, my intellectual mate, and we pressed on each other's vulnerabilities. We found in each other an equal, someone who both inspired us and challenged us mightily. We talked, we wrote, we learned, we fought, and we loved each other passionately. Our dynamic brought out the best I could be professionally, and I credit our relationship for teaching me to be more open about my needs and boundaries. He spoke most about the emotional learning he did with me, and the creative dimension that began to infuse his academic work as a result of our collaborations.

We were for each other the second spouse and each of us have two daughters from our first marriages. The road to becoming partners was long, gradual, and, at times, painful. With respect and care for our first spouses, we both divorced, committed to a life together, and spoke at the end of his life of our gratitude for having "gone for it" despite the challenges of geographical distance and blended-family realities.

He called the years we spent together "the happiest of [his] life." As academics, we traveled frequently and spent most of our time in Canada and The Netherlands. We visited many cities in Europe and the United States and spent long summers in Alberta. We also shared our family lives: I got to know his daughters and son-in-law and my daughters spent a year in The Netherlands with us when I was on sabbatical working on my PhD. Frans and I wrote more than 25 book chapters and articles together, and we were still working actively when he was diagnosed at age 67. We had just presented our career research work in Ottawa, Ontario, when the bad news came.

We got frequent visits from my family from Canada and Frans was a generous and cheerful host. I got to know Frans's siblings and nephews, and his friends and colleagues regularly came to see us. Frans also loved being in Canada. Having a whisky in the sunroom in Edmonton with my mother and stepfather, or with my first husband, Keath, were cherished moments that Frans reminisced about when he was ill. We felt blessed to be surrounded by so many loving people.

Death cut short the life we loved and had hoped to continue, but the way through illness and death was mostly blessed and Frans died with grace, making courageous decisions.

Frans used to say, "Except for the fact that I'm dying, I have nothing to complain about." He did not deny his illness and his death, and he went toward it openly, something that was both beautiful and meaningful to many.

***

I correspond with a number of people about my grief journey and I am grateful to those who make room for the range of feelings I have—not only deep sorrow and loneliness, but also anger, joy, and a sense of possibility. The ambivalence felt by those grieving is mentioned in the literature, but taboos against speaking about anything other than sorrow or positive feelings about the deceased are deep-seated and can block our ability to be honest, even with ourselves (Lengelle, 2020; Miller & Loring, 2016).

In addition, surviving spouses, as I have found, experience doubt and guilt over revealing the less-than-perfect aspects of a relationship. Doing so may be simultaneously freeing and burdening; speaking about the range of feelings we have is complicated. I, for instance, have noticed that the moment I utter a criticism about Frans, the tendency in me to defend him or to erase my potential trespass feels urgent. I realize I am true to two ethics and these don't always align: the writer's ethic to tell the truth and the partner's ethic to protect one's beloved.

It took gumption to write about our struggles as a couple, the things that felt unfinished, ongoing sexual desire after his death, and how several friendships have shifted along the road of bereavement. Yet, these are all important aspects of the grieving process; there is more to partner loss than the death itself.

Reviewing this manuscript, I am glad to notice that much has changed in the way I feel about our unfinished business. I am infrequently angry now and perceive a tender, positive regard between us. From an embodied and peaceful (and sometimes sad) place, I say, we loved each other, and we did not resolve everything I had hoped to.

This sense of healing, however, didn't simply happen as a matter of time passing. I did some active processing and will share some of what that entailed in the pages to come.

***

December 2, 2018

Vocation

I wake up and
the work calls
it is a constant
while the house sleeps
and you sleep forever
the field waits
anyone with a vocation
is simply lucky
it is the love that never leaves

During the last few nights, I have been reading Didion's (2005) *The Year of Magical Thinking*. Last night I had a vivid dream of a large warehouse where all the furniture was being moved. Frans was in the dream asking a colleague what she most wanted. This person values the wisdom of emotions; so, perhaps, I should take it to mean that I need to pay attention to my own feelings. I am no expert in dream analysis but am left with a feeling of things being reordered.

Yesterday afternoon, Maya, my youngest daughter, and I went out shopping. I noticed as we were walking through the mall that I was more present with her than before. Later, my neighbor Sue came and brought me hugs and conversation. My first husband and his partner came too, bringing flowers and more hugs. My mother sent pictures of her new paintings and we talked about how she painted when my stepfather died. Colleagues are sending their book suggestions and resources.

Jet lag is still getting me up early.

I would have told Frans all of this on the phone; now I tell it in my writing.

***

The Diagnosis

"I'm toast."[2]

These were Frans's first words when he called me from The Netherlands on April 12, 2018, to tell me the hospital had called and told him the tumor they had found was malignant. I had just flown back to Edmonton on the 5th, still thinking (and hoping) that his next appointment would reveal the nasty kidney stones everyone was talking about. The news was as bad as it could be. The tumor was already large with "unrestful areas beside it." It had closed off the left ureter—the tube between the left kidney and the bladder—and that kidney was not functioning anymore. I booked my flight back to The Netherlands immediately.

Frans had the rarest of the four urinary cancers and it was already inoperable. One to three people in 100,000 get this kind of cancer. I read about the prognosis in peer-reviewed articles that I studied until midnight the day before we went to see the urologist on April 19 to hear if there were metastases. There weren't, but although that seemed like good news at the time, we soon realized there were no good treatment options.

Frans and I had both taken statistics in university and the odds of getting better brought by the very toxic chemotherapy treatment and the potential follow-up operation they were offering were less than 10%. It was likely he would lose his health faster than he'd have any chance at gains.

When we did the math in front of the capable young oncologist, he nodded at our calculations, though we sensed some resistance to having it explained back to him this way. For doctors, it must be awful to realize they have so little to offer when their intention is to be helpful. We kept in touch with this oncologist every 5–6 weeks to ask for advice and he remained a source of support for us. We also developed a good working relationship with Frans's (new) family doctor and the young doctor-in-training in town, both of whom would be crucial to Frans's end-of-life decisions.

On May 3, 2 days before his 68th birthday, Frans decided that he would not seek treatment. Once he'd made that decision, he gained a sense of strength and agency again. His daughters and I could always hear in his tone of voice how he was doing emotionally, and we knew his decision not to do chemotherapy brought him peace. It also, of course, brought the necessity of admitting that death was on the not-so-distant horizon.

I remember the car trip home from the hospital that afternoon in the old blue Volvo station wagon. Time seemed to stretch and Frans and I, usually fast-paced in our banter, spoke about the no-treatment route slowly and with deliberation. It still all seemed surreal. It was spring, and everything was in luscious bloom; the juxtaposition almost made the news eerier.

In those weeks, Frans spoke of his diagnosis as a macabre dream—a theatre play that could hardly be his story. Although we faced reality head-on, it did not mean that there wasn't an underlying current of disbelief. We could and could not really fathom his impending death.

Joan Didion (2005) speaks about this form of denial in *The Year of Magical Thinking*. Her husband John died suddenly, which I believe makes this denial more extreme, but I too experienced magical thinking. One wakes up and remembers;

one wakes up and still feels inclined to pick up the phone to check for messages; it took me some time to become fully aware of his death, even though he literally died in my arms.

I can also relate to Didion's desire to keep her husband's things for "when he comes back," even though she had, like me, seen her husband die and looked at his body when his death was confirmed.

I too am keeping Frans's winter coat, partly because we bought it together, and partly, I know not why.

***

Witness of My Life

In the gaps

that naturally fall in conversations
the moments alone on the bus today
the silence in the room upon waking
the not-there-ness of you
is felt in those spaces
and amplified when my eyes fall
on the names and images of places we've been
an article about a designer in Madrid
the screensaver of the Golden Gate Bridge
the flight deal to Reykjavik,
That is where the eerie loneliness
opens the crack
to the source of my sorrow,
I followed every step of your leaving
held you in my arms when your eyes
lost their gaze
and I still ask
how can you really be gone?

November 25, 2018 (9 days after Frans's death)

***

Early Days of Illness

In the spring, no one would have looked at Frans and known he was ill. He had lost weight but now looked healthier than he had in the last few years. He was dressed in a pressed, long-sleeved blue shirt, his hands confidently on the steering wheel as he drove us home from the appointment with the specialists. We both expressed a sense of relief that there would be no hospital stays, no nausea-inducing chemicals that might destroy his skin and hair and so much more internally. We spoke of not having to live the yoyo of hope and despair we'd seen among close others.

The week after he'd made the decision, the oncologist phoned to tell us that the treatment he'd recommended to us for this kind of cancer wasn't even possible. I remembered that the urologist had told us that the left kidney was out of commission. The oncologist had conferred with the urologist and confirmed this was indeed the case. One had to have two fully functioning kidneys to even qualify for the suggested course of treatment. This news assuaged any doubt or guilt we might have felt about choosing to focus on quality of life and pain control instead of cures.

On his sunny birthday on the roof terrace of our Dutch house, family came and between the cups of coffee, tea, and birthday cake, Frans explained to everyone what his decisions were and why he had made them. My oldest daughter, Sophia, and her boyfriend, Caleb, were visiting, and I could see from the young faces that they were taking in the facts but that no emotions were flowing yet. Later, Sophia told me she'd cried on the way back to Amsterdam where they were staying with my sister Charlene for a few days.

No one seemed to argue or offer Frans other solutions. Even the naturopath who specialized in nontoxic tumor reduction was doubtful that anything we could do with food or supplements would reduce his chance of a terminal outcome. This had been our last hope and when we left that doctor's office, a quaint old country house with books to the ceiling and an old examination table, we faced the reality that we would be saying good-bye.

We cried together and Frans cried at the bag full of naturopathic supplements that could barely postpone the inevitable but made him feel like a patient taking 15 pills a day. I did change our diet completely in the next weeks, but in June, when he began to need opiates for pain relief, his appetite shrank to nearly nothing. The cancer had robbed him of 30% of his appetite already but the fentanyl patches robbed him of the rest.

Frans at first didn't want to know how much time he had left, but I had been reading the research and knew it would likely be a year or less. Our Belgian friends, one of them a surgeon, confirmed with me that it was likely Frans would not reach his next birthday. I remember thinking that this seemed too unhopeful—How could a man who was still walking 5 km a day with me die within a year?

What makes the writing about all of this bearable is that we got into the habit of being open about every detail, including our feelings about the illness. Frans often said, "I'm so glad I was open from the start… I did it for myself. I promised myself I would be open about everything right at the beginning." Many who visited us in the months that followed expressed their appreciation for this as it made any awkwardness there might have been to visit and engage with us disappear. There is a Dutch expression for this: *it took the cold out of the air,* which means it relieved any awkwardness that might have hung in the air.

In hindsight, I'm grateful for this Dutch-style openness. No one (at least not openly) judged us about his end-of-life choices, though I was aware not to share on forums like Facebook to avoid potential strain with religious friends and acquaintances in our circle. That said, I don't think negative responses by others would have fazed Frans. True to his character, in every adverse situation, one of his first questions was, "What do I want to do? What is my track?"

A new visitor would come up the narrow stairs to our second-floor apartment, take off their coat in the large hallway lined with books, and enter the living room. While they were on the way to sit on the grey couch, before they had even properly landed, or I had had a chance to ask "tea or coffee?", Frans would announce, "It's clear, I'm going to die. I'm open about everything; please ask anything you'd like to know." I smile now as I remember this; I appreciated his forthrightness and it allowed us to talk about our grief, practical and financial matters, and my future without him.

In those weeks, when regular Paracetamol (a kind of Tylenol) pain meds still did the trick, our lives seemed to go normally. We walked each morning, we worked on articles and book chapters, we made love, we argued, and we made plans to go to Canada for a few weeks. Frans called this last visit to Edmonton his "good-bye trip." He wanted to be able to take leave of everyone he'd gotten to know there over the years. He wanted to do that in person.

Last night, reading the first third of Didion's (2005) book, I stopped to make a note of this strange observation by author Philippe Ariés whom she quotes: "Death, even if sudden or accidental[,] gives advance warning of its arrival" (p. 26). Frans had dreamed of death and dying in the 2 years before his diagnosis. He also spoke more often about "being an old man" and "getting old now," while he'd rarely said those things before.

In the fall of 2017, I remember smelling Frans's breath and telling him something seemed off; it was the same smell I'd encountered when a friend had congratulated me with a kiss on the cheek at my PhD defense. She'd died of esophageal cancer 2 years later. Frans said, "Don't say that!" and I asked him what he was afraid of. He blurted out, "That they will tell me I'm sick with cancer and that I'll die!" It seems strange now that this did not wake us up to the possibility that he might truly be ill. We were both soothed by the hope of a kidney stone—he was the right age for a kidney stone, the right sex. His family physician had not thought to do any further tests. First, the diagnosis was diverticulitis, then it was kidney stones, and then it was terminal cancer. Hindsight is 20/20, as they say, and the part of us that can deny the truth of serious illness or possible death must also be the part that masks our fears and intuition with hopes of survival.

I wrote the poem below in March 2018, before we knew anything was truly awry; it now seems a strange foreshadowing of what was to come.

***

Omen

The body is a faithful dog
we might scold it, neglect it, wear it out
deny it water or exercise,
but it will stay loyal
it desires our connection more than
its right to live
Of course, it's imperfect
it has bad hips
or a snout that doesn't breathe well
or it might be too pure and trained to pose
which makes it awkward
or anxious,
But always
it waits for us
by the window
by the door
at the foot of the bed
looking for our love
sometimes bent in shame
and ever seeking us out
to play
to be touched
to be found worthy
ready to do our bidding
until it can't.

March 25, 2018

***

Community

Yesterday, I sent a request to 64 colleagues all over the world asking for support and inspiring resources on bereavement. The first e-mails are coming in.

This morning there was an e-mail from our Dutch colleague Tom Luken, in which he quotes a Dutch PhD dissertation by Riet Fiddelaers-Jaspers (2003) called *Verhalen van rouw: De betekenis van steun op school voor jongeren met een verlieservaring* [*Stories of grief*: The *meaning of support in schools for youths with a loss experience*]. In this piece, Tom finds a few key sentences that confirm what I wrote in the article Cures for the Heart, co-authored with my graduate student Patti McClocklin 2 years earlier, on healing poetry in the face of bereavement (McClocklin & Lengelle, 2016).

Here is my own translation from Fiddelaers-Jaspers (2003, p. 270): Recent research shows that the traditional way in which grieving is viewed cannot be maintained. Bereavement is a process of meaning-making and happens in a social context. It is an ongoing process that changes shape; there are peaks and valleys and one cannot at any moment really finish the process definitively. It is a case of letting go, but with a bond remaining with the deceased.

In 2016, Patti and I said it in our own words: "We note that grieving individuals 'write about' and 'write to' and thus evoke the person who has died. In this paradoxical way the bereaved face the reality of death by retaining the beloved" (McClocklin & Lengelle, 2016). Even though I am new to widowhood, I already see how this applies to me.

It seems strange and uncanny to me now that 2 years before Frans's death, I co-wrote an article on becoming a widow with Patti, who lost her husband to cancer as well. I cannot help but wonder, did life mean to prepare me? The signs I now recollect and weave together into my story feel like threads of congruence. Whether such expressions of alignment are an expression of spirituality or my brain's longing for security via pattern recognition seems to matter little.

Likewise, current e-mail and Facebook conversations offer me nourishing external forms of insight and connection. Sometimes the things people send even seem synchronistic, which strengthens my feeling that all is still right with being alive.

Yesterday, for instance, I was walking through the mall with Maya, who is almost 16 years old. She wanted to buy a sweater for Christmas and try on some pants. As we walked by a jewelry store on our left, I thought about the question of when to take off one's wedding ring. A title formed in my thoughts: "When to take off the ring and other widow questions ..." Then in my mind I added, a bit wryly, "Relevant and irrelevant questions of widowhood."

The same afternoon, an e-mail arrived from widowed career counsellor and colleague Roberta Neault, in which she actually pondered this question (without me having mentioned it) and responded to my request for resources.

> I read quite a bit as I grieved—but very little that I'd recommend. It was shocking (wearing my counsellor's hat) at how few "good" resources I found. However, one book that I found particularly useful was C. S. Lewis' *A Grief Observed* [1961]. I appreciated it for the rawness you described in *Final Negotiations* [Ellis, 1995, 2018].

> The kind of writing I particularly disliked (although I can't think of specific authors) was prescriptive; one example that really sticks with me was a statement about how problematic it was if a widow was still wearing her wedding rings after a year. In the midst of grief I was, not surprisingly, looking for answers and indicators. However, I didn't like anything that I found. In my own case, my wedding ring had been stuck for years and I was worried about needing to cut it off at some point. I took advantage of losing quite a bit of weight as I grieved and the first time I could take it off, I did—and put it into our safety deposit box. However, I had another ring made of gold from other jewellery that Gerry had bought me and a stone that we had bought together in India and I wore that on my wedding ring finger for many years (until I'd lost weight again and it had to relocate). These last few months are the first in years that I haven't had a ring on that finger, and the timing is good for me now.
>
> *(R. Neault, personal communication, December 1, 2018)*

I am still wearing my ring and Frans's wedding ring is in my purse on a gold chain—the chain he bought for me in Washington, DC, in 2009. I wore his ring around my neck on November 21—the day of his funeral—along with a pendant my older sister made for me years ago when Frans and I made our relationship known to our families. She called it "New Beginnings."

Again, I appreciate these external dialogues, whether by e-mail or in person. In Frans's and my model of writing through transformation (Lengelle & Meijers, 2009), we envisioned this internal and external dialogue as a kind of infinity symbol where we go inward (checking in with our feelings as well) and then reach out again, inspired and supported by others' perspectives, both in the shape of real people and from readings.

I cannot speak of my experience and make meaning of it without the conversations of others and their input. I need theories and fresh perspectives to look at my reality; my process is autoethnographic. I tell my own story, but in tandem, I am reading cultural perspectives on grief (e.g., what is known about grieving in North American and European cultures; what theories have been debunked; whether women grieve differently than men).

As a grieving spouse, researcher, and writer, I engage with all three dimensions of autoethnographic research: I share personal experience ("auto"), analyze and reflect on it using a variety of sources ("ethno"), and aim to create evocative stories ("graphic") (Ellis et al., 2011).

I may wake up in the night and feel suddenly fearful and then watch my fear ebb away. I feel less confused for having read Didion's (2005) and others' work about how grief comes in waves, and how sometimes the wave is fear, or terrible yearning, or deep sadness.

I also read that whatever emerges cannot be predicted, that the grief journey is highly individual (Neimeyer, 2016). It is comforting to know I don't have to adhere to any stages or qualify as normal depending on the length of my crying. There are patterns that widows and widowers might read about and feel comforted by, like the four "tasks" identified by grief researcher William Worden (2009, as cited in Hall, 2014),[3] but no rigid phases. My conversations with others seem to help me adjust day by day.

For instance, my friend Kashvi asks questions I never expect but that seem self-evident and necessary once she does. I call her questions "bonbons," and she seems pleased by the analogy. For me, bonbons are a luxury and usually, they are too sweet for me to eat more than one at a time. It is the same with Kashvi's questions: I savor them; they are rich; one at a time is good.

She asked me yesterday, "How is your body feeling?"

This is the answer I give myself after doing an internal scan: "I notice some burning in spots, a sense of having a thicker throat than usual, an ankle that may be asleep, and some slight pains by my collarbones."

Some compliment me on my strength and resilience, but I am doubtful about such labels. I am vulnerable. I notice any small triggers of stress (e.g., mostly practical worries) can have me ruminating, waking in the night as I wrestle with my imaginings and I find I can just manage to settle myself, grateful for more sleep.

In readings I do much later, I learn that the bereaved commonly struggle with insomnia and a variety of other physical symptoms, like waking up too early or not being able to fall asleep, sighing, eating too much or too little, being overactive or not active enough, and feeling tightness in the chest and throat, just to name a few (Luchterhand, n.d.; Utz et al., 2012). I found myself "pfffing" out air as if utterly deflated for months after his death, whenever I re-remembered he was gone.

***

Rhythms

In the 7 months while Frans was ill, my sleep was also disturbed. He got up at night to go to the bathroom and I would turn on the bedside light for fear he might stumble without it. Sometimes he'd lurch out of bed. Speed was something that characterized him in mind, work, and movement, but hearing him get up at night, my heart would kick awake from the adrenaline. I would say, "Easy does it," and he slowed a little near the end, realizing he risked breaking something if he fell. He had no more fat to cushion him; his muscles were so wasted that he couldn't entirely rely on them either. He did become more careful, but in the wee hours, I was often alert and my physiology hasn't yet settled down.

***

Thrown

The clocks are all set to summertime
The winter tires stayed on all year long
I'm thrown, I'm thrown
You described the news like a macabre play
A nightmare that you'd wake up from soon
You were thrown, so thrown
No clock can reset time again
And waking wakes me to this again
We're thrown

December 3, 2018 (2½ weeks after Frans's death)

Despite the surreal nature of time in grief, the daily tasks invite me back to some form of normalcy. This morning, I Skyped with a colleague overseas and later with my PhD student who will come stay and work on her first article in Edmonton next month. Afterward, Maya and I shoveled snow and went out for lunch at a greasy-spoon diner.

In the afternoon, I ran into a colleague in the aisle at the grocery store; she had flashed through my mind hours earlier so there was extra delight in seeing her, a kind of congruence. In the evening, my friend Liz came over and spent several relaxing hours with me on the couch. On the bamboo coffee table, I put the teapot, gluten-free biscotti, chocolate with hazelnuts, and a single white candle. Liz is a generous listener and thoughtful in her responses. I lie on the couch and ramble in neurotic fashion; she responds with a smile, or sums up what I've said, or nods in agreement, somehow affirming my need for myriad machinations.

I go to bed early and note that cooking is always the thing I find hardest when life gets full and life is full of this big happening right now. Empty and full. In the meantime, colleagues continue to send me their resources and thoughts on grieving. This morning messages came from Paris, Rotterdam, and Canterbury.

***

Talking to Frans

When I see a picture of your grave, the one I received this morning, I feel a mix of things. Of course, I understand why you chose to die in the country of your birth, why we chose for you to be left in the soil of your childhood. It's so that your children and grandchildren can visit that spot and know you to be part of their roots. You are not of my blood, so you cannot be my root, even if we shared so much so intimately. What is physically left of you lies 7,015 km away and others decorate your grave. That distance is bridged for me temporarily when a friend of yours tells me she has put a rose on the spot in my name.

"You were the love of his life," she writes. I sigh.

Here is the poem I shared with you in August the day after your daughters, your son-in-law, your grandson, and I spent the afternoon at the eco-burial grounds. We were there to choose your final resting spot on a very hot, dry summer afternoon. You cried reading the poem. We held each other on the couch. Our friends Deirdre and Robert were visiting from Exeter and they went out for dinner together so we could be alone for a few hours; they understood about choosing your beloved's burial spot.

Today

in tall grass
diagonally set between two oaks and
twin mountain ashes at the rear,
we found your final resting spot.
The sky had those friendly white cloud blobs
up against the blue,
the sandy soil of your childhood
crept into our sandals
as we moved through the scape,
checking the ground and
each other for the right feel.
Later, like a small group on safari
we went to learn your future
coordinates,
stood the ground
where your body will one day be.
They instruct us that
when the time comes
you must wear cotton, linen, wool, or silk,
this way you can return properly
from where you came.
But first, picture this,
the scene of our visits,
The place we will remember you
and love you
forwards:
Your view is a wide circle of trees,
like friends and colleagues
facing and surrounding you,
the horizon always in view
but never too vast as to be lonely

and a field with just enough room
for all your future visions.

August 2, 2018

On the fresh mound of your grave there are many red maple leaves. This brings you home to Canada a bit. It's good for me to look at the picture and know your body is resting in beauty, that the earth protects you and that flowers surround you.

In your sleeve, against your bare right arm, is the note that Sophia wrote for you on hand-made paper and her Corona typewriter. It's the message she included with the small shroud she hand-dyed in her fibre-major class. The shroud is decorated with an oak and mountain ash on the silk and we hung it on your basket coffin. It says:

Dear Frans, I am happy I could give you something. You always say a day not learned is a day not lived, or at least the Dutch equivalent. Well, I learned a lot while making this work. Rest easy with the mountain ash and the oak trees. Much love, Sophia.

***

I just got back from Tim Hortons, where I had tea. I cried as I walked through the snow, because we have done that walk together so many times. You would have been impressed by the 30 cm of snow we have. Everything looks like a Christmas card. I took pictures.

When I first stepped out the front door on my way there, I gave myself a grade, as I'm apt to do when I'm feeling shaky: to begin with, a wobbly 6 out of 10 on the scale of okay-ness. By the time I got back, I was a solid 7. The walking always helps. Now I'm back in my work chair writing again, with Debussy playing in the background and a lot of natural light in the living room. I am almost feeling a 7.5.

I did administration this morning and didn't enjoy it much, but such things also come with the reality of "life goes on."

***

So Fast

Yesterday evening, I read the article "Bird on the Wire: Freeing the Father Within Me," by autoethnographer Art Bochner (2012). In this article, Bochner tries to come to peace with the violent father of his youth, a man he was never able to reconcile with in life. Frans and my (now my) PhD student Kat sent me the article, and she and I spoke about dialoguing with the dead and why we might do that symbolically as a way of remaking "a self—myself—that can live not against the past but with it" (Bochner, 2012, p. 168).

What Bochner (2012) discovered is something I keep running across in different words: "Death ends a life, not a relationship and through personal narrative, I might be able to find a way to loosen the grip of the past and break free from my psychic inheritance" (p. 168). Wrestling with or maintaining a bond does not heal us in the face of loss, but rather research shows that "bonds with the deceased did not have to be deemed pathological" (Paxton, 2018, p. 111).

I have freeing to do too, as Bochner describes. I will get to that later.

It feels good to say "you." Right about now, at my 2:00 p.m. (your 10:00 p.m.), I would be calling you from this chair. I would be telling you all the things I'm writing about here. I would tell it in Dutch, of course, as that was our language of conversation—that is, unless I was very angry at you; then I would switch to English.

You will want to know that Daljit from the Tim Hortons had tears in her eyes when I told her you died. "So fast?!" she asked. She put her hand on my shoulder; she didn't know what else to say, but she said something that was meant as comfort, and I took it with me when I went out the door to get stamps.

The spruce tree across the crescent is gently waving its giant arms in the wind, its branches heavy with snow and the bright sun on it with some grey clouds behind. It is an Alberta blue-sky day. You know what I'm talking about. There is still so much beauty in living, Frans. I know you'd be glad I'm saying that, and you'll be glad to know I'm working on the *British Journal of Guidance and Counselling* with Deirdre and Anu. You'll be glad to hear that I'm working, period. I remember you said that going back to work is the thing to do after something like this; you hoped we all would.

***

The Illness

The complete journey from diagnoses to death took only 7 months. The weight loss continued all the way through—about two pounds every week. I kept track. I kept a kind of medical journal. I figured out Frans had low blood pressure early on: he'd lost weight and his heart medication had become redundant. With his doctor's approval, he quit taking the statins he'd been on since his heart attack in July 2003, along with the baby aspirin and the meds to lower his blood pressure.

The painkillers replaced those pills and he took sleeping tablets that kept his anxiety at bay and allowed him some normalcy in his day-and-night rhythm. In the early weeks after the diagnosis, especially in the days I was away from him in April, he went through some nights of terror. Who wouldn't? He'd call me once or twice in the middle of the night while I was still awake in Edmonton. It was comforting for both of us to talk. His youngest daughter stayed with him then so he wouldn't be alone. We longed to connect often. I had always said that a long-distance relationship is most vulnerable if something goes wrong or someone gets sick. We counted the days until I could fly back.

When Keath drove me back to the airport, only 11 days after I'd arrived in Edmonton, Maya said with a wry smile, "Well, it was nice having you here, Mom," as if I'd come home for a short holiday. We laughed. We could be lighthearted in those moments. But it was not easy being away from Maya for months. I didn't want to leave my 15-year-old, who was just newly in high school. I wanted to reach across to be present for her, but I also could be in no other place than with Frans. He and I decided our back-up plan to bridge the divide was to buy another airplane ticket if needed. Maya ended up spending the whole summer with us in The Netherlands.

***

Visitors

Over the span of those 7 months of his illness, we had many visitors. Our guests were mostly colleagues who had become friends over the years. We also had family visits in varying constellations. Frans scheduled appointments diligently so he would have company and meaningful distraction. He liked to say, "Dying is something you do alone, but it's so wonderful that there are people who are willing to journey with you." He considered the meaning-making process of dying a highly social and conversational activity, and I couldn't agree more, having gone through this with him. While he used to spend long days at the computer creating, he spent his last months deepening connections each day.

We sat on the yellow second-hand couch we'd bought at the recycle shop and visitors sat on the L-shaped grey couch. Our large square living room could easily accommodate 8–10 people at a time and sometimes the family group was that big. But most days we had one or two visitors, almost always one at a time and this made deeper conversations possible. These visits were one of the highlights of the whole illness-to-death journey. People asked me if I ever got tired of the company and I admit I sometimes did, but not very often. I continued my own morning walks near the end and sometimes spent an hour alone in the café on the market square where I could do some writing, but otherwise, I was at Frans's side and part of the conversation.

The house was always filled with flowers. We usually had two or three fresh bouquets at a time and many cards. Old students wrote; family and friends expressed their love and concern. The mantel above the fireplace was layered with cards with images of flowers, butterflies, and other natural scenes. People sent poetry that said what they wanted to say; some sent wise sayings; many sent appreciation for the ways in which Frans had helped or inspired them in their work or studies. His investments in corresponding with and supporting many people over the years showed in what came through the door and mailbox.

***

A Letter from Paris

This morning, I received an e-mail from career researcher and colleague Jean Guichard, who lives in Paris. He begins with the almost lyrical, "I'm very—very—sorry to learn of the death of Frans Meijers, who will be remembered as one of the major constructors of concepts—and a great observer—in the field of narrative identity."

Even the Garamond font Jean has chosen for the e-mail seems perfect. I feel I have received a real typed letter from the old world. Then he shares a Proust quote, which I first read upon waking, but that I had to read again before I could even begin to absorb it.

Jean introduces the quote by saying,

> In the book *Mourning Diary* by Roland Barthes (a book translated into English as paperback), there is a quotation of a letter sent by Marcel Proust to his friend Georges de Lauris, written in 1907, who had just lost his mother. I believe that what Proust wrote is so right that it can apply to the loss of anyone one is loving deeply:
>
> Now there is one thing I can tell you: you will enjoy certain pleasures you would not fathom now. When you still had your mother you often thought of the days when you would have her no longer. Now you will often think of days past when you had her. When you are used to this horrible thing that they will forever be cast into the past, then you will gently feel her revive, returning to take her place, her entire place, beside you. At the present time, this is not yet possible. Let yourself be inert, wait till the incomprehensible power… that has broken you restores you a little, I say a little, for henceforth you will always keep something broken about you. Tell yourself this, too, for it is a kind of pleasure to know that you will never love less, that you will never be consoled, that you will constantly remember more and more.
> *(Source: Barthes, 2010). (J. Guichard, personal communication, January 11, 2018)*

Dear Jean,

Your letter to me (yes, I'll call it a letter) was simply beautiful. I read it this morning upon waking and again just now, this afternoon, after writing and after my walk through the snow. I have almost finished writing on my widow project[4] for the day, but I will include bits of what you've written (with your permission, of course).

Poetry has been my solace in these past 8 months. I wrote almost 50 poems while Frans was ill and now the narrative reflections are coming as well. I will tell the story in various ways, in imagined letters to him, in my reflections on e-mails, and in recounting the facts of the illness journey. It is a narrative and dialogical and poetic process. When I wake up in the morning, I post my first reflection—it's the time I would have called him from Canada when we were on either side of the Atlantic. We spent 8 months of the year together and 4 months apart, so being "alone" at home here is not completely foreign.

I hear the bereaved, besides crying also sigh frequently. I am finding that. The bereaved also tend to not fully comprehend the loss; author Joan Didion calls this "Magical Thinking" and I confess that this too is what I'm experiencing. A friend of mine asked a few days ago, "how is your body feeling" and I've been paying more attention to this. I notice some burning and aching – around my throat and chest and, symbolically perhaps, my heel seems to be radiating some pain as well. Maybe the body knows more than I do.

The lines from Proust that speak to me most at the moment are, "When you are used to this horrible thing that they will forever be cast into the past, then you will gently feel her revive, returning to take her place, her entire place, beside you. At the present time, this is not yet possible." This gives me hope. At the moment, Frans seems very far away, though I sometimes write a dialogue with him, and our colleague Deirdre told me this morning that she wanted to ask him something and looked at his picture on her desk. He seemed to answer, "Get over it, Deirdre"! I told her I too had asked Frans to say something comforting to me and he "wrote" back, "Well, I was never very good at that, you told me ..." Deirdre and I both laughed about this on our video call.

I will send you a poem I wrote recently and thank you for listening/being a witness to part of this process.

Kind regards,

Reinekke

Later, I read in C. S. Lewis's *A Grief Observed* (1961) that the bereaved may be fearful of losing connection and the vivid memories of their loved one, but that eventually he or she does come back fully, just as Proust describes. This comforts me, as does some of what I'm reading in other books and articles.

***

Notes

1 Used with permission. The original Dutch by Gerard Wijers was, "Een uitzonderlijk belangrijke en intense psychische toestand in de relationele sfeer, die begrensd is in de tijd."

2 In Dutch, the expression he used was, "Ik ben de klos," which literally means, "I'm the spool (of thread)." In spirit, this means "I'm done for; I'm toast." The Dutch expression comes from the work of ropemaking, where the worker who holds the spool frequently has to walk long distances to follow the threads as they are spun together into rope. It is hard and tedious work; the most undesirable position to be in.

3 Hall (2014) lists Worden's 4 tasks of grieving: (1) to accept the reality of the loss; (2) to process the pain of grief; (3) to adjust to a world without the deceased (including both internal, external, and spiritual adjustments); and (4) to find an enduring connection with the deceased in the midst of embarking on a new life (p. 9).

4 "The widow project" was the name I called the manuscript as I worked on it.

2

UNFINISHED BUSINESS

In reading the first pages of Thompson and Neimeyer's (2014) book *Grief and the Expressive Arts*, I was once again relieved to hear that grief has no set pattern. The well-known Kübler-Ross stage model that everyone seems so familiar with is contested; the model was developed with the dying in mind, not the bereaved.

Thompson and Neimeyer (2014) write, "It is clear, for example, that roughly one-third of mourners experience few of the turbulent feelings associated with the classic stage model, instead responding with considerable resilience or even relief from the earliest weeks of bereavement" (p. 4). I cannot say I feel relief; if there is any trace of it, it is only that I could go home to Maya and not be torn between two sides of the Atlantic. Some people have reminded me that Frans is not suffering anymore; I am still not relieved.

A year later, I do experience relief, however, and I explain the reasons for this below.

Thompson and Neimeyer (2014) continue: "In stark contrast, roughly 10–15% struggle with intense, prolonged and complicated grief, characterized by extreme separation distress, preoccupation with the loss, and inability to function in major life roles across a period of many months or years" (p. 4).

Prolonged Grief Disorder, according to the World Health Organization (WHO, 2019), meets these criteria:

> Prolonged grief disorder is a disturbance in which, following the death of a partner, parent, child, or other person close to the bereaved, there is persistent and pervasive grief response characterised by longing for the deceased or persistent preoccupation with the deceased accompanied by intense emotional pain (e.g., sadness, guilt, anger, denial, blame, difficulty accepting the death, feeling one has lost a part of one's self, an inability to experience

> positive mood, emotional numbness, difficulty in engaging with social or other activities). The grief response has persisted for an atypically long period of time following the loss (more than six months at a minimum) and clearly exceeds expected social, cultural or religious norms for the individual's culture and context. Grief reactions that have persisted for longer periods that are within a normative period of grieving given the person's cultural and religious context are viewed as normal bereavement responses and are not assigned a diagnosis. The disturbance causes significant impairment in personal, family, social, educational, occupational or other important areas of functioning.
>
> *(6B42)*

I am functioning; I am preoccupied with the loss, but my grief is not terribly complex. There is unfinished business that preoccupies me, but it doesn't paralyze. I am aware that I have been angry at Frans.

My mother says that brilliant and driven people often have selfish shadow sides not always obvious to those who admire them from some distance. "Think of Picasso and Sartre. In their personal lives they could be egotistical and even cruel," she says. I would say that Frans was neither so famous nor so complicated as these others, and he was kind in many ways, but I did wonder if people who are particularly brilliant in one area, as Frans was, have failed to grow in others. Or that they are so single-minded about their work that they at times feel justified in running over others. Such tenacity often leads to good results, breaking down old structures of thinking, but there is collateral damage.

As I write this, I am reminded of Frans's own admissions. He often said he was "not good with emotions." He admitted that, "if triggered," he would sometimes "attack and insult someone right to the bone." He added, "I am not condoning it; I have a short fuse." I speak about this here, in response to what I've read so far in Thompson and Neimeyer's (2014) book, because I am looking honestly at this idea of feeling (some) relief after a loved one's death.

I remember a story told to me by my first husband about his German grandmother. After her husband died, she ordered Chinese food. He had rarely let her do that when he was alive. He counted their dollars as he had had to do as an immigrant fresh from Prussia, but later in their lives, they didn't have to worry about money anymore and he still discouraged her. She not only began ordering Chinese food after his death, but continued to do so once a week for many years. His death freed her to do this, and to me, this is a small example of how someone can be a "Happy Widow" when a spouse dies. I cannot say I am a happy widow, but I can admit that there are certain things I will not miss.

Recently, I told my friend Margot this. She said, "I bet you he was pretty tired of some of the conversations too …" and I laughed in recognition. "Yes, I can see that perfectly. He's probably on his cloud, looking down, saying, 'Thank God we don't have to talk about THAT anymore!'"

While Frans could be temperamental and reactive, I could be pointedly insistent. I pushed him to be clear and deliberate in his emotional dealings with his exes, which I believe he found emotionally taxing. His first wife had a difficult time letting him go, it seemed to me: in addition to hugging him, which I considered a normal part of their ongoing friendship, she would physically lean on him, sit with her arm around him on our couch while he was ill, pick lint off his sweater, bring him food, and openly express her continued displeasure at their divorce, even almost a decade after the fact. In the final weeks of his life, in our living room, she lamented that they had not gone to therapy to save their marriage, though Frans told her he didn't think it would have helped.

Sometimes Frans set boundaries with her and sometimes he did not; it was a difficult dynamic for me. While I wanted him to connect with all close family members and have a chance at resolution with her—I even left our house at times so they could speak privately—her visits were a source of tension. I acknowledged and respected her as Frans's first wife and the mother of his children, but she struggled, in my view, to accept my position as his chosen partner.

We did have family visits that were truly congenial, and she once said that I was the love of Frans's life. She and I even simultaneously growled at him when we felt he was saying something asinine. Our instincts about things were frequently similar and she did make genuine efforts at trying to accept me as part of the "extended family." That said, the strain of their unfinished business remained, and I believe she was driven by a deep wish to reunite her family. She would say that she did not agree with their divorce, despite the reality of his choice to leave and his clear reasons, of which I was not the cause.

I supported her visits to our home before and during his illness, and invited her to be present at his deathbed too, which she wanted. I suggested at the start of funeral planning that her name be included on the death announcement and the funeral invitation, while usually only the partner and children are named there. Not everyone would have been as accommodating under the same circumstances, but that she had played a vital role in his life was not lost on me. That her grief at his passing would be deep in its own way and should not go unacknowledged was self-evident.

I myself have a good experience of an ongoing friendship with my first husband, Keath, so I understand how love can be abiding and does not depend on how the relationship is officially framed. In the context of continuing bonds, I always deemed it possible to healthily navigate connections after divorce, but I repeatedly felt the struggle of Frans's first wife. When I told her that it seemed to me she was "holding on to him," she replied that it was up to her if she desired to do so, which of course was true. This, however, frequently complicated our interactions.

One afternoon, several months after Frans's diagnosis, when she came to visit him for an afternoon on his and my last vacation together in July 2018, she saw how little he was eating and said to me, "If I was the one taking care of him, I would be putting bits of food in front of him all the time." Frans came to my defense immediately: "You're not the one taking care of me and I don't want the food." I had read on the American Cancer Society website that food was often a bone of contention between cancer patients and their families; they advised not feeding someone with terminal cancer if food made them feel ill, which was the case with Frans. I had done my homework, and her comment seemed to imply that I was not caring well for him.

In conversations with him where I pointed out my displeasure, he would sometimes become belligerent or switch into a cold "academic mode" and deny that anyone could pick up on emotional truths intuitively. If his daughters or friends made similar points, he would sometimes revisit our conversation and admit that he might have underestimated the emotional impact of his divorce. He made strides in being clearer with his ex, hoping she would feel the freedom to move on, but this remained a source of pain for us all.

In part, our unfinished business had to do with this uneasy dynamic; however, more important was the way we communicated about it. Frans's fear of emotional situations, combined with his genuine appreciation for his ex, his loyalty to his family, and his long-time habit of not being entirely honest, made for a confusing situation.

Frans frequently denied my claims that her behavior represented a pattern of holding on and compared my friendship with Keath to his with her, though I pointed out the crucial difference: "I'm all for having peaceful family relationships and I acknowledge your bond with her, but she still wishes things were otherwise." I added that, while Keath could be happy for us, she didn't fully accept our relationship. Nor did she have to, but that made her visits awkward and at times stressful for me.

Frans would happily and proudly call me "mijn vrouw"—which means both *my woman* and *my wife* in Dutch—in the company of our friends, family, and colleagues, but in her presence, he seemed to find this difficult and called me his "partner." A few weeks before he died, sitting on our couch, he blurted out emotionally, "You are my respected ex-wife! Reinekke is my real wife!"

Several close friends of theirs acknowledged to me that I was not wrong in my observations: Frans and his ex-wife's divorce was emotionally incomplete. Frans admitted to being afraid of conflict and emotional outbursts, and she remained open about her ongoing disappointment in the failure of their marriage. The nonacceptance of their divorce was unfortunate. I believe that, had it been accepted, we could have been warm and relaxed together, just as Keath and I and Frans were in each other's company. I often felt I had inherited the unresolved marital issues Frans brought with him.

On the evening of Frans's death, my mother said, "It's time for everyone to go home now. Reinekke needs some rest; she is the widow." Frans's ex replied, "We are all widows." I remember thinking in that moment that I understood her comment and accepted that she would likely always feel that way.

Because Frans and I were matched in strength and intensity, we did what we deemed important and stood up for what we both wanted. That said, during his illness, I chose to more readily accommodate what felt like boundary-crossing behavior.

In his final letter to me, Frans said he admired and respected the fact we still dared to fight while he was ill. We took ourselves seriously, was his point. In that letter, he also conceded that all his life he had never opened easily and that he needed a "kick in the pants" to learn. He acknowledged that he had not been an easy partner for me in this regard. About his impulsive, sometimes temperamental nature, he said, "This can't have been easy for someone as self-reflective as you."

A few months before Frans died, he vulnerably said, "Maybe I had to get this sick physically before my ego could take a back seat." When I recall that moment, my appreciation for him returns and I look at him in my mind's eye with a huge tenderness.

I am learning to honor my anger, while also honoring him.

***

What Is Different Now?

Later in the grief process, I reflect on a question Bonnie, a fresh widow and one of my beta readers, asks after she has read an earlier draft of this manuscript. "What things do you do now, or no longer have to do, without the compromises and co-dependence of marriage? Like the Chinese food story of Keath's grand-mother?" I write her back:

1. I now sing loudly to music in the car. I sing out of tune and Frans was a very good amateur choir singer who often sung solos. He liked classical mostly. I like all kinds of music and definitely 80s pop. I turn the volume up and go with abandon, though I often don't know half the lyrics. I dance while I'm driving (well, mostly at traffic lights or thrumming with one hand on my thigh). I don't care what other drivers think and I no longer have to worry about Frans being embarrassed, gritting his teeth at my singing, or feeling inclined to micromanage my driving when I'm going at a relaxed Canadian pace.
2. I changed my diet recently to cut out sugar, starches, and most caffeine. I didn't need to think about asking anyone. I didn't need to negotiate with Frans or ask him to cook his own potato. I can put boiled water in the thermos instead of endless black tea.
3. I truly do not miss the arguments. He once said that I might. Maybe someday I will laugh and admit that maybe he had a point, that at least it was a form of connection that showed we cared what the other thought. But, truthfully, reacquainting myself with my own rhythms these last months, I

don't think I ever will. Looking back over this past year, I am glad to notice I have not raised my voice to anyone since Frans's death.

***

December 3: further reflections

I stop to ponder something I read in the book *The Five Things We Cannot Change*, by poet, psychologist, and Buddhist David Richo (2008). I use his list as a kind of self-check:

1. Everything changes and ends—*check*
2. Things do not always go according to plan—*check*
3. Life is not always fair—*check*
4. Pain is part of life—*check*
5. People are not loving and loyal all the time—*damn it!*

Richo (2008) writes that, as long as we are resisting any of these five realities, we are going to suffer. If we resist number 5, as I realize I do, we will hurt and reject others and cause our own suffering by doing so. It makes sense.

Frans died in my arms and his last words to me were, "I was so lucky with you." Those words were loving and loyal. They do not cancel out some of the other words, but they do help me look back with love.

Thompson and Neimeyer (2014) complete their initial inventory of mourners by saying, "Between these extremes fall a large number of adaptive grievers who come to terms with their losses after a period of upheaval, often without the benefit of professional therapy" (p. 4).

I think I fit into this large group and my homemade therapy so far is writing, walking, corresponding, and getting enough sleep. Upheaval, yes. There is some noise in my body; it is holding some of the pain for me.

***

Moods of the Day

My body is like a quiet animal

a good dog left along a roadside
not by neglect
but simply because the car
stopped there
and the door opened
and there was a field to step into
and when it turned around
to try and go back

the scenery had changed,
the car had gone—
it was not intentional.
A body knows how to grieve
like an animal spent
it simply curls up into itself
or, when safe enough, keens
into the air.

***

December 4

I am walking again and had two nights of fairly normal sleep. That is progress. Yesterday, in the morning after doing some administration, I wrote about 1,000 words but then I wilted.

The snow and sunlight were gorgeous, so I went out. When I got back, I wrote another 2,500 words by 5:00 p.m.; I didn't expect I could or would, but I did feel stronger from having gone out.

I took pictures of the Mountain Ash trees on my walk. Frans is buried near two, which is symbolic for me. I have one in the yard here in Edmonton that he could see from his chair. The second one is near the neighbors' fence and is large and lush and we would walk past it on our way to Tim Hortons.

Tea scheduled again today with my neighbor and my "third daughter" Colleen (my daughters grew up with her and she was often in our home). I welcome people coming to visit at midday or early evening—that is, during my writing breaks. I am guarding my writing time. I incubated this writing project over the span of Frans's last 8 months, while I was sitting beside him almost constantly. So, the work needs to be written as the muse prompts. The more I write at the moment, the more that seems to want to be written.

On Mondays and Thursdays, Maya and I are off screens after 5:00 p.m., and that makes for reading, conversation, and music time. Yesterday, I started reading a book on art, mourning, and psychoanalysis by Esther Dreifuss-Kattan (2016), and I am almost done Didion's (1995) story. Massage is also on the agenda so I can get my body more mercifully engaged with the process. I know on Amy's massage table I will talk, and I will cry.

I did laugh a little yesterday, thanks to Maya and her fun and dry wit.

There is so much more going on in the world that needs attention, like the scary movement to the far right; the environment; wars still raging. At the moment, this is what I can contribute; I hope it is more than a personal pilgrimage. I hope in writing this grief journey, I inspire awakenings that ripple out and offer comfort to others.

***

Work

Frans didn't like hospitals and his motto seemed to be "work hard every day and keep the doctor away." He used to work 6 days a week and even answer e-mails on Sundays. He was a happy workaholic, as many researchers are. My older sister Leo, who works with researchers, had warned us. She said, "I've often seen researchers retire and then drop dead within two years." Frans took his leave from his position as a professor at The Hague University in November 2015, though his consulting business was still going. He and I were also still working very actively together, and organized a conference for 300 delegates that was held in November 2017.

I sometimes think Frans believed he could escape death by working. "I'm too busy working to die" is something he'd uttered more than once. This too, of course, is a kind of magical thinking.

We were busy with many projects and sometimes I complained about the intensity of the pace. Did we need to do six or eight or even 10 publications a year? Why not do two or three and consider a bit more carefully what else we wanted to spend our time on?

Byron Katie (2002), a self-help author with a powerful writing exercise called "The Work," once said (I'm paraphrasing here) that when you lose a partner to divorce or death, you've been spared in some way. No exceptions. This sounds like a rather uncharitable thought, but it has stuck with me over the years since I heard it. Not to rationalize death and try to "find the upside," as Didion admits she tried to do, and couldn't, but to listen in and hear the whisperings of your own soul that might have been ignored by the presence of a strong partner.

Frans was used to leading. This applied to his own research projects and many others he guided and supervised as well. He was used to "applying soft pressure" (as he called it) and, quite frankly, when it came to my own life and projects, so was I. Two driven people, proactive and in charge of themselves—an alpha male and an alpha female. Although this created the fruitful and equal dynamic we had, it also inevitably led to some friction regarding priorities.

In May 2017, I stopped to seriously consider whether I was giving enough time and energy to my poetic and creative self. I had completed my PhD in 3 years and we were still going at a breakneck pace the 2 years following. I'd also been hearing myself say that I wanted to write for "normal people," not only for academic readers. Was a hybrid form possible? I imagined a book on expressive and creative writing for teachers and counsellors, as well as laypeople, while Frans talked about Springer, Sage, and Routledge, and saw a textbook.

In a poem I once wrote about our symbolic children, I said, "I want our Claire (our academic work) but I also want our Joe (our more creative work—something that could reach the Joes of this world)."[1]

Frans went on to edit two academic books in the last 2 years of his life. These texts included our own chapters, and I'm glad for him that he got to enjoy this. I also appreciated his dedication, but another voice was calling to me.

I began to persevere on an inner level and I finally decided to stop waiting for his understanding or blessing and say no to some of the projects that were on offer. Instead, I wrote an accessible manuscript called *Happy: Poems and Reflections for Writing and Healing the Self* (Lengelle, 2018a). I incorporated it as a syllabus for one of my graduate courses and then asked if Frans would ask his Dutch publisher to consider it in a translated version. We got the go-ahead and I started translating it in the fall of 2017. I completed the translation in March 2018, just before Frans's diagnosis, and he edited the Dutch version in the first weeks after the terrible news (Lengelle, 2018b).

He used to tell our visitors that this work gave him something to ground him in those early days. I was and am incredibly grateful and moved by the fact that he had immediate faith in the project and even sold it to some of our visitors when it arrived in print. We proofed the final pages on our holidays in July 2018. This was no small feat as the fentanyl patches tired him—he could barely write anymore, but he could still edit others' work. He finished one last article with our career-research colleague Peter den Boer—a final meaningful piece critiquing the blind faith in so-called career competencies in The Netherlands, something he had worked on earlier with another colleague, but which he felt had ultimately failed at being anything more than another instrumental career intervention.

Now that Frans is gone, I determine what my projects will be and when I will be embarking on them and when I need to rest. Have I been spared? Spared the pressures of an ambitious partner? Yes and no. Yes, I do notice that my physiology is calming down as I trust my own rhythms and he is no longer here to nudge, cajole, and convince me we should say yes to yet another book chapter. And no, he was the best work partner I ever had. He might not have initially seen value in some of the projects I spoke about, but when I went ahead and did them, he championed them with me.

I cannot blame the ambitious researcher in him that he didn't always see the poet in me.

No, that was my responsibility.

***

To Cry and Not to Cry

"Grieving is a healthy, protective process. It's an evolutionary adaptation to promote survival in the face of emotional trauma, one where the injury goes undetected since daily function is preserved" (Shulman, 2018, p. 142).

I did not cry a lot in the early days back in Canada. I cried while Frans was ill. We cried together. I cried deeply when he was on the brink of dying and when I held his dead, still warm body in my arms. However, right after his death, there was a funeral to arrange, and his daughters and I carefully and competently navigated the work of seeing to those next steps. We had had conversations together about this prior to Frans's death and we'd also met with the funeral director at home. After that, there were my things to organize and pack so I could come back to Canada.

I had to function and organize, and in the meantime, I cried quietly.

Just as I'm writing this, I get a message from a widow, a former student from a course I first taught in 1996. Coincidentally, she's just reconnected with me in the last few weeks. She tells me that, eventually, the deep pain comes. She sent me a few snippets of her journey in writing and speaks about the torture of losing a husband suddenly. I can't really imagine the shock of that, and I feel grateful again for having had the time with Frans.

I am skeptical at the moment about crying and what is needed; I trust that mourning will show me. I'm open. When my stepfather and then my father died, I cried with sorrow and gratitude. Theo, my biological father, and I were close; we were also intellectual companions. He died suddenly of a heart attack; I found him dead in his home and could accept it as a fact immediately. He had diabetes and had had a stroke 2 years before; he had started to look very fragile.

Rudy, my stepfather, a very loving man who actively helped raise me, died of cancer over a span of 3 years. Both deaths happened as I was working on my PhD and I kept on working. Yet, that didn't mean I didn't grieve: I grieve them still and that sorrow is soft and full of love.

I'm not sure if it is my sober Dutch upbringing or my penchant for being intellectual, but I notice I accept death as a reality of life (that said, I probably wouldn't be so bold as to say that if it applied to my children). With my fathers and Frans, I can bow to the reality of death and the fact that there is so darn little we can do about it. People get sick and die. My beloved and I are no exception. We are not special. No one is actually entitled to "grow old together." There is a reason death is called the great leveler. When people asked us, "Aren't you angry—that it's happening to *you*?"—we did genuinely think, "Why *not* us?"

There is no use in overanalyzing it. I cry when I hear a sad song about loss. I cried when my sister and I watched a silly romantic movie that featured meeting loved ones at the airport. I will never again meet Frans at the airport or be met by him. Just writing that makes my stomach sink, but that is only because in writing that sentence, I am at once in the past (he used to … I used to …) and in our nonexistent future (poor me, he will not be there). Both of these thoughts—past and future—are simply thoughts, little movies of remembrance and projection. They are not real. Real is me sitting in this chair writing. Real is the fact that my feelings are mixed.

A strange but perhaps logical fact: when I was pregnant, I noticed pregnant women. When I had my miscarriage and told others about it, women who told me they too had had a miscarriage suddenly surrounded me. Now that I am a widow, widows are coming forward. There are so many. Of course, there are!

What was I thinking? They even appear without my prompting. We see what we are focused on and what preoccupies us.

On the plane trip in September 2018, flying back to Frans after a job interview in Canada, I happened to be seated next to a beautiful woman of 29 who told me that she was bringing her husband's ashes back to his family in Scotland. He had died in a workplace accident in November 2017—Frans would die almost a year to the day after that.

"... you are not alone, ha, ha, ha ..." As I write this, I imagine the cackling voice of Vincent Price saying these words.

I cry and I also laugh at the macabre reality of life.

***

My Love, I'm Angry

December 5, 2018

Yesterday, I went out to dinner with "Coco" and Maya. Coco (Colleen), who I call my "third daughter." She notices a lot and Maya and I feel cheerful in her company. We went to the Boston Pizza that Frans and I used to go to once a week, especially on days when our writing left us no time to contemplate what would be for dinner. He usually had a half rack of ribs and a Canadian beer; I would have gluten-free Mediterranean pizza with Caesar salad.

Dear Frans,

Coco remembers fondly your political debates and your upbeat banter. She also noticed that over time you were more and more open to others' viewpoints and were less apt to interrupt or dominate the conversation. She didn't let you get away with much and that makes me smile. It gives me hope for the young women of the future.

My father taught me to openly challenge him on any point if I felt he was exaggerating or off the mark, so I was lucky. I carried this over into my relationship with you; my parents did not condition me to be convinced by any other voice before checking in with my own, and that included the voice of the white educated male. You weren't always appreciative of my feistiness. You say the last 10 years of your life were the happiest, which tells me you did love an honest challenge.

Your friend Janus who knew you for over 45 years said that in the years with me, you changed a lot, and that the conversations felt more open and connected; that you listened better and didn't offer your opinion first. Two nights after your death, he and Els made dinner for me and my mother. I felt deeply quiet inside—it seemed like a combination of being simultaneously at peace, deflated, numb, and grateful for their company. Your body was still lying at home in the guestroom with a cooling element underneath and a funeral upcoming.

When Janus said that I was one of the only people who had been able to stand up to you, I realized why I had sometimes felt tired and strained, but that I'd also been braver than I gave myself credit for, and you more open. You were a good debater; your arguments were very convincing. I learned so much from you about making the argument; however, when it comes to the heart, some of the arguments you made were downright unfair.

After dinner, all of us sat around a glass table near their old woodstove and remembered you—always with a mix of heartfelt appreciation and admiration for your help, inspiration, and steadfastness, and also with question marks. There was hurt and honest critique in some of our memories, and I'm glad the evening made room for that, too. As I write this now, I suppose this is the way of it with passionate, single-minded people on a mission to bring new ideas to the world. And we all trespass. We are sometimes admired. We are also seen in our shadow sides. The stories and feelings around someone else's woodstove after my death someday will likely be similar.

What sometimes softens all of this for me is that you often spoke of having an "inferiority complex"—being a boy from a small town, having to be a chameleon to fit in in higher circles, and frequently making yourself bigger than you actually felt. This was a keen bit of self-awareness. It doesn't justify certain behaviors, but it does bring understanding. We both had our weak spots: mine was feeling threatened when spoken to harshly. I felt our relationship was in danger and I needed reassurance. I would become fearful and my urge was to seek validation. This put a burden on you to help me in ways that made no logical sense to you and tried your patience. Your weak spot was feeling insecure when you were questioned in your intention, autonomy, or expertise; this made you feel uncertain of your value and your fear reaction was expressed in anger. Fear and anger do not make good housemates. We hurt each other. You called it "stirring in the other's wound."

You and I had signed up to go to a nonviolent communication course at the end of September, but you were too sick to go by then. Nonviolent communication is something you first introduced me to via online videos. Remember, you sent me one of Marshall Rosenberg's films about 5 years ago and I was intrigued. We both began to study it off and on. He talks about the violence of diagnosing someone, or trying to educate them, and the use of "big words" like "You never …"; " You completely …"; "You always …"; "It's totally …"; "It's absolutely …"

Your sentences were punctuated by these words and that did not change. At your funeral, I spoke warmly about our love and devotion and dedication to our research and writing work. I also said that you were no saint, that you were impatient, and that when challenged in your authority, you sometimes resorted to verbal violence. Sometimes your critiques were accurate, and rightly you challenged some of your colleagues' assumptions on career concepts and instruments. The issue was not that you didn't frequently make a damn good point; the point is that you could make it damningly. A colleague you later apologized to says it this way: "Frans could indeed offer critique well, but he did at times let his ego and insecurity play too great a role."

What I am saying now—imagining you might hear me—is that I am admitting to anger. I am no longer afraid to say it. Not always singing your praises makes me feel guilty as well. This morning in the shower, I thought about what Joan Didion says about how anger and guilt are related, how feeling angry at your deceased loved ones causes guilt. Aren't you supposed to say only good things about the dead? After all, they can't defend themselves anymore.

Your long-time friend Ellen says that I was simply a "mirror to your feelings of disempowerment," and that your emotional growth really only started in earnest in the last decade of your life. Your daughters said they could finally speak to you and you told them that they had me to thank for that. These reflections now remind me of what Tilly Warnock says in her reflections on writing and healing: people are "not evil, but mistaken" (as cited in Anderson & MacCurdy, 2000, p. 49). We misunderstood each other; it's not that we were really out to hurt each other. I do believe that. I will eventually likely feel that, too, but I am not quite there yet.

Saying all of this, the iceberg of my resistance melts a little. Eventually, it will merge with the sea in harmony. In the meantime, I hold all of it as gently as I can: I love you, I feel angry, I feel some guilt, and I trust the process. In future letters I may not even recognize the "self" I am now at all.

At the moment, I do not miss you.

That is not to say I wouldn't want you to be sitting with me, here, right now.

***

When I asked Frans several months before his death if I might be losing him totally, as he is an atheist, he enthusiastically replied, "No, if you need me, you need only call and I'll be there for you." He saw himself as being part of me, part of a set of internal voices. I would likely feel what he would really say; I need not feel alone, even though he "will never again be physically present to touch, smell, hear or see …" (Neimeyer & Konopka, 2019, p. 3).

R: What do you think of all that I'm writing about you/us so far?

F: I support it, my love. I see you are doing well. I also feel that you are sad underneath your strength. How is your day going? Ordinarily, you would phone me around now and tell me about it.

R: (I notice in my response that I skip from feeling to what I'm doing. It seemed safer; it was usually the safer answer if I was feeling down and I got on the phone with Frans.) I've been writing on Whyte Avenue. I was in the café working here and when I got up to go to the washroom, a man asked, "Aren't you worried about your computer?" You could have said that. You were always asking about the car doors being locked and double-checking things. In those six words, I could hear that the fellow was Dutch and I started speaking Dutch to him. Nick is 86 and worked in editing and reads about health. He's very smart and my little wish to speak some Dutch with someone today came true without any effort.

F: Well, it's not completely unthinkable that you would meet a Dutch person in Edmonton, with 40,000 Dutch immigrants having landed there.

R: Yes, that's the logical explanation for these things. I thought you would say that (half smile). I need food soon. I'm going to walk to Café Mosaics. It's like my inner battery loses its charge suddenly, and then after walking or speaking to someone who uplifts, it does a bit of a turbo charge, but that's temporary.

F: Yes, take good care of yourself, my love. And know that it's true what I said in the letter, that I want to be close to you.

R: I've been studying and grief theories have caught up with your thinking on that. Freud and his colleagues used to think people had to let go of the loved one, but how can you really? They have become part of you. The new grief theories talk about "a continuing symbolic bond to the deceased" (Neimeyer & Konopka, 2019, p. 2; Paxton, 2018). Big sigh. Time to walk.

Can you say what you said before, about my future?

F: You are too young, too beautiful, and too intelligent to remain alone. I know you will do well in life and work. Is that what you wanted to hear?

R: I think so. I was remembering some of the kind things you said, and I don't want to forget those things. The sun seems to be coming right in the window now.

***

Deep Dialogues of Healing

My friend said, "you seemed fragile"

and I rejected the word
too quickly, it turned out
later after walking home, head down,
I admitted it to the mirror
and then to my friend
maybe a confession would clear it
make fragile less true
and less scary

December 6, 2018 (3 weeks after Frans's death)

Yesterday, I wrote in familiar cafés; 3,000 words in two locations. I took a walk in between. Coming home, I gathered my books and papers and music to sit in bed and read more on grief and creative forms of healing.

This morning I felt fragile. Each sensation seemed like it would discombobulate me.

I try to welcome the discomfort of my feelings. I relax into them and keep saying to myself, "Okay, come on then, whatever you are." Usually, doing that dissolves whatever is tugging. Though sometimes a thought feels particularly heavy. For instance, when I remember what didn't work between us and what we can never hash out together anymore. I literally feel pressure in my head, as if two thumbs are pressing against my brain from either side, right above my ears.

Walking helps to settle the clench in my body that those thoughts seem to produce.

On the way to Tim Hortons this morning, I meet a neighbor Christine, the mother of a little girl who comes and visits and picks apples from my tree every summer. I tell this neighbor that Frans died on November 16. She opens her arms. She holds me for several minutes. Then she looks at me, her scarf over her face so only her eyes are showing.

"Now, I remember why you went over …" She hugs me again. Then she looks up, "I don't know what to say." These are actually the perfect words.

"There is nothing to say." I smile at her.

She hugs me a third time and says, "We'll be around."

In a book chapter my friends and colleagues Robert Neimeyer and Agnieszka Konopka (2019) wrote, which I was reading last night, there is a story about a mother, Darla, who loses her college-aged son to cancer. She is stuck in her grief and comes to the realization that she suffers and is simultaneously afraid of suffering.

The counsellor places "suffering" in an empty chair, as is done in Gestalt[2] and other therapies, and invites Darla to speak to suffering and have suffering reply. She discovers that suffering is not as threatening as she first imagined and that it has been the bridge that keeps her connected to her son Kyle, but that it need not be the only bridge.

This idea that we can talk to "suffering" as if it's a voice or entity in and of itself is explained using the theory of the dialogical self (Hermans & Hermans-Konopka, 2010). In the theory, the self is defined as dynamic and multivoiced, and each voice (called an I-position) represents either a part of ourselves (e.g., me as mother, me as writer, me as liking a clean house) or something we might consider as other or outside, but which is also experienced as a voice accessible internally (e.g., Frans, wisdom, the place I feel is home, Buddha, God).

Reading the Neimeyer and Konopka (2019) chapter, I see ways to work more creatively and actively with parts of my grief. In particular, the places where I am suffering from the edgy parts that I sense won't simply disappear with time.

It seems there is passive grieving (i.e., surrendering to the waves of pain that come and go without leaving residue) as well as the desire for active grieving when the pain is made of past scratches, gripes, and frustrations that threaten to harden into a kind of grief plaque. I am aware that I don't want to keep walking around with unresolved issues. I also don't want to stay downhearted out of a skewed sense of loyalty to Frans. Nor do I want to avoid what is irking me out of fear of social judgments.

The bereaved are frequently judged (or feel judged) about their grief. If they seem too sad, others tend to point out or radiate the need for a kind of "chin up" attitude. If grievers are angry, they are counselled to forgive and forget—in my view, often prematurely and without useful ways in which to process salient issues. Conversely, research shows that if someone who has lost a loved one seems to be doing okay, others question whether they are in denial or perhaps only loved superficially (Bonanno, 2009).

Just after Frans died, our colleague and friend Tom called and reminded me of a passage in psychiatrist Irvin Yalom's (2012) book *Love's Executioner*, where he talks about our suffering as proof of our love for the deceased, and how the internalized belief that we must suffer in order to prove our love can prolong bereavement unnecessarily. Grief counsellor and expert Therese Rando (2012) asks a pertinent question in this regard: "Is it okay for you to be okay?" From whom do we need permission to be "okay"?—For instance, to laugh while in grief, to experience moments of well-being, to notice a sense of relief or hope for a new opportunity?

Later in the process of editing this work, Bonnie, the widow I mentioned before, comments on the complications that social pressure can cause:

> I had this arise for me when a lay meditation teacher suggested my coping well was spiritual bypassing. I am grateful that I have my own internal wisdom voices, and my primary external teacher, to counter this. We do not need to meet the expectations of others.
>
> *(B. Ryan-Fisher, personal communication, July 2019).*

As I consider what Tom shared with me, I notice there is "good pain" (e.g., my sorrow, missing conversations with Frans, noticing my sexual desire for him still arising in my body) that I need only receive and let flow through. There is also "bad pain." The latter I associate with unpleasant pressure in my head, thoughts that verge on rumination, old worries, revisiting angry memories, and a general resurfacing of "issues."

When I feel my body tightening, I know I am in the landscape of "bad pain."

After reading Darla's story, I intuit that by speaking to and with I-positions (and also inviting the witness position—the so-called "meta-position"), I can loosen the "bad pain" and have it flow through like the "good pain" does.

In short, I feel compelled to heal in some of those places that I can no longer work on with the living Frans, so I must do it with the imagined Frans and other internal resources.

Artists often have an intuitive understanding of these dialogical processes. They will say things like, "The tree spoke to me and I had to paint it," or "The painting told me it had to be left alone for a while," or "The poem was dictating itself to me as I walked through the open field, and by the time I wrote it down I realized it was the advice that I needed." Many authors perceive the voices of their fictional characters speaking in their minds, "Some authors even said they could enter into dialogue with their characters and that their characters 'talked back' and argued with them" (Foxwell, 2020, Para 2).

I read the following lines from the Neimeyer and Konopka (2019) chapter: "Some people seem to hold keys to important areas of one's inner landscape. When they die, or they are gone, the key seems to be lost and this area is hardly accessible" (p. 110). Through imagined dialogues, we can build new bridges within the self so that we need not abandon those places in us that were opened by keys that others held or hold.

In order to begin healing, there are a few steps that Neimeyer and Konopka (2019) suggest, and I turn these into a writing exercise for myself. I begin with the prompting questions the authors provide and embark on a written dialogue from there.[3]

1. What is the special quality of the loved one?
2. His unique role in relationship to me?
3. How did I experience myself in relationship to him?
4. What are my dominant feelings in the wake of his death?
5. What would help me with a specific issue around this loss?

(p. 111)

1. Frans's special quality in our relating was his dialogue about life, love, and work. That is pretty general though. Can I get closer and more specific about that? We spent at least 2 hours a day talking about life, work, and personal growth, and in that conversation, we developed a lot of our ideas for research and writing. Dialogue was also a source of our troubles; this sounds ironic, but in a dinner conversation we once had with our career colleagues, someone mentioned an insight that Adler had. I'll paraphrase it here: the thing you at first love most about your partner is the thing you might end up despising most too (e.g., she has a great sense of humor, turns into, all she can do is joke around).
2. Frans's unique relationship to me: lover, spouse, research and writing partner.
3. How did I experience myself in the relationship? Loved, loving, inspired, cared for, challenged, and dismissed.
4. Dominant feelings in the wake of his death: sadness and anger.
5. The specific issue I would like to work on through writing: feeling dismissed in conversations and being angry about this.[4]

After writing out the answers to these five questions, I build in a kind of inner pause. I sit with the responses while postponing any tendency to find answers or draw conclusions. For a less-experienced writer, such a step may require a facilitator who invites the participant to sit for a moment and become acquainted with any bodily sensations and underlying feelings. Then such a facilitator, in my case an inner counsellor, might ask questions like these:

(INNER) COUNSELLOR: Are there any sensations, images, or words that are coming up as you sit with the responses you've written down?

REINEKKE (SENSING): I am getting a sense of a big muddy, oily pile of goop that I will call "the problem."

COUNSELLOR: Let's put a chair out for "Goop"—the messy problem you felt was never resolved between you. There is a chair for the part of you that really wants to be heard on this over here. You can sit here and address Goop. Let's start with these voices and we can add positions as needed. I'll be here with you as a witness.

The mass seems to gurgle and shift a bit like Jabba the Hutt. I note the pile kind of makes me giggle inside—it's so ridiculous-looking and not scary.

REIN-WHO-WANTS-TO-BE-HEARD (RWH): Holy shit, that is a stinky pile of stuff!

GOOP (GURGLES AND BURPS): Yes, that is exactly what this is. (More burps and gurgles).

COUNSELLOR: Take a closer look. What else do you see?

RWH: I see straw mixed in there. Oh, jeez, I can hear Frans saying, "Yes, yes, Reinekke, didn't I always say love is the ability to transform shit into fertilizer?"

Frankly, I don't know whether to laugh or cry. I am seeing this huge pile of shit and Frans's perspective on it. He's excited by it and I thought it was really just a huge pile of unwanted crap. I'm looking closer and I see there are also the sharp points of pitchforks hidden in there. When I tried to clean this up with him, we hit those sharp edges. Sometimes we did move some of the pile with the pitchforks, actually.COUNSELLOR: Is this the same pile of shit it always was?

(This feels like an important question.)

RWH: It looks the same, but I see there is fresh manure piled on top each time, and some of it has ended up in the field.

COUNSELLOR: What happened to the shit you did manage to clean up or use as fertilizer?

RWH (I LOOK TO MY LEFT AND HAVE TO CRY IMMEDIATELY): Oh, my. I see that there are huge fields of golden crops! Gorgeous fields! Our books, our thoughts, our love! It's very stunning. Very stunning what we've created out of that pile of shit and the ground that was there waiting already. (Crying, tender, grateful.)

FRANS: See, my love, it was never the same old shit, different day!! (He's standing right next to me, beaming.)

COUNSELLOR (TO RWH): How is this for you?

RWH: I am feeling his compassion and love. My mind is trying to barge in and judge me for not having the "growth mindset" in this area, but most of me is just grateful to see this. (To Frans): It doesn't mean I liked the way you shouted or got ugly about things we argued about! (To the counsellor): I note a holding on to something—a kind of grudge.

COUNSELLOR: Let's put the grudge in a chair too. What can you tell me about "Grudge?"

RWH: Grudge is like a version of me in the shape of ropes that are tightly wound—especially rope arms tightly across the chest. The words that go with it are . . .

GRUDGE: Damn you for your rude, belligerent, asshole behavior! What gave you the right to be insulting?! (Tightening around itself.)

COUNSELLOR (TO FRANS): So, do you recognize this? This immense frustration, the anger? What is your sense about it?

FRANS (SIGHS): Yes. I see it; I felt it. I was rude at times. I was frustrated. But I never meant it the way that she took it. Well, sometimes I did mean it, but I thought she would forgive and forget. I have a short fuse and have always been a hothead.

GRUDGE: He has very poor manners when he's challenged! I'm not the only one who has said and experienced this.

RWH: I didn't expect perfection, but kind words are really important to me. And if unkind things are said, I want that to be acknowledged. Then I can move past it. My need here is to be heard and to be treated respectfully.

GRUDGE (GROWLS, FACING AWAY, ROPE ARMS STILL CROSSED): He didn't fight fair! And he knows it.

COUNSELLOR: What would help untie you a little, Grudge?

GRUDGE: She DID NOT deserve that shit!

FRANS (SITTING IN A CHAIR NEARBY, LOOKING DEFEATED): I knew she was very angry with me. Yes, I knew. I told her the evening before I died that my own fear had often provoked my reactivity. Negative emotions often scared me.

RWH (SADDENED): He did own his part. But, are there even such things as "negative emotions"? Aren't there only emotions and negative ways to respond to them or painful ways to act them out?

GRUDGE (ARMS SO TIGHT THERE IS SOME TEARING OF SMALL FIBERS OF THE ROPE NEAR SHOULDERS AND ELBOWS): (Mumbling something about injustice in a terse voice.)

COUNSELLOR (TAKES A LONG, DELIBERATE BREATH AND LOOKS AT EVERYONE IN THE DIFFERENT POSITIONS AND CHAIRS): Let's sit with this for a moment. RwH didn't feel heard and wanted to be included and trusted and not blamed. Frans was reactive in an attempt to deflect his fear but was also well-intentioned. Grudge tightened around the problem and Goop got bigger and bigger. What is needed for you to move more of Goop into new fields?

RWH: I'm doing it by writing, like just now. So, I think I can clear Goop over time. It is a kind of harvest, actually, and I look positively on that. Grudge is the one that needs attention.

COUNSELLOR: Grudge, what do you need? What would be good for you? What would the best rope-life look like to you?

GRUDGE: Being woven into a hammock where the tension across the whole of me is even and in harmony. I'd like to hold Reinekke in that hammock so she can feel my firm embrace. I'm the one who holds and rocks. This was about justice!

COUNSELLOR: Tell me more about justice and what that looks like.

GRUDGE: To be fair! To speak kindly! To be honest about agendas.

COUNSELLOR: I'm noticing another voice who wants to speak to this.

JUSTICE: For Reinekke, this is about truth and kindness: the two trees (pillars) of justice. The space that is needed for a dialogue of equals requires an interaction where the intention is to leave the dignity of each speaker intact—always. This is a basic premise in Reinekke's book of Laws for Living. This is not a topic of debate for her, but a basic rule for loving. That it cannot always be achieved, especially with loved ones, is difficult for her to accept.

COUNSELLOR: This insight could reveal a fundamental dimension of this problem. In some families, voices can be raised and insults can be thrown around in the privacy of the home. Members may not like it much, but they can move on and sometimes don't think much of it. They do not necessarily see it as a threat to their bond.

RWH: Whoa! It scared me. It left scratches. It did feel like a threat to our bond!

FRANS: Dear, love, to me it never was! I didn't know I'd frightened you so. I don't condone it, even! But after we'd fight, I'd forget all about it five minutes later as all the good new experiences with you flooded my mind.

RWH (SAID LIKE A SAD REALIZATION): I know, that's what you told me, even in your letter. I see that we were both afraid.

FRANS: Yes, my dear. We were both afraid, mostly because we wanted to be together so much! Remember my last words to you, "I was so lucky with you!"

COUNSELLOR (TAKES A DEEP, RELAXED BREATH AND NODS): It sounds painful and beautiful. Grudge, it sounds like you defended Reinekke from some of the pain.

GRUDGE: That's my job. But (sadly) I didn't do it very well. (Ropes loosening with a sense of futility and surrender.)

FRANS (SAD AND OPEN-HEARTED): Growing up, I never learned how to be or deal with emotions. That's what I learned with Reinekke. I'm so grateful for the last 10 years of my life! Our life and our work were so vibrant because of this!

Some of my friendships with colleagues and others were much deeper in those later years because I learned about having and allowing feelings. My life was always good, but my years with Reinekke were the best! That's what I told everyone!

COUNSELLOR (TO FRANS): What I'm hearing was a need to control emotions and situations that challenged you. And not having experience with emotional regulation, sometimes things got out of hand. (To RwH and Grudge and Goop): Often when someone tries to shut down emotional situations with expressions of anger, they have been taught to not express their needs and they have been doing it to themselves for a long time too. (To RwH): What I'm hearing about you is that unkind words are really scary for you and you associate them with losing love and connection.

RWH: Actually, I associate them with damage and destruction of the relationship, not as a way of blowing off steam. When someone is aggressive like this, to me it is a sign that love cannot be trusted.

COUNSELLOR: How do you feel now?

RWH: I am deeply sad. And filled with love, too. I feel heard. I feel his good intentions as well (deep sigh).

GOOP (LARGE PIECES OF THE SHIT AND MESS ARE FALLING ON THE FLOOR BESIDE THE CHAIR; THE WHOLE PILE IS SHIFTING AND BECOMING A BIT LESS OF A MESS): I'm shaking loose here, don't mind me! There, I feel less heavy now. Ahh . . . yes. Wonderful, more air! New things will grow!

COUNSELLOR: How are you doing over there, Grudge? (Using a very compassionate voice): How are you? What do you need?

GRUDGE: The acknowledgment helps. I would like to give up my job, if you don't mind. I'd rather go hang in the garden on those trees. This was not an easy role and I'm tired and a bit threadbare. You can call me Mr. Curmudgeon now, it's a much nicer name. You can call me at any time you really need me, of course. Consider me your safety net.

Reflections on the Healing Dialogue

Once I'd written the dialogue and let it sit for several days, I began to feel a bit lighter. I also turned the piece into a scholarly article 6 months after Frans's death, doing a full analysis of how I'd changed the narrative in order to reduce my suffering (Lengelle, 2020).

The edgy bits of bereavement turned out to be the unfinished business of our living (not his dying) and it was like pipes had clogged up over the span of our years together. The time and space following Frans's death felt like an opportunity to wash these lodged bits down and out, and to name what they were made of. In the heat of our lived relationship, we were too actively engaged with each other and would become mired in a patterned argument.

If Frans had written about our conflict, I think he would have said this: "I loved Reinekke so much and I don't think she really GOT that. My relationship with my ex was something I honored but didn't think much about. Yes, I did feel guilty and obliged. I wanted to be loyal and my ex had given me a lot. I also didn't want my kids thinking I was some spineless wimp, so I stood up to Reinekke to show them that she didn't control me. In the end, I see she wasn't trying to control me. I was in a tough spot. I had made a mess of things with my marriage and around the time of my divorce, too; mistakes I ended up paying for right until the end." (He said all of these things at various times and I've created a composite of them in this paragraph.)

Death meant aloneness, and aloneness meant time and space for embodied reflection. Indeed, the irony of writing this healing dialogue seems to be that I can posthumously re-engage Frans in a dialogue to "work out" what was creating strain and tension for me, while in life such a dialogue may easily have added to our troubles.

I dare say, "bad pain" clogs the drains, but it can be transformed into "good pain," and then it seems to wash through like the benign waves of grief.

Notes

1 Frans and I had spoken about having actual children together and Claire and Joe were the names we had decided on.
2 Gestalt therapy is "a humanistic, holistic, person-centered form of psychotherapy that is focused on an individual's present life and challenges rather than delving into past experiences." Source: https://www.verywellmind.com/what-is-gestalt-therapy-4584583.
3 A version of the following exercise was published in Lengelle (2020).
4 A note to the reader: "dismissed" is one aspect of a range and richness of relating. All of the dialogue written here is imagined, though some of it is based on things Frans said to me and wrote in his final letter to me—in which he also mentions our conflict and his perspective on it.

3

OUR HISTORY AND PHYSICAL LONGING IN GRIEF

Frans and I met in 1993. I took several education courses with him at the University of Leiden, in The Netherlands, where I did my Masters. I researched and wrote my thesis project in Calgary and Edmonton and he supervised the project at a distance. We faxed many messages back and forth about the work I was doing.

I was inspired by his lectures. I liked how he broke rank with a lot of conventional thinking in education; he was not politically correct. He'd been a hippy in the first student protests in the left-wing city of Nijmegen, where coincidentally I was born around the same time he was raising hell there with his comrades.

I had a kind of "rock-star crush" on him. I felt it while in class and forgot about it on the way home, knowing it was unrealistic to have any serious interest in one's instructor. I usually had a boyfriend anyway.

Frans eventually let me know he had feelings for me as well. This surprised me and was a bit confusing. On a street corner near the social science faculty building of our university in Leiden, he once said, "If I wasn't married, we would already be living together"—which at the time made me angry, as it seemed both a full and a very empty statement.

His first gift to me was a CD of Fauré's Requiem which he was singing with his choir at the time. I still have it 27 years later, and now it seems poignant that he gave me music that is intended to offer peace and sleep to the souls of the dead.

He often phoned me in those early years and would tell me he loved me; he was expressive and enthusiastic, but there was no way forward for us. I was in my 20s and hoped that after my studies, I would return to Canada and settle down to have a family. He was in his forties, with two young daughters. I once visited his home and met his then 2- and 6-year-old and his wife. I did so deliberately so I would see the reality of his life.

His learning about relationships had happened in a paradoxical context: the way he lived seemed to combine old-world models of lifelong marriage (with mostly traditional gender roles) and 60s experimentation. Relationships, he would own, were not his priority, and he enjoyed his freedom while being taken care of by a steady first girlfriend who had become his wife. He was much more interested in politics and education than in personal relationships, and pursued his studies and later his work diligently.

In 1995, I left for Canada, and I met Keath in January 1996. We married in December of that year and Sophia was born the following October. Frans would reach out to me twice a year, but it was difficult to maintain contact. What would start as a friendly exchange and mutual update would always turn into Frans expressing his love and sexual feelings. Although I felt attracted to him still, I wanted to honor my marriage, and it made me mad that Frans didn't seem to honor either his or mine.

Near the end of his married life, Frans used the metaphor of a tree that had become hollowed out over the years but still looked good on the outside. "She and I had stopped communicating about things that mattered years ago. A good storm was enough to blow it down," he said. My married life with Keath was a safe haven for me, but it too had fatal flaws, related to my career drive and a restlessness I could not name. I would say to Keath, "I feel un-bloomed," and with Frans, I would bloom, both professionally and intellectually. The latter was the fuel for our sexual passion too.

Some might say Frans and I were the storm in each other's imperfect world, but I believe it is more accurate to say that our mutual desire to grow personally, professionally, and emotionally ultimately drew us together. He used to say, "You had the key that opened me up," and I too felt I had opened with him. Despite our strong and abiding appreciation for our first spouses and the happy family lives we had both led, we were undeniably drawn together. I divorced in 2009 and he did so a year later.

In the fall of 2006, Frans and I began work on our first scholarly article, he from The Netherlands and me in Canada. In those early months of our steady correspondence, he e-mailed me a history of his love relationships and he asked for mine. He wanted us to know each other; in his view, one's partner relationships and lovers held a world of information about how a person is and what they value. This seemed ironic, as by his own admission he had reflected little on this domain of his life. I saw his request as an invitation to go into the depths together. It was as if he indeed wanted to know himself and me in a new way; he had never shared the full history with anyone. I sent him my history as well.

As the years progressed, we liked to describe what we had as a connection of "head, heart, and belly." While our other significant relationships had been a combination of two of the three, with each other, we felt we had found all of them. I think now of these words by C. S. Lewis (1961) about his wife, Joy: "The most precious gift that marriage gave me was this constant impact of something very close and intimate yet all the time unmistakably other, resistant—in a word, real" (p. 18).

Frans and I had our symbolic marriage ceremony on September 16, 2018, 2 months before he died. We finally toasted to our love in this more official way and we recorded it for our closest friends and our four daughters. We were already common-law spouses and felt married, but we did not marry in the church or legally. Frans was my life partner, he was my big love, and he was my spouse, but he had not become my husband on paper, though he had asked me many times to tie the knot.

Over the years, when I asked myself the question, "Would I like to legally marry Frans?" I would feel for the answer inside. We did not share biological children and there was no need for this step, but I felt Frans's first marriage was not completed emotionally. I encouraged him to go talk to his ex-wife several times, in part to give her what I felt was her proper due. I felt he had, in key ways, been half-hearted in that relationship; he admitted to having been reliable but not fully committed.

Though I did not doubt his devotion to me or our commitment to each other, instinctively something inside me said, "No," and I stayed true to that. Like all relationships, ours was imperfect, fulfilling in many ways, and our trust was shaken at times. (I revisit the topic of trust near the end of the book; new insights grew as I wrote and moved through grief.)

In the 10-minute movie we made of our wedding, Frans was very frail and spoke tearfully of his gratitude for our years together. I spoke through my tears as well, beginning with all our work accomplishments, showing the pile of books, and thanking him for all we had shared in our partner love. We toasted to our love with watered-down Orangina, as that was the only thing he could still drink in those final months.

The things I miss most now are our animated dialogues and the intense passion and deep affection we shared.

FRANS: I remember how we used to get into bed with one another each evening. Skin to skin.

REINEKKE: Every piece of clothing seemed like one too many. You once said making love to me was like the first time every time.

FRANS: Yes, that's how it was.

***

Grief Observed and Physical Longing

C. S. Lewis (1961) writes as I feel, "For those few years she and I feasted on love, every mode of it—solemn and merry, romantic and realistic, sometimes as dramatic as a thunderstorm, sometimes as comfortable and unemphatic as putting on your soft slippers" (pp. 10–11).

What will happen to me because of this? The question scares me. I feel the void it opens viscerally: my head is suddenly hollow; my adrenal glands pump out their fear.

I sit longing for physical touch. In the not being hugged or held, an existential shudder arises.

The next poem happens as my mind reaches beyond now. The words began to emerge after a conversation with a friend last night. We spoke about not knowing.

On futures

My imagination
throws spears into the future
possibilities on fluttering ribbons
they don't hit any targets
they aren't meant to
in fact they find no spot to land at all
but that is what imagination is for, my love
we learned that together
it is the invisible space between hope and despair.

I was able to buy an e-version of the book *A Grief Observed* by C. S. Lewis (1961) for $0.99, and began to read. Friday nights are apparently bad for those recently bereaved or single (both divorced or widowed), and I was alone and a bit worried about what the evening might bring or not.

Lewis (1961) writes about the death of his wife Joy. I highlighted bits of the text. In the first third of the book, there are many lines I want to leave a digital margin note on. Unlike Didion, Lewis expresses his hurt and yearning in physical ways. He writes, "No one ever told me that grief felt so like fear. I am not afraid, but the sensation is like being afraid. The same fluttering in the stomach, the same restlessness …" (p. 7).

In response, I write, "I will never hold his warm body again" and "He has been silent for days now … For days."

I reread the lines in Lewis's (1961) book that have the most resonance:

> There are moments, most unexpectedly, when something inside me tries to assure me that I don't really mind so much, not so very much, after all. Love is not the whole of a man's life. I was happy before I ever met her. I've plenty of what are called "resources." People get over these things. Come, I shan't do so badly. One is ashamed to listen to this voice but it seems for a little to be making out a good case. Then comes a sudden

> jab of red-hot memory and all this "common sense" vanishes like an ant in the mouth of a furnace." (p. 18)

Yesterday. I went for a massage. My shoulders and neck are stiff. I need more of this and it reminds me of not being touched. The kids hug me, but no one touches me.

C. S. Lewis (1961) again: "There is one place where her absence comes locally home to me, and it is a place I can't avoid. I mean my own body. It had such a different importance while it was the body of her lover" (p. 13).

He also writes, "By writing it all (all?—no: one thought in a hundred) I believe I get a little outside it" (p. 12).

There are many bridges to the beloved. One of them is sorrow, another is sexual yearning and fond memory. And then there is poetry.

I note an observation about the dialogue I fear(ed) missing most now that Frans is dead. (I have to write "Frans is dead" sometimes to see it in print.) The observation is that the dialogues I am having are still rich. The internal one first off and the external ones too. And there are moments of intense gratitude.

> A neighbor
> passes me a card
> through my doorway,
> wordless
> the hand of generosity,
> reading it now
> an afterthought.

Such poems can create from gratitude something quite tangible. I imagine I might give instruction on writing poetry, but then I stop myself.

I don't want to provide exercises or things to try. This seems paradoxical because I am a writing teacher. Why don't I want to?

I don't want to be prescriptive. I don't want to act like my way through grief is in any way "the way." I imagine readers will end up writing their own medicine and follow their own hunches, whether my story has compelled them to or not.

Some people have been dropping me little notes, wanting to know how I am, sometimes adding suggestions on how I might grieve better and I am a bit averse to anything prescriptive myself.

The Zen masters say it well: don't speak it to completion.

I don't know how I am supposed to grieve but I trust my intuition and my body. If I am writing too much and crying too little, my body will begin to hurt. I trust that. I am not expecting or rejecting anything.

I do know that, right now, I would like to be held in an intimate embrace.

***

Sex

> Drifting away
>
> This morning you talk about your leaving again
> then go on to proof our last chapter
> and check the flight tracker
> waiting for the other beloveds to get home
> In the afternoon you nap in a holiday chair
> it's more upright than the one at home
> but you make the most of it
> In the evening we almost make love
> but stretched above me
> you look down at your body
> and cry seeing this frail and ugly stranger

The last time Frans and I had sex was in June 2018. I miss making love. In July 2018, on our last holiday, we tried to have sex but it was not possible. I held Frans as he cried about the way his own body looked to him; he was horrified by it. Nothing about our naked closeness turned me off; I felt compassion for his suffering. On that summer night, I accepted that having sex was over, though our intimacy continued until the end.

My memories of our passion and my sexual desire have not ended with Frans's death.

Yet, this is not something you read about in most widow books. Sex is surprisingly absent from the bereavement literature too. Is this another vestige of implicit and misplaced decorum?

After completing the first draft of this manuscript, I looked again for grief resources to analyze and reflect on my experiences using pertinent and up-to-date information. I found Joan Price's (2019) book, *Sex after Grief: Navigating Your Sexuality after Losing Your Beloved*, which was published in August 2019. She begins the book with a quote by two other widows who acknowledge this gap in the literature, "I read Joan Didion's and Joyce Carol Oates's classic memoirs about mourning a beloved husband. They are lauded as unflinching, but in their combined nearly 700 pages, there is no mention of the type of sexual bereavement I was experiencing. The unspoken message, as I received it: Keep your mouths shut about sex" (p. 9).

Don't speak ill of the dead seems an important internalized rule, as does *Don't speak of desire*. You are supposed to be grieving, not horny. Yet, is this not also a central part of having and being a spouse? The physical relationship. Whether it's a passionately sexual one or something else, we long for our partner and the body does not forget. I at times feel the intense pain of loss when I am aroused. It is difficult to be grieving while fully alive. My mind automatically goes to memories of Frans when in wordless terms I ask, *Where is my lover?* And it feels both utterly natural and tragic to fantasize about him.

This morning, I awaken after a partly broken sleep and feel a yearning and sexual desire for Frans. In my mind, I go to scenes of us as lovers. We had strong sexual chemistry that was fed by our impassioned conversations. I fantasize about him as I lie there; I imagine we're in an intense embrace where we want to consume each other. Images from memory and fantasy mix and flip back and forth in my mind. I am not surprised I can still be so aroused by images of him, as all our years together this desire never waned. Yet, now, knowing he is dead, my desire is part of the most visceral heartbreak.

Of course, I cry loudly after I come. I say his name and reach to his side of the bed. There is a heart pillow there that used to grace our bed in The Netherlands; the velvet fabric is somehow always colder than I expect it to be.

Doctors don't tell you that opioids kill many a desire, not just for food. When Frans began to take the opioids in June, his once active and playful sex drive disappeared. He was a very sexual man and took lots of initiative with me, so this change felt very much out of character. I asked him if in his mind he was still sexual, but he said no, though he could still look at me and perceive me as attractive, and we were still able to share sexual intimacy. Even in the final months, I told him of my desire and he lay beside me, speaking to arouse me as he'd done many times. Wonderful kisses and warm smiles followed.

Who speaks of this?

In the stack of over 20 books that I read on grief and loss in the first year after Frans's death, authors touch on the physical pain of grief and the yearning for connection through a sense of smell or visual objects (like sleeping in a spouse's clothing or kissing a photo), but again, virtually nothing is said about ongoing sexual desire. It is only in Ellis's (1995, 2018) autoethnography and later in Price's (2019) book that I read of a couple's intense physical attraction being remembered and mourned after death.

Fortunately for me, I find out I am not alone in my experience of ongoing sexual feelings during Frans's illness and after his death. The widow on the plane in September 2018 told me that on the Facebook group she belongs to for widows, women do speak of this continued arousal. She explained, "Of course many of us were sexually active and engaged with our husbands before they became ill (or died suddenly), and so we miss that."

The man in my life is gone, but I am still very much alive and life is stronger than our opinions about what we should or shouldn't feel when we face our beloved's illness and death, and the aftermath. I spoke to several female friends about my desire and was heartened to find that none of them were surprised.

In the months that followed this writing, I also got up the courage to ask a kind man to hold me, which he did.

I will write about this later.

***

Going to See Friends

December 9, 2018

Saturday, Maya and I drive to Calgary in the afternoon. The roads are clear of snow and we decide to surprise Sophia and meet at our friend Ellie's party. It's a housewarming, Christmas potluck dinner. Her new apartment is a suite in a 1909-built home across from a historical building and museum called the "Lougheed Mansion" in the middle of downtown Calgary.

Ellie's place is like an English teahouse with books, proper silverware, a long table filled with food, a friendly fat black cat named George, and Ellie's chiming voice and good cheer. We love Ellie. Being there feels like being home with family.

I thought I would fade by 9:00 p.m. (my regular bedtime now), but new energy arrives as I stay present and allow moments where an inner void seems to pass through me like a ghost. The eerie echo comes and goes. I cherish the listening, hearing others, being heard, sturdy hugs from Ellie's friends. There are about 15 people at the party who come and go in different shifts. One is a bald, smiling 1-year-old girl who reminds me of my own girls at that age.

A mutual friend comes to sit with us later. He is an introverted and soft-spoken man. I met him first in the fall of 2017 at an art opening. He asks the girls about their lives. I notice he listens well. Even Maya, who is generally quiet, opens up to him.

I tell my friend Marlene about the visit later by text and she writes, "It sounds like this encounter is healing a piece of you." I notice I felt warmed by this man's presence and at ease.

Ellie's girlfriends also ask me how I am and talk to the kids—they've heard that I am newly widowed. I take time to also get to know each of them a bit better. I ask where they work, if they are partnered, whether they are originally from Calgary.

Later I can't remember any of it; this is apparently normal for grieving brains.

I do remember their names and their hearty hugs.

***

Maya and I stay in a hotel two blocks from Ellie's and we meet her for breakfast again in the morning. We take some pictures at our table, the shots are of the girls, me with the girls, Ellie and me, Sophia sewing at the table, and Maya drawing in her sketchbook. Today is a day off writing (mostly) and driving back to Edmonton in the afternoon.

I am conscious again of living in the moment—not in the past where we were, not in the future where we will not be, but now where living invites me.

Driving past the Edmonton International Airport on the way back into town, I cry for a few minutes. That's where I would have picked up Frans in another week or so.

Maya rubs my head and neck.

"This car is a safe zone for crying," she says to me.

***

We stop at Boston Pizza as we drive into Edmonton, though we have promised each other we will start cooking at home after all this eating out. We get home before 7:00 p.m. and both retire to our cozy rooms.

My room is now the corner bedroom. I no longer sleep in the master bedroom. I arranged this on purpose in August 2018, months before Frans died, when I flew home to Canada for a job interview. In those weeks away from Frans, knowing he would never be returning to our home in Canada (and I would only be returning after his death), I switched the bedrooms. I gave Maya the largest room with her own sink and toilet. I cleared Frans's office, desk, and desk chair and stored his papers and computer in the smallest (guest) room.

I didn't want to come home to the utterly familiar in the desolation of his gone-ness. I didn't want the geography of my house to confront me in every hallway wander with the way it had been. I took his underwear and t-shirts out of the drawers and put them neatly on the shelves in the laundry room. I hung his winter coat downstairs where I kept and would still have his shoes, even a year after his death.

I didn't want to come home after a long flight and unpack my clothes into the teak dresser and shock myself with the sight of his clothing. I wanted to come into fresh spaces. The fresh spaces of a woman's life; a single life; a life that would be filled with enough grief.

I go to bed, still writing.

In my journal, this appears: "He would have been here in the middle of the month and that feels stolen from me." I note that the word stolen is a victim word. It seems to imply that something or someone did this to me.

> No, it happened.
> The world owes me nothing.
> Again, no one and
> No-thing promised a long life together.

I meet the feelings of emptiness. One can be bereft in an open and nonresistant way. I feel very grateful for my daughters and the Calgary friends.

And I am thankful for one month of leave from work. I keep up with the house, I do the laundry, I even e-mail some students who are waiting. The only thing I seem to not be able to do is to cook for myself.

Frans joked that I would support us financially once I got a tenure-track job. The first, and last, time he said that, I replied, "Yes, and once that happens, you can cook for me." It was one of the rare occasions that he seemed dumbfounded and didn't reply. In Dutch, when this happens, we say "he had a mouth full of teeth." I believe his having lived comfortably for so long in traditional roles but being, at the same time, fully aware, as a sociologist, of gender equity that he was genuinely stumped at what to say.

Occasionally I still joke with people about his dislike of cooking and the fact that my job started on January 1, 2019, and Frans had already died 6 weeks before. In the middle of October, we knew I had gotten the full-time job; in the middle of November, he was gone.

It seems he really didn't want to cook.

***

Reflections and Friends

December 11, 2018

Yesterday was a heavy day of writing. I wrote about a difficult time in my life with Frans and later saved it in a separate file. It had to be written. It makes sense of our bond and what I am learning from some of the struggles.

After writing, I went to dinner with my friend Angela. We shared 2 hours of conversation about life, loss, and growth. I vented a lot. She lifted my spirits by listening non-judgmentally.

I drove home carefully on the icy roads and went to bed early as I tend to do on weeknights.

My friends bring me much joy these days.

Earlier in the day another friend visited. This reminds me to be here now: present moment, present moment, present moment. While writing the past and future is part of this project, living happens here and now, and there is peace in that.

***

> The sun on winter tree
> brought back the memory
> of another season
> That season is over,
> but the light remembered it.
>
> December 12, 2018

This morning I thought of the Sufi poet Rumi who talks about a place where we no longer have to speak of the dualities of right and wrong, but that we can meet and embody a place where we have transcended such ideas. I also think of my friend Margot's "Sawbonna" and the idea of seeing the other and recognizing our shared humanity instead of forgiveness, which she calls "the other F word". I aspire to more enlightened perspectives but know striving to get there is futile.

My sister Leo's friend Debbie from our women's Tribe group visits. She brings a book, a meditation CD, the essential oil "Release," a sweet card, and mainly herself. We speak about the way in which we talk to ourselves—how inhospitable communication from others can reflect something back about ourselves.

"How are you talking to yourself?", she asks.

I notice a question that recurs: where did I go wrong? Where did we go wrong? I mean in those places we had trouble hearing each other.

The answer to my question is not the interesting part, but rather, why I would ask this question and not a different one? It's a refrain under my questing about the unresolved.

If I'm trying to do things right and think in those terms, there is bound to be a wrong in there. What if I asked a question beyond this duality—for instance, what did I most want, in the end? If I had received that, what would that have given me? How can I give it to myself—not just as a thought or intention but as a felt experience?

As I speak with Debbie, an image of a strong woman comes through—a form of me that stood and witnessed my struggle. It seems to be affirming, "What you went through did not go unseen and unnoticed."

Self-compassion, you might call it.

Empathy, even.

Later that day, ordinary life and its simple goodness calls.

I go out with Maya to Ikea in the evening. She is looking for Christmas decorations for her little artificial Christmas tree that she has named "Firdinand." We find three golden hedgehogs, three red-breasted little birds, and wrapping paper that tells stories. The veggie hotdog she has at Ikea tastes surprisingly good, she tells me. When we get home, I heat the chicken soup I made in September and froze for my return. I did groceries today, but real cooking still waits.

Before bed, I indulge a little in answering more cheerful questions, like where did I go right?

> Where did we go right?
> We loved each other.
> We did superb work together.
> We smiled a lot.
> We kissed a lot.
> We gave each other a lot.
> We always returned to the conversation.
> We stayed together until the very end.
> We wanted to stay together—even when it was hard.
> We could own some of our blind spots.
> We learned.

> We argued. We debated. On some things, we simply did not agree.
> There was much gentleness too.
> We had many wonderful people surrounding us—still do.
> We have beautiful daughters—two + two.
> We had plans—they didn't all come true—but we had them.
> The happy ending was, "I choose you … even though I have to go."
> The happy ending was, "I choose you … even though you had to go."

Dear Frans, do you have anything to add?

FRANS: No, that's about it, my love. I'm still with you. Keep writing. I know you will edit the book with all your new insights in mind. It will be a book of love. There is nothing wrong.

***

By late evening, another light bulb burns out. This time, it is the one in the lamp above my work chair. This is the third bulb gone since the day of his death. It's a special large bulb and I order three replacements online. I am a bit superstitious: lights burning out as a sign that Frans has been to visit me, as if to tell me there is a shift of some kind happening. This one feels big. Almost a year later, I read Paxton's (2018) book on grief and continued bonds. As a social scientist himself, he struggles with the idea of "signs" like this, but then concludes that, because they are experienced as meaningful, even by the atheists and agnostics among us, they should be included in studying bereavement.

I walked in the bright sunshine today and felt strengthened. I woke up half scared, half angry. I stayed with it and that helped me cry so some of the pressure released.

I have called Frans my "Imago relationship," a term I read in the work of marriage counsellors, authors, and married couple Harville Hendrix and Helen LaKelly Hunt (Hendrix, 2007). It is the dynamic in a spousal relationship in which you become entangled because of childhood wounding. It often means one encounters one's parents and the unresolved issues one has with them. This doesn't mean the relationship is dysfunctional, but that suffering ensues as people act out their childhood wounding with each other. One encounters one's self and the rules that were tacitly made about living that, clearly, the other person does not always share.

My mother could be harsh with her words; my father could be vague with emotional/relational boundaries and had weird and interesting theories about how relationships could be. In my relationship with Frans, I encountered both my parents at once—also the good parts, like his *joie de vivre*, his curiosity, his being organized, and having a clean and tidy home like my Mom. His being intellectual, loving dialogue, being fun-loving, original and unconventional in his thinking, having visitors of all kinds, and exploring ideas are exactly how my Dad was.

Although we did go to two different counsellors for a few sessions to look at some of the issues we were encountering, we never got the chance to do in-depth couple's counselling to untangle and understand what didn't work in our dynamic.

I store my wedding ring with Frans's in a small bag with a lock of his hair that I'd asked for when he was in Edmonton for the last time. As I put things away, I come across a letter from him, from June 2018, that he left in my night table knowing he would never be back in our Canada again. He writes, "You have given me a chance to really love and that is something I'll be eternally grateful for."

***

December 14, 2018

I slept 9 hours last night. Maya had a fun time decorating her "Fir-dinand" tree yesterday evening. We will all decorate the big one together in the next few days. Sophia and her partner, Caleb, will also be home for Christmas.

I was about to start on the writing this morning when I read my latest e-mails. There was a long one from Ellie and I wanted to respond. I wanted to tell her about my anger and how it is shifting. She too is processing a relational loss and we are the same age. She writes,

> I've read recently that more and more women are single in their middle ages and choosing to be so and are happier for it. We give so much to our partners, spouses and children that we forget who we are and how to discover ourselves and blossom within ourselves. That's not to say that there is no benefit in being coupled because obviously there is, but that there's also a depth to knowing oneself. Isn't there whole industries dedicated to finding oneself? Let's hope we discover until the day we die because the story is so interesting!
>
> *(E. Talbot, personal communication, December 14, 2018)*

I recognize the promise of Ellie's words, but that didn't happen fully until August 2019 when my life seemed to flower open, fueled in part by grief's collateral gratitude. The idea of being single began to feel wholly comfortable by then and it was a refreshing surprise I could not have imagined at the end of 2018.

I began in August to consciously note a number of advantages of not having a partner: I could plan my own trips, I could sleep undisturbed, I could make my own decisions, I didn't have to worry about financial entanglements, I did not have to think about ex-wives and blended families, and could spend uninterrupted time with my girls.

***

The Ego

There is a part of me that wants to believe in Heaven. Is it possible for an agnostic to do so with conviction? I spend a full week of evenings late in the spring of 2019 watching YouTube videos on near-death experiences. It was soothing to do that. It gave me hope that maybe Frans's death is not the end. That we might meet again or that he can send me messages from the "other side." I allowed the hardcore scientist in me to take a break and imagine.

I want to believe that the dead are without ego. That they get things in a nonjudgemental way; that their anguish is over and they want ours to be over too. It may just be a back-to-the-womb dream, but I will borrow it as a source of comfort.

Leonard Cohen's song, "Bird on the Wire" seemed like the perfect ode to me yesterday. I imagined Frans singing it to me. It wasn't about him getting down on his knees to apologize but about me remembering his humanity and ultimately mine. I could have sung the song to him as well.

REINEKKE (R): Frans, now would be a good time to talk. Are you there?

FRANS (F): I've been wanting to interrupt you all morning, because I see you have been suffering. I don't want you to suffer! I do see how you've suffered. I see how fear made us both reactive. The pattern we had was very painful. I do see that, *liefje* [darling], I do!!

R: That is a relief to hear.

F: You don't have to keep worrying about "Frans was good, Frans was bad, or I do appreciate him, but I didn't appreciate that about him."

R: Well, that's what's showing up. Anger, acceptance, gratitude, and nonacceptance. That's how it is. Dual mind. I'm not there yet, so I'm trying to accept the here.

Now it seems he's sending me a picture of the trip we made on the ferry to Staten Island.

F: I see us just going back and forth to Staten Island on the ferry. Back and forth and back and forth over the water.

R: Yes, we didn't stay on Staten Island but we had to make the trip if we wanted to see the Statue of Liberty. We went back and forth once and it seemed futile, but we did get a taste of liberty. We didn't actually make it to the statue, but we had a taste. We knew it was there and that it was meaningful.

F: (nods thoughtfully): Yes, my love.

R: I am a bit afraid to admit that I miss you.

F: Why not admit it? I miss you too! I miss our life. I had to go so quickly. I wish I could have stayed longer.

R: Yes, I read that today in your letter—about you wanting to stay longer. [In his actual letter to me, he said 15 years longer.] You were sorry you had to go.

F: I didn't want to leave you alone. I want to comfort you.

R: You're doing that now. You always gave me lots of attention. Lots and lots—that was nice—very nice. I did feel wanted and special and yours.

F: You were mine. I was yours. That all really happened for us.

R: I feel a little more courageous. Less angry.

F: Yes, I can feel it too.

R (THROUGH TEARS): I'm vulnerable, sad, just letting that be there too.

F: I'm holding you.

Soft tears as I type and reread the dialogue. Sorrow.

***

Moments of Normal

I cooked again last night! I went grocery shopping and there is fresh fruit in the bowl this morning, too. Equilibrium is returning along with sorrow and tears.

I could finally write, "I miss you."

A successful good-bye is paired with good memories, is something I once heard said by German psychotherapist Bert Hellinger.

Writing was very tough at the start of this week and I at times wondered why writers torture themselves in their drive to be honest and clear and carve some meaning out of the human condition.

In the end, I believe writer Anne Lamott (1994) has the answer to this question and says it more eloquently than I can:

> Becoming a writer is about becoming conscious. When you're conscious and writing from a place of insight and simplicity and real caring about the truth, you have the ability to throw the lights on for your reader. He or she will recognize his or her life and truth in what you say, in the pictures you have painted, and this decreases the terrible sense of isolation that we have all had too much of. (pp. 225–226)

Or maybe it's best to use her better-known and less self-important quote on the matter: "We are a species that needs and wants to understand who we are. Sheep lice do not seem to share this longing, which is one reason why they write so little" (Lamott, 1994, p. 3).

***

Ingredients for Living and More Ordinary Days

December 15, 2018

Suzanne, a former student of mine, sends me a few scans of a book chapter by one of my own first writing teachers, Eunice Scarfe. Eunice has been widowed twice, and writes that

> The ancient Greeks believed there were three stages of grief: the death itself, the burial, and the reintegration of the bereaved. The coming away from the edge of the grave is another way of putting it. The return to the living and to living … How do the bereaved return from the grave? Through story, I believe. "Turn and return" I call it, a cyclical process of remembering death and turning from it.
>
> *(Scarfe, 2002, p. 270)*

Yesterday I wrote in a steady and relaxed fashion and read the reflections on Eunice's losses. She writes beautifully and unsentimentally; she too mentions a first wife not recognizing the relationship she had. My colleague Katrin Den Elzen sends me her full-length widow story later in spring; I begin reading it.

When I consider again whether I will join a widows' group, I read Eunice's and Katrin's words and see that I am already part of one. Other widows I speak to and read about and many other authors and researchers on loss are part of this group. I do not even need to sit with them in physical form to feel I have benefited.

The kids are all home for Christmas now and the house bubbles with energy and joy. I feel blessed and very clear and present.

Today mother chauffeur duties call as well as dinner plans with a friend and the kids. Sophia, my oldest, has decided it is going to be shepherd's pie. Frans would have loved to be here now for these simple moments.

I imagine his presence and smile.

***

4

GRIEF'S EBB AND FLOW

During the 2 weeks before Christmas and the 2 weeks after, with kids at home for the holidays, the work of writing and reflecting is interrupted. When I revised the book sometime later, I noticed this section seemed more fragmented and some of the pieces were more like logbook entries than the story or my reflections on grief and writing.

There were days I could do deep work and there were days when I couldn't. Nonetheless, I decided to leave in the shorter snippets to show grief's ebb and flow and how life continually called me back to normal living.

Journal Entries

December 16, 2018

Frans died exactly a month ago. I type that line and just look at it for a bit. One year ago, he was flying to Edmonton and Facebook reminds me of that fact. "Happily into the new year together," I wrote in December 2017.

I am glad the children are home with me, though, at times, I am suddenly very tired and relish going to bed early. In bed alone, I can be with my sorrow, and that fosters a kind of closeness to Frans that I am still longing for. If I cannot meet him in real time, I can meet him in dreamtime.

There are many rituals for remembering the dead. The Irish get together a month later and hold a kind of wake again. The Japanese do something each week for 49 days. Some say that we must remember each year on the day or every third or seventh year. I read all of this in Eunice Scarfe's (2002) chapter.

In the (secular) West we have few set rituals, it turns out. What do we do?

Over the next several months, it turns out, I will visit Frans's grave. I will light candles for him on his birthday and put photos on a makeshift altar in the living room. I do a number of things that could be considered "ritual," as if to create a frame for grief. It's like grief needs room to be displayed and to be contained.

Yesterday, Marlene, one of my oldest friends, came to visit. We laughed and spoke candidly, as is our way. There are days that almost feel normal.

The self-talk goes like this at the moment: Rein, these are difficult times. If you accept them as they are, they make you stronger. A sense of humor is a must.

The kids and their friends didn't know I could do accents. I did a Scottish one at the table last night. Dynamics change when someone leaves the table of life and there is more room for our "other" voices.

The shepherd's pie was wonderful.

We added Red Devil cheese to the mashed potatoes.

***

December 17

This weekend the house was filled with activity, good cheer, and food. The university kids are enjoying their break and everyone is enjoying each other. The kids play frequent card games and their friends come and go. Sophia works on a number of sewing projects that I find lying on the kitchen table or on the couch, and that I carefully put aside. I call myself a "micro-cleaner" (as opposed to waiting for things to pile up and then binge clean). This act of constant tidying seems to keep me sane. I like clean surfaces. Eventually, I collect wayward socks, sweaters, and the sewing project into a laundry basket at the top of the stairs so that all the chaos is in one place. I see a parallel here with writing.

In quiet moments I sit, and always Frans drifts back into my thoughts. Before bed, I write a short conversation with him. What comes out of it is a simple version of what he would always write: *Ik hou van jou lieve vrouw van me.* (The felt translation goes like this: I love you, sweet woman of mine.)

I re-realized something in conversation with a Dutch colleague of ours yesterday. When you lose a spouse to death, they are still such a part of you. You don't feel like you're un-partnered. No love is lost.

Today is for reading and studying and taking notes. I continue to look for resources on grief. Both those that speak to someone's personal journey as well as the more analytical kind that reflect on the process itself. Reading a part of the expressive arts and grieving book by Thompson and Neimeyer (2014) is on the agenda today.

***

December 18

Morning

I start with a cup of tea
and self-compassion
slowly does it

Afternoon

The sunshine, a walk, my neighbor sanding my driveway, the kids hanging with me (me with them, actually), a colleague's kind voice, my Mom's loving words, a conversation with a Dutch friend of Frans's—all of these things raise my spirits. I also did a little work and was the chauffeur for kids' Christmas shopping.

Mornings are the hardest for me, though frequently still productive. I think it's because when I wake up my mind immediately begins to scan for things that are "not in order." Reflective-writing expert Jenny Moon (1999) refers to using writing as a form of reflection as "mental housekeeping" and I see that my desire for keeping my house orderly is a direct result of my desire to feel and be ordered inside. Anything that feels incomplete with Frans now, I seem to perceive as "out of order." The moment I take in that insight, the need to get it "ordered" feels less acute.

Advice to the bereaved (to myself, actually): do not try to change life retroactively with misguided thought experiments. There are downsides to being a creative intellectual. I am again referring to the residue of unfinished business. I admit that I am still wrestling with bits of it that float through my consciousness.

Best not to draw any conclusions but just let whatever worry there is be there and also watch it drift past again. Since writing the Goop, Grudge, and Rein-who-wants-to-be-Heard dialogue, I note I speak about the issues as more loose, floating, and drifting past, instead of stuck. That's progress.

My friend Margot reminds me, "Consider one's humanity …" An internal voice chimes in almost immediately, "But isn't that just copping out?" The microcleaner doesn't easily release her post.

There are pitfalls to self-reflection when there is a major life change. Especially when that self-reflection also involves blaming someone (and myself) or a desire for some perfect understanding. I am reminded of an article I wrote with Tom and Frans about the dangers of self-reflection as applied in a careers context (Lengelle et al., 2016). A common issue is that self-reflection can easily lead to rumination, and in the article, we report on researchers' findings that "people who have a tendency to self-reflect find it difficult to disengage from this process in the face of adverse circumstances, unfavorable outcomes, and negative events in their lives" (Elliott & Coker, 2008, p. 101).

There is still some part of me that imagines I had more control than I did, and if I sit in that half-comforting illusion, I also touch on guilt in the form of the would-haves and the could-haves.

Could I have seen his illness earlier and got him to a doctor?

Was my way of viewing the situation too perfectionistic?

Did our stress give him cancer?

***

December 19

I slept well last night. Mostly, I'm able to keep the inner dialogue to "follow the out breath" and "what is here and now"?

This is how the self-talk sounds: what will the next thought be, let it emerge, you don't have to believe anything you think. Just watch the passing clouds.

Instead of focusing on my inside world to the exclusion of what is happening around me, I deliberately make note of a few things I see around me.

1. Sophia, making her own socks (I joke with her that this saves us a little now she is off on a student exchange in Maine in the new year).
2. Noticing the bounty of food: chocolate, cheese, potatoes, and the willing hands of the kids who are cooking for me when I don't seem to be able to.

I am still writing short dialogues with Frans in quiet moments. I go back in time and remember how we met, how we reconnected, and how it has come to this.

***

December 20

Frans and I had first reconnected in person in April 2007, and in the spring of 2009, Keath and I separated and began our divorce. Frans announced his own divorce in July 2009, but didn't show signs of actually following through until a year later. He continued to live with his wife and for several months after his announcement, they even slept in the same bed. His words and his actions did not line up, though he tried mightily to convince me otherwise.

By November 2010, having struggled for over a year to communicate with him about what our possible future might look like, I broke up with him. When we got back together in the summer of 2011, I remember him saying that he at first didn't know what I was referring to when I spoke about having an open dialogue, making decisions together, and whether we might have a home of our own.

His own words were, "I realized sitting upstairs in my home office for those months, and at first wanting to blame you for leaving, that I had never fully committed to any woman in my life. That is what you were asking of me. Finally, I crossed the emotional bridge to commitment. I am so glad I did."

A few days ago, I wrote over 30 pages about the period of our relationship when we were apart for 10 months in 2010–2011. I cut the pages out of the draft manuscript afterward. I saved them in a separate file. They felt ugly and disheartening. I don't want to visit that chapter of our lives now, especially not in light of his death after having had good years together.

I had embarked on writing this part of our history in an attempt to be complete in my telling of our relational past, but I see now that it was counterproductive. In reflecting on the process of doing this, I learned something firsthand about unhealthy writing.

Writing this struggle out in vivid detail and revisiting how I coped (and didn't) made me feel quite sick. The mere act of taking out that section was already a relief and I began to understand how writing can be toxic.

It was the kind of writing that expressive-writing researcher James Pennebaker (1990, 2011) warns about. He calls it a form of rumination that can even lead to feelings of depression.

In his book *The Secret Life of Pronouns* (Pennebaker, 2011), he talks about what markers (i.e., word use) signal a beneficial narrative. First, pronoun switching, which means someone might start with "I did this" and "I felt this," but switch to "he told me this" and "they think that … ," instead of solely sticking with the *me* or *I* or other references to oneself. A writer or poet who uses a lot of "I" pronouns is often more honest, but also more prone to depression. A therapist would likely intuitively pick up on this; for instance, if a client speaks a lot about themselves, the counsellor might ask, "And what did your friend say about what happened? Have they responded to your letter?" If the client were instead to talk about another person a lot, the counsellor might ask, "And what do *you* think about it? How did you feel when they said … ?"

The second marker of a beneficial narrative is that it includes not only positive emotion (mostly) words but also some negative ones. Someone who writes using only positive emotion words is likely ignoring parts of the story, and someone who writes predominately using negative emotion words (e.g., upset, frustrated, mean, awful, depressing) is not likely to be engaged in writing a beneficial narrative. This is where my troubles lay in writing the piece about our history. It was filled with mostly negative emotion words and negative interpretations. Moreover, it was repetitive, and I had told the story repeatedly in the past. This all showed that this part of my story about Frans and me was frozen in time, just the way that trauma is (Van der Kolk, 2014).

The third sign of a beneficial narrative is an increase over time of cognitive words:

> Two of the cognitive dimensions included insight or self-reflection words (such as think, realize, believe) and another made up of causal words (such as because, effect, rationale) …. People whose health improved the most started out using fairly low rates of cognitive words but reported increases in their use."
>
> *(Pennebaker, 2011, p. 10)*

Pennebaker further argues that these are the words that signal meaning-making processes. I believe in my own writing about that difficult passage of our relationship that I was not making meaning, but instead had fallen into the trap of lamenting.

In Pennebaker's earlier book, *Opening Up* (1990), he warns against three downsides of writing. The first way in which we can be unhealthily over-reliant on writing is if we use it to talk about our problems instead of taking action. In my case, I was writing about a past that I could not alter literally, and which had also frozen in the narrative sense. Pennebaker notes that, "After a death or other trauma, writing helps to sort out complicated feelings and memories" (p. 194), and that we must not over-intellectualize but use writing for self-reflection that also includes our emotions. In the difficult section that I removed, I was mired in a host of negative emotions with the false belief that if I reflected enough (i.e., did enough intellectual work), I would fix what had gone wrong retroactively. The third danger Pennebaker describes, which I believe applied most to me as I wrote, was "using writing as a forum for uncensored complaining" (p. 195). Finally, Pennebaker also touches on writing not being a substitute for friendship and conversations with others who may help loosen our frozen perspectives.

My body told me that how I was writing as I wrote about our break-up and separation was unhelpful, and this was confirmed when my friend and colleague Tom read the raw manuscript and said, "In this portion you sound like you are ruminating." Later, he and I spoke about the impossibility of perfect relationships.

***

Reading this all again, more than 9 months after Frans's death, I have concluded that if there is such a thing as closure, it's more likely to be found in understanding our human needs and ingrained habits. The combination of both seems to underlie our persistent responses and behaviors.

What has preoccupied me in grief is a mixture of yearning to still be close to Frans, the impossibility of undoing what I believed had come between us in life, and the strange and recurring shock of dealing with his disappearance, regardless of also experiencing him as an undeniable and abiding part of me.

I believe I will always miss him and our world.

***

More December 20

Yesterday was a good day: I counted my blessings before sleep—just things from the day itself. At least five was my goal: I am healthy, the kids are alive and well, I have enough money, I like my job, and we loved each other. It was soon 10 things, and I am no Pollyanna.

Top three: kind-hearted friends at a lovely family Christmas party; singing in the car with the kids on the way to another party; a very good deal on new phones from the guy at the mall's Wireless booth.

Dear Frans, life goes on, as you always said it would and should. Here's an update you would really like. The "human" (nephew Colin) has grown quite tall and asked me how I was. You would have been impressed.

On my night table is a book about surrender—a gift from Debbie. I read one or two short chapters each evening. This morning she also sent me a small film she made entitled, "Are you finished with suffering?" The question lingers and I feel a hint of laughter in my body.

This morning I also woke to an e-mail from Ellie. She sent me this most appropriate and heartfelt poem, which she wrote in 1998:

Dear Soul

With every beat of my heart
I will celebrate your life.
With every tear that betrays me
I will moisten my memories
to keep them growing.
And never shall I forget
the quiet times
when silence was comfortable.
Who is to say that we cannot always exist?
The earth welcomes the ashes of long-gone fires,
allowing the grass to grow again.
The ocean will dance to the moon
and Selkies will shed their skin
in the shadows of rocks.
And I will take comfort in the safety
of impossible notions.
You will never really leave my side.
Love will always bind us together.
I will walk barefoot in the sand
for you
And, for once,
you can follow in my footsteps.
Dear Soul,
You will never be lost.

(Eleanor Talbot, 1998)

***

December 21
Yesterday, I wrote the poem "Chasing Grief" in the café where my nieces work. I wrote it in response to a conversation with my friend Margot about how we approach the questions that life brings us through loss and uncertainty.

Chasing grief

Like a good girl
I have been chasing grief,
out I go to meet my tears
and they don't come

out I go to read the literature
and all I need comes to me.
I wanted to marry the sorrow
but anger flared instead
I walked with the anger
and then it went its own way.
I needed to do, and do nothing
the hot pursuit always
makes the essential elude the doer
I cannot say or write it
to completion,
Again, here, here, here
surrounded on all sides by love
and grief comes to me
like a tiny bird that lands on my hand
when I have sat long enough
and have foregone all my plans.

The message to myself seems to be, make more room for the passive surrender to grief, especially when you notice you've been very active. Frans's singing teacher used to say to him when he was too eager to sing beautifully, "Don't go to the music, Frans. Let it come to you."

***

Dear Frans,

Your desk is about to get a new destination in the house. It is in the living room now for whoever wants to visit to work. Maya eventually moved her computer there as her room is crowded with artwork and clothes! Your chair is inhabited by different visitors at different times—sometimes it collects the backpacks, coats, and scarves of the tired.

Your wooden bread plate has turned into our cheese platter. We took inspiration from Ellie and her great afternoon snack spread of exotic cheeses, chutneys, and jellies.

Kat, our PhD student, sent a package with gifts which included Maya Angelou's poem "When great trees fall." It describes how your loss is felt by me and many others.

Yesterday evening, as I was eating dinner and listening to my favorite Christmas CD, I suddenly stopped breathing and had to remember to start again. I realized it was time to retire for the evening, though it was only 7 o'clock.

One of my nieces spoke right to me yesterday—like a woman, not like a girl.

She knew exactly what to say.

She said your name; she looked me right in the eyes and said, "Auntie Reinekke, I heard that Frans died. That must really be affecting you." She didn't add any polite or fake condolences.

She spoke simply and I could feel again how my heart is full of tears.

Your pictures are always near me—where I sleep, where I work.

Grief is so many things.

This clean grief that comes unbidden is love.

***

December 22

Frans, our thick, straw-colored curtains from our Dutch abode have found a home here in Edmonton. The girls and I agree they are both cozy and classy here in the house. The ceilings are lower here by about half a foot, so Sophia hemmed them. She skillfully managed a perfectly straight stitch along the expensive material; nothing was wasted or cut. Keath helped me mount the curtain rod above the living room window.

Yesterday evening, eight of us went to a stand-up comedy show by Mike Delamont, who plays God as a Scottish Drag queen explaining what Christmas is and where some of the actual traditions come from. A lot of it is wonderfully absurd.

I laughed again, and watching Keath and his girlfriend laugh and the kids and their friends enjoy warmed me. I had bought the tickets while you were still alive, knowing that I would need to do things like this and that I would.

Yesterday morning, I joined in "Breakfast Club" with my university colleagues. It was familiar and good. This weekend is about relaxing together and enjoying visits and more Christmas preparations. The social and domestic activities of life give ground and aesthetic pleasure. You would have been here, so I write to you instead; in some way, that makes it feel like you are.

***

December 23

On Facebook, I come across a picture of Frans and me from 3 years ago, on our walk through the snow to Timmies. Today I will walk the same route on my own. There will be beauty and memories.

Sleep didn't come easily last night. "There will be times like that," I tell myself, and I close my eyes and watch my thoughts. You know, the monkey mind offering up its concerns and preferences. I keep just watching my mind's antics. I am calm but not quite restful enough to sleep.

Yesterday my friend Leanne visited in the living room and we talked for several hours. I served tea and ginger cookies, and we spoke about life, loss, and struggle.

Mike Delamont, the comedian we saw on Friday, said, "You can say three wise men came, but you don't say that about women. Women are wise."

Women know what to do at a (re)birth, if they trust themselves, so wise need not be added. I feel this to be true when I speak with my friends.

I smile and am grateful for the women in my life.

***

December 24

By our bed, there is a bookshelf of comforts

The other comfort is telling you the mundane:
Sophia hemmed the curtains
she had exactly the right color thread
A Christmas card arrived from your friends
they spoke of their visits and our love
The kids went skating
I worked and folded laundry
There is no fresh snow,
but I am hoping for some
We walked to the store in the dark
to get two dozen eggs and bananas
it was windy still and crisp
I hope to sleep better tonight
I very much miss your arms around me
as you will well understand
and the winter shoe claws my Mom left are very good
I would have had to get you a pair.

***

December 25: Christmas with loved ones

This morning we are making brunch together. The young people get up at 11:00 a.m.; I have been up for several hours already.

Friends near our Dutch home lit a candle for Frans today. They sent me a picture of it. Other friends put flowers on his grave for me and also sent pictures. I am really moved and grateful (and crying as I write this).

Soon I will have a phone conversation with Frans's twin Jan and his wife and sons. The conversation is pleasant, even heartfelt in moments. When I say to one of Frans's nephews that I'm writing a book about Frans and our life together, he says, "At least they can't take that away from you." That comment lingers in my mind as I consider that I have lost regular contact with Frans's daughters, and I imagine his ex-wife might prefer me to be erased from the family record.

A few things I have discovered since losing Frans:

1. Some people truly feel connected to you—more people than you realize—while others fall away suddenly and perhaps necessarily. (I reflect more on this later.)
2. There is peace and beauty if you focus on what is right in front of you.
3. Everyone is protecting their own wound(s) through their story of meanings.

4. One day at a time is very good advice. Thank you, Vicky in Canterbury.

***

December 26

There are many voices to grief. As I have written before, we are a dialogical (multivoiced) self. There are many perspectives and feelings and they are all part of the mix. Here are the "parts" of me that take their turns to speak.

1. Deeply sad: he is gone forever, what terrible tragedy is this?!
2. Lover: a longing for his touch, his eyes; memories of our passion hurt and soothe.
3. The worker: this pace is better for me, I am studying even more now, cultivating flow and sharpness. I will miss his perspectives.
4. Mother: look at these beautiful children around me: what do they need to flourish? They are home!
5. Friend: I am more present, I am surrounded. What dear good people there are in my life.
6. Wonderer: when I ask myself if I would have done it differently, whether I would have changed my history with Frans or other choices … and … more wondering.
7. Inner wise woman: no, I would have done it this way, it was all worthwhile, and it is and was my life. It still feels like my life, even though he was older and got ill, and I am "alone" now. I would have done it the same. This is so deeply felt and trusted. You are brave enough to live this, Rein, I say to myself.
8. Content: Yes, this is my life and I love it! Good morning.
9. Practical: some fresh air for you today—get out walking.
10. A witness of all the voices: amusing, isn't it?

***

December 27

Today we will cook our turkey. I call this day "Friends' Christmas." It's my former wedding anniversary, of my marriage to Keath, and as we have stayed good friends, I use the day to celebrate accordingly. The evening isn't limited to family members, Keath doesn't always pay a visit and sometimes it's partially potluck. Everyone seems to like to come.

Sophia and I were back on the cross-country skis yesterday after many years. The snow was a bit crystallized, but we made it work. Caleb took photos and short videos of us on the field.

A small insight about marriage and widowhood: during my partnering with Frans, I grew in many ways. I am enriched. Now in widowhood, parts of me from the past blossom again, like my outdoor athletic self. Some things receded into the background when I was with him, like the part of me that dances spontaneously when I hear music I like, or that suddenly decides I want to go away for the weekend to Calgary and book a hotel room for Maya and me there. Author Jeffrey Berman (2015) refers to the widowed reconstructing themselves as a "new post-widowhood identity that turns out to be remarkably consistent with her pre-widowhood identity" (p. 203). I would add that it may return in ways to the pre-marriage identity, while being enriched by the married identity.

***

December 28

A lovely evening with friends and family on "Friends' Christmas." Fifteen young people came to hang out; the rest of us are over 45. Lots of laughter and activity. Our friend Peter carved the turkey, quoting Aristotle before he did—something about joints!

Again, inside there is a mix of feelings and thoughts. Part of me steps in and enjoys it all more fully than before, while another part of me is quiet. Words that resonate just now as I write are "water-logged heart."

Later in bed, I listen to Joni Mitchell. Music helps emotions to flow and I remember how this human journey has always been both joyous and sorrowful.

***

December 29

"Nevertheless She Persists"

These words are an embroidered gift from my friend Heather Von Stackelberg. They are now pinned up beside my work chair. She tells me how the phrase applies to women in politics and glass ceilings and speaks about American politician Elizabeth Warren. The words apply to me too, she says.

Another friend reaches out for support as she is contemplating divorce; she wonders if she is not burdening me. I write her a poem to confirm she is not; it is good to feel I can still be present for others too.

Another friend sends me a link to David Whyte's work; I have followed his writing since his book *Crossing the Unknown Sea* (2001) came out many years ago. He combines poetry—both the writing and the reading of—with meaning-making in life and vocation. He talks about the "conversational nature of reality." He likes to say, with a chuckle, "the conversation IS the relationship."

In Frans and my work, we similarly saw the value of dialogue for meaning-making and growth processes in life and career. I have been to hear Whyte twice in person, once with Frans in January 2017 in Asilomar, California.

I remember now that in one of his talks Whyte said that we are used to seeing our lives in terms of progress, performance, building things, and succeeding, but that we also need to consider the other half and "apprentice ourselves to loss." He also says that we don't go it alone; I take that to mean we aren't victims. In his collection of poems *Everything is Waiting for You* (2003), he writes, "Your great mistake is to act the drama as if you were alone. As if life were a progressive and cunning crime with no witness to the tiny hidden transgressions" (p. 6).

These ideas seem useful for me to remember now. I think poets have a bit of a head start on this because we have a melancholy streak. We contemplate death (even our own); we seek out the places where we hurt or where we see others hurting. We are drawn to other artists and courageous teachers who share this strange journey of faith without dogma.

Artists and spiritual people are alike: they seek to co-create their own responses to what life brings. They aren't satisfied with someone else's answers, though they can be inspired by those.

Poets can be heartbroken, listen to the saddest music, and feel in that some kind of blissful bowing to how it is. It's the place where we accept the unfixability of everything, I wrote in a poem months after this early writing.

The human condition is the poet's field of interest; we want to deepen it, experience it, taste it, name it, surrender—do the soul work.

Frans's dying invites me to do my soul work. To know life better; to hide even less. Conversations with others are necessary for this process of (re)acquaintance. Time alone is needed for the internal dialogue; the sitting with; the cultivating patience and receptivity.

I persist
Nevertheless

December 30

A few blessings worth counting. I write this list:

1. Good relationships
2. Healthy kids
3. Long walks
4. Fresh snow
5. Work that matters
6. Friends to eat at a large table with
7. A good night's rest
8. Stubborn gladness as inherited habit
9. In-the-moment living
10. Places I feel welcome
11. Sustained hugs
12. Moments to experience new things

December 31

The day begins at a coffee shop and artisan bakery in Calgary, across the Bow River from Sophia and Caleb's studio apartment. We walk there in the crisp cold, almost blinded by morning sunlight and blue skies. We meet up with our friend Darrin. Caleb and Sophia have brought their sketchbooks and are planning out their next creative projects. Darrin talks about what he should consider reading in the new year. Out of my purse, I grab Michael Singer's *The Untethered Soul* (2007). Darrin is surprised that I hand it to him as a gift, and later tells me it has helped him a lot to stay in the moment and worry less. It has done the same for me, reminding me often to be where I am and not to get trapped in the past.

The kids go to the bakery counter and order chocolate-covered croissants and expensive coffee. This is where I like to spend money; some of our best family time is spent in cafes with our notebooks. Sophia sits next to me, hip to hip. I notice Caleb's big happy smile and it always makes me smile too. He tells me about his latest project.

My journal scribbles at the moment are to-do lists, though I almost convince Darrin that I knitted my Norwegian Dale sweater when he compliments me on it. "I spend most of my time writing; I don't have time for knitting. The only thing I ever knitted was a navy blue scarf that I didn't know how to successfully take off the needles when it was scarcely three feet long." Sophia explains how to complete knitting; she is a fiber major and has skills that I marvel at; she did not get them from me. We all laugh as we take our turns joking with each other.

"We go forward well in the same measure that we honor and embrace the past," Frans used to say. He also used to say, "The best thing about the past is that it's over." His voice always feels close, his remembered words enrich my quiet moments and conversations with others. His internalized thoughts remind me of the way Dutch idioms consistently arise when I am speaking. "The Dutch have an expression for that: better to turn back halfway than to get lost all the way."

Yesterday, I wrote another dialogue with him and I felt his love and *joie de vivre* in his replies. It made me smile and cry. He just kept saying, live, be you, and I will be there with you when you want and need me.

My updates on Facebook go from daily to a few times weekly. Teaching begins soon and I will be concentrating on more writing and research. The first 6 weeks of widowhood have felt raw, intense, yet also merciful in ways, and I see I have written half a book. However, the writing pace slows steadily, which I think means the rawness of the experience is becoming less edgy, the need to process and keep Frans close less acute.

What will 2019 bring? I tell myself it's a matter of openness, surrender, getting on with work, allowing emotions to come and go, being gentle with myself, and being truly present with others. I keep repeating a number of key insights like this, which tells me what I'm doing is consistently useful.

What Frans might say now: "You cannot predict the future, my love, but keep trusting your process. The best decisions start in the belly; you check them with knowledge [he points to his head], and then you go with your gut."

***

5

WRITING AGAIN AND IN TOUCH WITH FEELINGS

January 3, 2019

Came home to a Turner sky

sat calm and empty in my soft chair
My girl and I took down the tree
wrapped each decoration carefully
made the bed downstairs for guests
We watched the day go by without agenda
Friends called.

In grief, you are saddest
and most alive and
when someone can
hear your tears
without offering platitudes or advice
just a yes, and another yes
you remember again what it is like
to be embraced.

January 4

"Grief can be the garden of compassion. If you keep your heart open through everything, your pain can become your greatest ally in your life's search for love and wisdom." Rumi

Yesterday I sat working in a Starbucks at the mall. As mother chauffeur, I got busy reviewing a book chapter on the use of theatre in community learning.

While sitting there waiting, I phoned Margot. She and I discuss the precision of language, what drives and guides our vocations; she asks about my grief.

M: The way you use language is different than how I do it. You're precise. I don't consider myself an academic.

R: You always say that.

M: I feel things in my body. In my arms. That's where I can tell.
How are you today, Rein?

R: Tender mostly. Though sometimes grief comes sharply into view. There is an intensity to it. Grief follows you around.

M: You? (She's pointing to my use of pronouns)

R: Me. It follows *me* around. It's like the ring in a teacup that the dishwasher never gets clean. I can still drink from life, but everything is marked.

M: Tell me more about *marked*. What do you mean?

R: That it's here. That it's always with me, not like a heavy weight, but like something that keeps knocking at my consciousness. Reinekke, be awake to it, that's what it seems to be saying. Frans would ask, "What do you want to learn from this?"

Later that day, I read a passage in a book I've had for many years on stoic wisdom. It's an interpretation of the work of Epictetus, the Greek philosopher (born 50 CE), by Sharon LeBell (1994), an author I later reach out to thank for this work:

> Every difficulty in life presents us with an opportunity to turn inward and to invoke our own submerged inner resources. The trials we endure can and should introduce us to our strengths. Prudent people look beyond the incident itself and seek to form the habit of putting it to good use. (p. 17)

I tell Margot, "It's like there is also something really good here: something that happens through the combination of pain and awareness of the facts. I see others more as they actually are—not as a matter of routine and patterned response. For instance, I look at a complexion; see the way a shy note passes over a face; I hear the sound of someone's longing in the way they open up about suffering."

It's as if everything beautifully fragile in someone's mood or demeanor becomes accessible. I find myself truly wanting to look behind the doors someone hints at, instead of politely skipping the discomfort that might arise. Melancholy becomes joy's identical twin. It only makes perfect sense!

Who are you, is what I ask someone else in the way I look and listen and ask. Because to stay in balance, I ask myself this and the old labels don't fit. Microscopic truthfulness, a term I borrow from writing teacher Brenda Ueland (1938), is strangely comforting.

On New Year's Day, I write to Margot, "Today I was shaky and scared at various moments of the day; I was comforted by and at the same time trapped in my chair; probably in all it was an hour's worth of uneasiness and body pain."

Maybe it's comforting to say these things because I notice it passes. The next moment, I say, "I felt energized when I opened the roll-shutter and took a picture of the clean kitchen; I want to set up my office this week."

The two poems below I wrote as I was sitting waiting in a café yesterday. They are a part of the ongoing conversation with and about Frans. As I write his name, a little fear erupts in my stomach. I have not yet written about his death, but I know I will go there soon. Which thoughts are foremost in my mind?

Might it be that the longer I live on without him, the less he will still be real in my imaginings? Will he turn into a projection of my memory, always skewed by my opinions and preferences? This thought plagued C. S. Lewis when his wife Joy died as well, though he, like Proust, comforts me by affirming that their beloveds returned in a way that felt full and abiding. This idea, at the moment, sounds like a Zen Koan: something I hold as a puzzle and have to live and ripen toward understanding.

Will I remember Frans's clear conceptual voice, his energetic joy-vibe, his common sense when I need more than just my own? I remember his advice in December 2011, when I almost lost my job as my university embarked on cost-saving layoffs. He counselled me how I might keep my employment. He was calm, he asked me what I wanted to do in my working life, and if it was to continue with what I loved and was doing, to make a case for that. He had faith that I could argue for my position, even despite the fact I was teaching in a graduate program with only a Master's degree at the time.

That conversation took place by the woodstove in Edmonton, both of us in our chairs, he asking me questions, me writing down reasons why I was the one they needed to keep. I wrote the case, he gave me some final pointers, I submitted it, and I kept my job.[1]

Sunset

Another day ends
without you in it
there were even moments I forgot,
ordering coffee after a short line-up
looking for a light bulb in the top cupboard
noticing the car covered in road salt.
I wake up and my heartbeat's a judder
sometimes it goes to a hundred for no reason
and there is a thing called broken-heart syndrome
I wake up to you gone again
get into bed, the same thing.
Everyone knows you were not a quiet one
and this IS quiet

like you did some magic trick
promised not to talk anymore
and pulled it off.

I Google quotes on bereavement and find Kübler-Ross's "Denial helps us to pace our feelings of grief. There is a grace in denial. It is nature's way of letting in only as much as we can handle." It seems fitting.

I begin to be able now to write about Frans's actual death. It comes out in bits and pieces as I continue daily writing and posting on Facebook.

Where

I washed and dressed your still-warm body
therefore, of course, I am not looking for you in the crowd,
but inside my own crowd of voices
I listen for you
in a moment of desire
your eyes still seek mine and I seek them
how does one NOT turn arousal into tragedy?
I will tell me how—don't reach into the future
and for a moment forget all the street views you ever shared,
then tell someone who won't shame you for still being this alive.
Some say the widowed are afraid
of aloneness
I don't believe them
because that's where I still feel you.

***

January 5, 2019

Bereavement is a curveball, the twilight zone, a Dalí landscape.

The bereavement zone is both living and waiting to live. It's getting on and also feeling faithful to the past. Throughout the day I feel like I'm going back and forth.

I make notes—that is, observations—about my inner state and questions that arise. Writing a list of notes turns out to be useful. Perhaps it is a way of micro-cleaning my mental landscape.

1. The bits that hurt most are also the best parts of the life we had (well, duh!). What do I miss? Touch, being together, the plans we made, and the dialogue about everything.
2. I have not only lost Frans but the world we created together. It was a place where we tried things out, worked, hoped, built things, learned, surrendered—the place we both came home to, not literally but internally. A common language. This is the part that freaks me out sometimes. Yes … a

common language that created a world we were at home in. (That kind of loss is enough to stun you and my thoughts here trigger some separation anxiety.)

3. I read that breathlessness is a symptom of grief; so are heart palpitations. (My heart seems to have stopped juddering around in the last two nights.)
4. In the book, I also want to write about widowhood and desire. Desire doesn't end with the illness and death of a spouse. (I have mentioned this earlier and end up writing about it in more detail later.)

Yesterday afternoon I spent an hour cleaning the closet where Frans's things hung. A turquoise shirt, Ralph Lauren, shirt size XL is one of the three shirts that belonged to Frans that I keep. Why am I keeping these? No idea. Will they come in handy? Probably not. Will I take them out often to look at them? I don't think so. Does it feel less empty than if they were gone? Certainly. "The heart has her reasons, which reason knows nothing of," as Blaise Pascal is known for saying. When I pick up the shirts and smell them, I smell Frans. Of course.

Keath phones me in the middle of my cleaning, just as I finish putting a bunch of things in a recycle bag for the Good Will store. He asks me how I'm doing and I can hardly get a word out.

I brought Frans's new winter jacket with me from our home in The Netherlands. I also have the old one we bought 7 years earlier in Valemount, British Columbia, while on holidays there. I put them on the table along with a pile of his sci-fi books, a stack of scholarly articles on leadership, and printed emails. I also look at several pictures of us and then consider the three shirts. I leave them on the table for several hours, still not yet knowing what I will do with them. I read once that there was a widow who kept clothes for more than a decade until finally her friends convinced her to donate them. I have been reading about minimalism and practicing getting rid of things more and more in past years, so I have practice in considering stuff as stuff, taking up space, and the dangers of being sentimental if one truly wants space to live and breathe.

I end up giving the books to my Mom, who likes reading in Dutch; she's very pleased with them. I recycle the printed articles and put them in a large blue bag that will go out with the garbage on Tuesday morning. I keep two of the shirts and hang them right back in the closet. Almost a year later I give them to Caleb, Sophia's boyfriend, who is happy to wear them and knows they are Frans's. I store both winter coats downstairs.

Today, I worked on revisions of a book chapter Frans and I drafted just as he was getting ill. It tells the story of our lives and career stories and how our work came together (Lengelle & Meijers, 2019).

Writing that, I'm reminded of Buddhist teacher Pema Chodron's book *When Things Fall Apart* (2002), and how we can never really get ground under our feet, or rather that it's always temporary, though we are always striving for that.

Last night I watched the movie *Truly, Madly, Deeply* with actors Juliet

Stevenson and Alan Rickman. Rickman died of cancer at 69 in 2016. My friends Liz and Peter lent me the movie a few weeks ago because they thought it might speak to me. I haven't really dared to watch it yet. The story is about Nina, played by Juliet Stevenson, a young widow struggling with her loss and coping with regular visitations from Jamie, her deceased husband, played by Rickman. Two places in the movie made me cry: their intense embrace as he comes back from the dead and the moment in the end when he lets her go for good.

Bereavement looks mostly like normal life, though it continually feels weird as well. It's like being reminded every few seconds that something is not right with the world but that there is no fixing it either.

Any energy one spends on retrieval is tragic and exhausting, and, of course, futile, but it also feels like loyalty and sometimes even closeness.

***

The World We Create Through the Language of "Us"

While Frans was ill, I read an article by a young widow, Christine Frangou of Calgary, who published her story on widowhood in the Canadian newspaper *The Globe and Mail* (2016).

The article became newly relevant right after Frans's death, especially these lines:

> The desire to talk to your spouse after they've died is a recurring theme in studies in scientific journals and online support groups for the grief-stricken. I understand why: My brain has not yet caught up with the reality of my life. I am accustomed to reflecting on the world through the language of Chris and Spencer—what we find funny, sad, interesting. Now that he's gone, I'm the only one left who speaks our language.
>
> *(Frangou, 2016)*

I shared this passage with Frans when I first read it. Doing so once again felt like I was throwing a ball over the fence into my future where I could pick it up later and shout back over the fence, "Now I'm there and it's true! We knew this. WE!" As I mentioned before, this trying to bring him with me into the future is something I did with my poems as well.

Revisiting the manuscript almost 9 months after his death, I still miss the "Frans and Reinekke" dialogue. I likely always will. As I reread Frangou's (2016) article for the third time, I feel compelled to reach out to her and say, "You can still talk to Spencer, write him …" But it seems trite, even cruel to say this without the full context of all I've written in this book. It sounds like I am rationalizing or buying into magical thinking without a fuller explanation of what I've experienced through my writing. Or, I'm arrogant in thinking she hasn't already figured this out herself.

As I learn more about grief in my readings by Bonanno (2009) and Neimeyer (2016), I consider that Frangou (2016) may be suffering from complicated grief, as her suffering has seemed to endure and remain very intense, even after 6 months. I don't consider my grief complex or prolonged.

I send her a message via her website; I thank her and tell her the lines and ideas in her writing that stood out for me.

Frangou writes about the so-called "Widowhood Effect," which refers to a 22% increased chance of dying after one's spouse dies. She writes that widows lose about 75% of their network without necessarily knowing why. People drift off; it seems some cannot deal with the feelings they see in the griever; social networks shift.

Maybe a single woman is threatening in the former couple's world. Maybe grief changes us in a way that makes the old conversations and connections feel trite. My sense is that grief does two almost paradoxical things simultaneously: it makes us too tired to deal with additional stress and it makes us vibrantly aware of what we no longer want to experience (e.g., superficiality, lack of empathy, drama). A griever's tendency to isolate is not always a bad thing: being alone can be time with the internalized beloved; being alone is time to rediscover self; being alone, as Frangou tells her readers, you don't have to pretend that you're okay when you're not.

As I was editing the manuscript, Roberta, one of the widows I mention earlier (and who is one of my beta readers), prompted me to elaborate on why Frangou's article had made an impression. I realize it's the way she can speak about the intensity of her feelings and offers the reader a glimpse into her personal life, even in the fine details of where she keeps the notes her husband left her.

I revisit her article a third time, and now the part that stops me in my tracks and brings tears is the description of her leaving the hospital room in haste just after her 36-year-old surgeon husband dies. As she closes the door, she says to her father, "I don't know where to go."

Then, she writes, "In a shining moment of dad-wisdom, he responded, 'We'll just go forward.'"

***

Into the New Year

School is about to start up again and this means I'll be home alone to write.

I have a feeling of being intensely focused: I am driven to put words to what I shared with Frans as a way to work with this rich life material. All the good we shared humbles me.

It's a privilege to have been so close to someone; to have created so much together; to even have had the chance. I want to go toward that fullness, absorb that, integrate all it might have to offer. It's a harvest, like a garden in fall: on the outside, all seems over with, but the crop is there, ready to nourish and take us through the winter (of grief). It just takes work to unearth and bring it inside.

Yesterday one of Frans's friends, Joseph, a widower, wrote to say that he believes the work I'm doing now (both the book and a recent tribute I wrote about Frans's career-research) is important, because it is a "conscious way of reconciling with the new reality." He himself has put on an art exhibit of his partner's early artworks and found that going into the new year was easier this time. He is a year ahead of me with the loss of his spouse, who was also 20 years his senior. He was a professor (now retired), his partner a well-known Dutch painter.

In the afternoon, after doing a plethora of editorial tasks, including drafting a tribute to Frans, I take out a CD of one of his concerts and listen to him singing. The music I listen to is from a concert he sang years ago with his colleague and an accompanying pianist. He sent me the CD of that concert at the time. "One of the love songs is for you," he wrote. As I've mentioned earlier, he was a good amateur choir singer. I loved his voice as many others did.

How can I be hearing him and never hear him again? It does not compute.

We did research and work jointly, creating the career counselling method "career writing" and writing and publishing many articles, as well as presenting together at conferences. A very vital part of what brought and kept us together was our intellectual partnership, which was fuelled by the way we could connect creatively.

What grew overtime was a commitment to each other and to our own growth, which was fuelled by our mutual desire for learning. There was no walking away or even wanting to; we had maturing to do and we did it together. We learned how to be wholehearted. This is also part of the legacy; our life together has changed me for the better. In some ways, we had been selfish and closed off in our sacred tower of "autonomy" in our other relationships. We mostly knocked that out of each other.

We (finally) allowed ourselves to say, "I need you."

It's good to cry; it softens everything. It's the water that life drifts on. Grief is not only a weird lonely echo—sorrow is love, plain and simple.

I want to say to others, "If you ever wonder if you're courageous enough to love someone because you might lose them someday, I'd say, you likely will (or they'll lose you), so what is there to lose? Aren't these the inarguable conditions of life anyway?"

There is life after (a partner's) death; it involves reinvention; a new lesson in surrender.

Frans would say, *"Er zit niets anders op dan doorgaan …"* [There is no other option than to keep going …]. Anyone who knew him will hear this in their own head,

" *… ja, schat, het leven gaat door …*" [Yes, dear, life goes on]. I've written that several times now; it's as if he keeps wanting to remind me.

And I keep writing.

"Give sorrow words; the grief that does not speak knits up the o-er wrought heart and bids it break," as Shakespeare said.

January 6, 2019

Saturday morning, I talk on the phone with Tom, who visited us regularly while Frans was ill. He admired the way Frans faced the inevitable and made end-of-life decisions. The three of us had co-written and published an article on self-reflection a year before the diagnosis.

Tom, who is in his late 60s, tells me he has lost three friends in his age group this past year. We talk about what this means for how we might live now. I tell him how I'm doing day by day, about how I continue to observe my thoughts and feelings and write them down. How I sometimes weep to music, then get active again; how my body is feeling; what I should make of the well-meaning suggestions others make as they follow my process and show their care.

He's an active and good listener and repeats back the things I say in a way that makes me feel really heard. These are also the fruits of death: a conversation with Tom that I likely never would have had had this not happened. There is an affection in our friendship that I appreciate.

After the phone call with Tom, I take Maya to see one of her friends and then head to a café for coffee and book browsing, laptop on my shoulder. This is one of the first days that I am really alone. My children are both doing what they want to do and there aren't urgent household duties to tend to or work to finish that can't wait until Monday. The Christmas holidays are nearly over, and everyone is busy.

Today would be a day I would likely be home with Frans, reading and chatting, or phoning each other overseas in the morning and early afternoon to update each other on the day. This silence and time to do whatever I might want to do feel both luxurious and, in moments, unsettling.

There is a mild tendency in this moment to go into the past and remember what was or to fuss a bit mentally about the future: what will it be like, knowing Frans won't be there? If I live as long as the average woman does, I have more than 30 years to go.

I shift my awareness back to the present moment, which has been a place of solace, both during Frans's illness and after his death. Frans helped me practice this in the 7 months he spent on the couch each day. Our "world got smaller," he would say, but it also became more open and relaxed. There was a kind of thriving going on as we met with our visitors, served cups of coffee and tea, put fresh flowers in vases and allowed each seemingly patterned day to open itself to new meanings and conversations.

Here is the insight: the reason I believe I am doing well given the circumstances is that I am living here and now 90% of the day. For about 5% I dip into the past and 5% I look ahead with hope and trepidation.

I will tell you where I am now: local bookstore café, eating cheesecake, drinking chai, and writing. More than 100 pages of writing and Frans has been dead 50 days. My work is a devotion to our love and a daily companion. (I will say more about the various benefits of writing later.)

Everything in the past is done. Though memories are wonderful and inform our daily moments, they are gone. And the future does not exist.

5% Past … *Lieve* (dear) Frans, I remember your insistence on getting to airports early, how you liked to eat on time, your love of the *Volkskrant* crossword puzzle, your waiting at the station to welcome me with a smile and a hug, your fast and noisy slamming on the keyboard as you wrote articles and emails (a three-finger-typist), and your jolly whistling and oom-pah-pah-ing as you walked through the house. In those moments, you reminded me of Mr. Arbuthnot from the movie *Enchanted April*. You were a great kisser, just like he was.

5% Future … In some distant tomorrow, we may meet again. I pretend and find unscientific proof in light bulbs that burn out in the house.

I am open to new conversations, new adventures, and I'm seeing every day, in all kinds of small moments and interactions, as a gift.

Twenty-five years of personal development and poetic living has got to have prepared me for you dying, dammit!

"How do you stay 90% present and not drift into the past?" someone recently asked me. The first thing is to just notice when I drift off into the past or the future. I feel that in my body because it feels like strain or clench or fear. If it's a precious remembrance, something that uplifts me, I allow myself to go there. It's a relief that not every good memory equates with tragedy. If it's hope for the future, I go ahead and imagine, but if it's a place of suffering, then I make a point of noticing and breathing and reminding myself, "this is a movie of the past" or "this is the movie of the scary, unfulfilled future … and I can't know my future yet."

The advice I give myself after noticing I'm doing too much tragic time traveling is *Breathe, look at your surroundings, name three things that are supporting you right now: the table, the barista that offered a refill, the scarf against the wind.*

***

Generation Gap Reflections

Not to say that looking back or forward doesn't have its purpose in grieving. Healthy grieving is considered by some researchers to be a kind of "dual process" where we go back and reflect on the loss and feel it and then look to the future with some degree of openness and hope. The two terms for this are "loss orientation" and "restoration orientation" (Stroebe & Schut, 2001, 2010). We oscillate between both and move forward doing so. A year after Frans's death, when I respond to editors' feedback on the manuscript and discuss my findings with a friend, I say, "I have found a second oscillation, it's engagement and detachment, moving between being 'with grief' in the emotional sense and cognitively reflecting and observing."

I do see that the processing of a loss takes into account the reality of the present moment and includes a kind of life-review. This is not the kind of dip into the past that hurts, but one that notices what was and learns from it. One of the things, I have, for instance, reflected upon off and on since Frans's death, is our age gap of 20 years. In talking to a friend about it not too long ago, I named three advantages and three disadvantages that all feel meaningful to me. They erupted spontaneously when I was talking about how I like to crank the music loud in the car.

Advantages were: his wisdom and ability to advise me having gone through many cycles of political and bureaucratic change; he wasn't too easily ruffled by the goings-on at the university. He was also quite mellow and there was room for me to do what I wanted and needed to do (e.g., travel on my own, visit friends, schedule my own work, and all this without considering him too much). He had built a life and career, and more and more he focused on how to help me do the same. His wild years were also behind him.

There were also disadvantages and I name them here because I also noticed some shifting in the way I view my life without him. An age gap of 20 years for us meant we didn't share youth culture. He grew up with a mix of 1950s tradition and Bob Dylan, and he was a hippie. He also grew up in a prosperous era for educated white males; in his generation, all of them got jobs, usually had several offers, and were made permanent in short order.

I grew up with *Back to the Future*, Michael Jackson, and on my first date I saw *The Breakfast Club*, a movie he'd never heard of and didn't "get" when he watched it with me later. If I cracked a joke, his daughters and son-in-law "got it" (15–20 years my junior), while Frans would stare blankly. He didn't like loud music in the car; he liked dinner at 6 o'clock, and mostly expected it to be cooked for him. In visits with friends, there was regular talk of dental crowns, operations, friends dying, and retirement trips.

Listing the advantages deepens my appreciation for Frans; perhaps this is part of healthy loss orientation. The disadvantages make me appreciate the spaciousness of now; perhaps that, too, is part of healthy restoration orientation. Interestingly, without deliberate intention, I wrote these reflections and my conclusions before considering the dual-process described by grief researchers Stroebe and Schut (2010).

This might be an interesting writing exercise, to focus on one theme (e.g., age gap, religious differences, other notable differences between a person and their spouse) and write out three advantages and three disadvantages honestly.

When I turned 49, 2 and a half months after Frans died, I felt I'd turned 12 years younger. I am returning to my own generation. Now I see life as perhaps lasting another 35–40 years, instead of a rush to do everything in 15–20.

Of course, one never knows what time will be given, but this being in my own generation feels congruent and refreshing too.

As I delve more into the grief literature and print another handful of scholarly articles in March 2020, while editing, I find out there is a term for what I am doing with these generation-gap reflections in the wake of Frans's death. It's called "benefit finding" (Hall, 2014, p. 10), something grieving people do more and more of as time goes on, while the process of sense-making (e.g., of the death or of unfinished business) becomes less salient. "It is not so much making sense of loss that alleviates distress, as it is becoming less interested in the issue. The finding of benefit on the other hand grows stronger with time" (Hall, 2014, p. 10).

If a grief counsellor were to diagnose me, they would, I believe, scribble the following on a piece of paper: "Normal resilience, a sense-making griever, with 10% stress-inducing unfinished business. Sense-making mostly focused on unresolved relationship issue with the deceased. Benefit finding expresses itself in both gratitude and relief. Administered self-therapy through writing, tends at times to be too cerebral; however, uses humor and is able to access and surrender to adaptive emotional bereavement strategies."

***

Pondering Day-to-Day

January 5, 2019

The next writing exercise I try is out of a chapter by Jane Moss (2014). I think I did it just to play and then to reflect on my playing. The fact that I can use the word "play" tells me there is some light entering my being. Grief is less persistently sad and my desire for resolving the old issues wanes bit by bit.

When it comes to writing-the-self processes, a direct question, "Where are you at?" is impossible to answer. But playing with fictitious scenes brings up metaphors where I might make new discoveries about where I'm at with grieving.

The instructions for this exercise called "The Furniture Game" are to write 30 seconds on each of several items with the intention of expressing how you are each of these things at this moment (Moss, 2014, p. 71).

A piece of furniture: I am a long red chesterfield with soft fabric. I am kind of a chaise longue, I lie there like a dramatic opera singer stretched out for the final tragic scene, with black hair, white handkerchief, and a bosom that looks good in red fabric. Tearstained. I have strong oak legs that maybe no one notices, but they are solid and slightly overshadowed by a trim of ribbon and brass tacks. Because of those legs, you can move me through the room easily and I will not collapse or tip over. People like to lie down and read books on me—they bring blankets and fur. There are cozy lights by me and end tables, as many as you need for putting books, cookies, and cups and saucers for tea. I look fancy but I'm a comfortable and practical piece of furniture to come home to. I am in a warm room with a wooden floor and a mantel and a fireplace. There is literature here and a kitchen off to the side where you can melt real chocolate for hot cocoa. Classical music plays in the background—sometimes deeply sad tunes, sometimes polkas, other times the voice of Joni Mitchell, Kathleen Battle, or Alannah Myles.

An animal: I am a golden retriever that has been trained to do the work of a bloodhound. It doesn't fit. I'm resting from the ordeal. I'm a friendly beast that just wants to come home to loving hands and a fun family. I've been racing through the world with an eager sheepdog who sometimes pretended to be a German Shepherd police dog. He was just insecure. He was a very jolly, hard-working sheepdog and I saw that part mostly. When he was doing the other act, I got kind of scared and tried to crawl away or bark back but he was better at the act.

A flower: I am a rose. A red rose. I live for love. I am thorny too if you don't handle me carefully. I smell sweet and droop if you let me "dry up." I am still beautiful dried, but much more fragile.

A time of day: I am 4:00 a.m. No one is awake yet and I am there wanting to know what the meaning of life is. I'm too tired and have to go back to sleep.

A type of weather: I am a blizzard outside the window. But I am also cozy and happy indoors witnessing it. The blizzard is everywhere and it's gorgeous to watch. Sometimes I shiver, but it's out there beyond the window. I'm safe inside. If I had to go out there in the blizzard, I would be sure to use a light and a rope and come back home. I am not afraid of the blizzard and can totally dress for the weather. To one person this would look like a dangerous situation but not to me; I've grown up around blizzards and I know what to do.

An item of clothing: I am a wizard's cloak that allows the wearer to appear and disappear at will. I am protective and warm.

A song: I am a song of heartbreak and transcendence. A total eclipse of the heart song, but it ends well. The dramatic dance is part of movement and life.

Yes, these little descriptions tell me where I'm at. They let me feel it. They bring in some fun. They're easy to do. After the first sentence or two, they wrote themselves.

Later, when I revisit these creative snippets, I see the kinds of themes a Jungian psychologist might pick up, but as I am no Jungian psychologist, I draw no conclusions. I do try on my own interpretations though. Could staying inside while the blizzard is threatening but familiar outside my window mean that being inside my own psyche is safer than confronting the cold pain of death?

Of all the reflections, the dogs seem to say the most. In one paragraph, it paints the edgy parts of the emotional landscape between Frans and me, but in a way that has humor and is blameless and leaves me with a smile. I suppose that's why this exercise is in a book on grief and the expressive arts focused on creative meaning-making.

***

Living in the Now

January 7, 2019

The hopeless now

They say cherish hope
but 'hope-less' is cherishing too
no hope for what can never be
is the peace of the hope-less now

On Sunday I visit my colleague Adien who lost her brother young. We talk about our dead beloveds. It feels good to do that; "They stay alive that way," she remarks, and I feel the value of that paradoxical statement.

Later, I speak with Els and Janus, Dutch friends who will visit me in Canada in the summer. It was good to talk about Frans again and to reflect together on what bereavement looks like. I tell them that the grief experts (e.g., Bonanno and Neimeyer) I have been reading keep reiterating how the bereavement process is different for everyone.

There is an inquiry-based writing exercise I use for inquiring into stressful thoughts that I share with my students too. I find it allows me to stay in the here and now. It's part of my HOW of not getting stressed out about every thought and opinion that is offered up by my own mind, or by others.

This useful process, which has become a mental habit over the years, is something I first encountered in 2002. It's a four-question inquiry method developed by a woman named Byron Katie (2002).

Whenever a painful thought arises, the idea is to start by writing it down. Then one begins by asking the first question about the thought: "Is it true?" The answer is either a yes or a no, though the mind rushes to give its opinions and offer evidence of its beliefs.

Today, the exercise is useful for working through this stressful thought:
Frans shouldn't have become ill and died at 68.

1. Is it true, Frans shouldn't have become ill and died at 68?
   (Additional instructions based on Katie's work are to sit and feel for the answer. It can be Yes or No … just one syllable.)
   My answer is, "YES! He should not have …"
   I notice the whole dialogue in the mind goes something like this: yes, damn it! Doctors should have figured out sooner what was wrong, the medical system failed us, he wasn't even 70 yet. We were eating healthily. He quit

smoking at 37 .... What the f ..."

The second question helps one pause again ...

2. Can you absolutely know that it's true, Frans shouldn't have become ill and died at 68? (Can you know more than reality ... more than "God"?)

   I sit with the question. Close my eyes. Really ask it with sincerity. Let myself feel it in the body.

   No, I can't absolutely know ... (My answer here could still have been yes.)

3. How do you react, what happens when you believe, "Frans shouldn't have become ill and died at 68"?

   Messed with. Angry. Treated unfairly by the universe. Ripped off. Pissed. A bloody mess. I want to find out who is responsible for this unnecessary rotten tragedy. My stomach is in a knot; my head hurts.

   This is the question that makes you observe what the thought is costing you—also physiologically. You don't have to drop the thought or try to drop it at any time. You can keep the thought. You're allowed to declare yourself "Right."

   Now, question 4 always feels like a cool thought experiment:

4. Who would you be without the thought Frans shouldn't have become ill and died at 68? Just imagine, and know you do not have to drop or get rid of the thought, just imagine not having it, right here and now, or think if you didn't have it in the painful situation you might be remembering (e.g., the moment of his death). Imagine your brain synapses momentarily not firing off the thought, "Frans shouldn't have become ill and died at 68."

Who would you be without the thought, Frans shouldn't have become ill and died at 68?

Woman sitting in chair, in my safe home, listening to daughter's music coming from the shower. Woman who just talked to a friend. Woman who is tired just now and will crawl into warm bed soon. Woman breathing, sitting, being. Fresh memories today of dear friends, good company, enough to eat.

What you find is that you can either believe a painful thought or question it.

The next step in the process is writing "the turnarounds." The most obvious and daring one is "Frans should have become ill and died at 68 ..." How do I know? He did.

At this point, the idea is to come up with answers to why this turnaround is just as true, if not truer than the stressful thought I began with.

Katie would say, "Reinekke, tell me how it's true that Frans should have become ill and died at 68; give me a reason."

REINEKKE: He did.

KATIE: That's right. He simply did. You can argue with reality, but you're only wrong 100% of the time when you do. Is there another reason?

REINEKKE: He chose to go when he did. He didn't want to suffer into his 69th year.

KATIE: So, you're telling me you can see ways in which it was better he died at 68, than any older?

REINEKKE: Yes, given the circumstances.

KATIE: Ah, and how does that feel?

REINEKKE: Like a relief, actually.

KATIE: So, he didn't have to suffer one more day. He didn't have to get older, for you or for anyone else. Is there another reason why this thought is as true or truer than your original thought?

REINEKKE: He had kidney pain a year and a half earlier. There were already signs he might become seriously ill, but we ignored them and assumed they were kidney stones. It wasn't entirely a surprise when he got diagnosed.

KATIE: So, "he should have ..." also means, he was already sick, but you didn't know, so in hindsight, it makes sense that he died when he did.

REINEKKE: Yes, it makes sense.

KATIE: Does that thought bring you stress or peace?

REINEKKE: Peace, actually.

I realize by writing that I cannot know if my thought, "Frans shouldn't have become ill and died at 68" is true at all. By questioning it, I see how such a statement is wishful thinking. I don't chide myself. I don't try to rationalize. All four questions are required to bring me to the clarity I need to do the turnarounds. They involve feeling and they do not mandate that I think differently.

I wait for the next stressful thought to arrive; they always come unbidden.

"Frans getting ill and dying at 68 means" (fill-in-the-blank: horrible or scary) ... I will always be alone, I lost the best partner I could ever have, I will not be able to ... (fill in the blank ... more scariness).

Try any of the above. Can I know any of my future scary film projection thoughts are true? Generally, no.

The moment a thought like that arises, this is what comes to meet it:

1. Is it true? You will always be alone ...
2. Can I absolutely know it's true? (Can I know more than reality?) Can I know the future? That I will always be alone?

Shakespeare says, "Why then 'tis none to you; for there is nothing either good or bad, but thinking makes it so. To me it is a prison."

This exercise has been likened to the Socratic dialogue and Cognitive Behavioral Therapy strategies. It has been proven to reduce stressful thinking (Nye, 2011; Smernoff et al., 2015).

That Frans died is enough to live with. The sad and scary thoughts I might heap on top of that take me out of reality.

Here are a few other thoughts that also arise and that feel kinder:

Wow, life gave me an amazing opportunity to love. I took the chance. I am still taking the chance. The love remains.

With that thought, I can end the day … start the day … or be with life now.

And this morning, I'll start the day with a Happy Birthday to Maya, who is 16 today. And I'll start with 19 new graduate students, in my new full-time, tenure-track job.

I'm available for living.

***

January 8, 2019

"The secret of health for both mind and body is not to mourn for the past, worry about the future, or anticipate troubles, but to live in the present moment wisely and earnestly." These words, attributed to the Buddha, hung in the room where Frans died in our Dutch home. It was on a poster one of the girls had bought the year we were overseas on sabbatical.

When I sat with his body in the days that followed his passing, I put flowers on the table there, had candles burning, and sometimes I would notice those words.

Predictably, their wisdom didn't keep me from pondering the often-unanswerable questions of life and death. As I write this, I hear Frans reciting Wittgenstein, like he did in life "Whereof one cannot speak, thereof one must be silent" (it sounds better in German, with a Dutch accent, of course).

Death brings up all kinds of questions about existence and meaning. We ask, "Why"? and "Is there more?", which is a question generally answered by academics with a firm and sober "No." They can agree that humans just fabricate meaning to deal with the pain and the mystery of loss. For me the questions related to living well and loving well are things like, Did we spend our time well? Was I present enough? There is no definitive way of knowing or assessing this, and one question tends to lead to another in an endless chain.

Sitting there with his body, I talked to him as if he could still hear me—sometimes in my mind, sometimes out loud. His physical mass was there, but it was like an odd-smelling wax copy. Death on a cooling element, I have learned, smells like a strange deodorizer that should not make it to market. I smelled it once before at the crematorium where my father's body was, and I thought it was a scent they used in the funeral parlor.

To me, Frans felt far away, though internally the connection to him remained close and the first evening of his death, I wrote a dialogue asking him where he was.

R: Where are you now?

F: It's all much stranger than I thought. I'm traveling. There is much to do. Much to do.

R: Is all forgiven between us, Frans?

F (with few words he communicates by waving gestures and this message is: *It's not even a thing here*): It's all okay, my love. Gotta go!

Does she believe these are real communications?, a skeptical reader will want to know. And my answer is, who knows? And is it important? I don't need to believe the dialogues are real, but they feel true.

Caleb, Sophia's boyfriend, made a series of turtle pins during his last semester at art school. The turtles were inspired in part by the mythological story of life (i.e., our existence) as held up by a giant turtle or tortoise. There is a story about the turtle(s) relating to the principle of infinite regress (that one proposition depends on another, and another, and another … infinitely …). And such are the questions of life—one on top of the other, many of them impossible to answer, though they look intriguing and seem to go somewhere. But, as the saying goes, it's "Turtles all the way down."

Artists and spiritual people are kindred, I like to say. They both try to tease out the reasons for existence, but artists are not satisfied with the answers passed down or prescribed, though they often have a healthy respect for the symbolism and wisdom found in religious stories.

Artists want to make their own representation and integration. That's what I think I'm doing with my writing and the dialogues I have with Frans. They are just as imaginary as one turtle on top of another: there are no answers, but I am temporarily soothed by looking for the next turtle.

***

January 9, 2019

I started working with a very enthusiastic group of graduate students, created a new workspace in the sunny part of the house, and went for a physical. The sun did me good yesterday.

Today "our" PhD student Kat arrives from Ontario to work on her article, a literature review. Conversations on career writing and narrative identity development will be happening in the chairs in the kitchen.

Frans is sorely missed on this project, which we began together last year. He would have loved to be a part of it.

Now about getting Maya into a good post-holiday sleeping schedule!

***

January 10, 2019

I had a beautiful dream that you visited.

They say that there are dreams about people we know and there are "visitation" dreams. This was one of those where I felt it wasn't just images and dreams, but I felt your presence.

In the dream, you looked at me with a loving and penetrating gaze. It seemed like you were saying, "What I have given you is for you and I want you to have it fully and without reserve."

***

January 12, 2019

These last days my heart is full to the brim with a feeling of sorrow that pours over in spurts like an overfull pail. This week my sister Elke was so beautifully present and sincere that the pail of sorrow tilted and flooded out over the edges.

> If you want the bereaved to grieve,
> do not tell them how to be
> what to do
> love them as you would a tender thing
> name their loss with an open heart
> expect nothing
> then they will tell you how it is
> in the most tender moments

Today I reassured a colleague who was a little scared to approach me that this sorrow is not dangerous or scary, that it is living. It is still me! It is me living with a full heart.

I missed Frans dearly this evening. It made me shaky and quiet at first, then I spoke of it to my sister Elke, then I wrote it down, and then I cried it out.

> I am not depressed
> our kind of living was too alive for that
> our attitude in life had a lot of music to it
> and music sometimes expresses the most formidable beauty in
> the saddest pieces
> it has its pauses
> its full stops
> its baritone whole notes

The only sadness that would be wrong is if people and moments that mattered went unnoticed or unremembered.

In one of my Facebook posts I write, "Emotions are like a weather system that keeps the surface of the planet clean. And sometimes they ravage portions that will never look the same, but they too restore themselves in a certain way to become different landscapes where new birds come to sing their songs (never that rare, special bird, but other ones that belong in the landscape, nonetheless)."

What I am saying is that I am alive, at work, breathing the day, helping others, and taking care of myself on this unknown shore. When asked to make loudly the sound of joy, a wail comes out instead.

These things are equal: a wail and an ecstatic scream.

Later, that same day, I visit an old book in my collection. The work of Kahlil Gibran (1923). "The deeper that sorrow carves into your being, the more joy you can contain" (p. 29).

> In the morning
>
> while sorrow was sitting
> on each lower eyelid
> a hum of something
> sang its way into my mind
> a message in the shower saying
> " … happiness is the truth."

I didn't know the exact name of the song with the lyrics, "Happiness is the truth" that started humming in my head, nor did I know the artist. I found it on YouTube. It is called "Happy" by Pharrell Williams. I played it on my laptop while I put the kettle on and made coffee in the French press.

We spent the day working. Kat and I sat in our chairs and did what we like to do: study, read, and write. In the early afternoon, she and I walked through the snow and sunshine to Timmies. Frans's chair is well used; Kat is at work, I want to tell him. Later, I cook roast potatoes and beef and make romaine lettuce with blue cheese dressing.

***

Note

1 Part of this story became the introduction to my PhD dissertation on career narrative work and a scholarly article called *Narrative Self-rescue: A Poetic Response to a precarious Labour Crisis* (Lengelle, 2016).

6

BEGINNINGS AND ADAPTIVE EMOTIONS

In April 2007, Frans and I both went to the National Association of Poetry Therapy (NAPT) conference in Portland, Oregon. It was the first time we'd seen each other in almost a decade, though we had been corresponding daily since the fall of 2006. Our main topic of conversation was what change processes and dynamics underlie our ability to have agency and feel whole both personally and professionally.

Frans spoke about concepts like identity formation and narrative identity. I spoke about creative, expressive, and reflective writing, my own experience with writing and healing, and stories from the years of working with students. We also talked about attraction, sex, and our feelings for each other.

I remember sitting with Frans in a Starbucks in the middle of downtown Portland and him explaining cognitive learning steps that we would later use in our model. I explained to him how changing a narrative usually resulted in a shift in perspective, acceptance, or new meaning found (or a combination thereof). I insisted on the observer in the model, which, at first, he could not place.

Our conversation was always engaged and animated, and it turned us on. We also went to the Portland art gallery and found we were drawn to similar pieces of artwork. For instance, a sculpture of grandmothers on the lower floor of the city's gallery struck us both as exceptionally beautiful. We sat close, we walked hand in hand, as we had done those many years before.

We went into a jewelry store and Frans bought me a gold ring, which I requested be sized for my pinky finger; we are not ready to call our relating a marriage, I said responsibly. We were, after all, married to other people. It was clear, though, in our impassioned and inspired conversations and in how our bodies sought closeness and touch, that we were embarking on something that we likely wouldn't be able to keep from pursuing.

When Frans left Portland a few mornings before I did, I remember sitting in the lobby on one of the couches where we had just said good-bye. It seemed for a moment that I didn't know what to do or where to go—that I just had to wait until my body would decide. He had gone out to the airport shuttle bus that was waiting for other hotel guests. I remember standing up and walking out the glass doors just to see if I could wave one more time, and as I stood on the sidewalk outside the hotel, trying to make out if I could see him, he came out of the bus with fast strides, crossed the curved road by the doors, and held me. It was in that moment that I trusted that his affection for me was as deep as mine was for him. Although we had just spent several intense days together, sleeping in the same bed, but without fully consummating our love, this embrace felt like a turning point. When I got home from that trip, my friend Marlene asked—assessing where this might be going and what it might mean for my marriage to Keath—"Would you ever give Frans up?" I remember, to my own surprise, answering definitively, "Only when he is dead."

That statement was made truthfully and soberly. I didn't feel the decision was of my own making. It was like I was hearing myself say something so I would come to know how I felt.

***

When I returned to Edmonton, we continued work on our article, which was published in the *Journal of Poetry Therapy* in 2009. While writing that article, I also wrote a new book of poetry called *Blossom and Balsam: Poems that Reveal and Heal* (Lengelle, 2008). I dedicated it to both Keath and Frans using the name "Grysard" for Frans so as not to reveal his identity. I still feel a debt of gratitude to Keath, who also did the cover of that book.

Frans and I met again in London in the fall of 2007, and the following spring at the Poetry Therapy conference in Minneapolis. In 2009, we also co-presented our writing toward the transformation model at the NAPT conference in Washington, DC. We had a group of about 15 conference delegates who came to listen who were all sitting with us around a large round table. One of those participants, who did not know of our personal relationship, asked, "How in God's name did a researcher and a poet meet up to do this kind of work together?!" That question amused us, and we explained that Frans was looking for more creative methods in his work and I was looking for concepts to create more conscious foundations for the work I was doing.

In 2012, when I went to the NAPT conference by myself, this same woman (a widow), who by now knew Frans and I were more than research partners, said to me, "You know loving someone that much older than you means that you will likely lose him." It was as if she wanted to know if I could handle the idea of him dying; she talked about the horrible loss of her own husband. It was as if she wanted to be sure I knew what I was getting myself into. I simply said, "Yes, that's true. I may well lose him one day."

It was not really about choosing; her question was, in that sense, not compelling. What could we do but live the life that we were both strongly drawn to live? Our intellectual life and compatibility were at the heart of our physical and emotional (and sexual) attraction, and we were compelled to learn more together. We were of the same caliber, or, as Frans would say, "cut from the same cloth." It is something we had not known with our first spouses, as both his ex and mine had been in supportive roles and had focused more on the domestic aspects of life. Both of them were loving, but neither of them was interested in the intellectual life or tried to find fulfillment in a career. They simply could not be dialogue partners the way Frans and I were for each other. Frans and I were always in search of the next internal challenge, the next intellectual horizon. And perhaps we were also selfish.

I recently read this online quote by Sam Shepard and it resonated: "There can be a real meeting between two people at the point where they always felt marooned. Right at the edge" (2017). Frans and I wrote about our personal lives in a final chapter on our career choices (Lengelle & Meijers, 2019). In it, we speak about what leads people into their careers and that it also involves an element of what pains us. We describe both feeling like strangers in a strange land for different reasons: he as a small-town boy becoming an intellectual, me as an immigrant child of divorced parents. We wrote the stories with a desire to understand ourselves and each other. Our drive to learn was equally intense; once he said to me, "We are doomed to one another."

He was right, it would turn out. And that meant that I was doomed to see him die. Frans being dead makes writing about our passionate and engaged life both poignant and sorrowful. Our experiencing together on this earth is done, and I literally and even physiologically reconstruct the memory and touch its associations. These memories collide with thoughts like "He is dead now, so that is over," and "That was then, but that will never be again," and "Now see how precious all of that was, even in moments when I didn't appreciate it fully."

Time travel (i.e., being anywhere but the present) is painful, the Buddhists say; it is attachment to what no longer is. There is truth in that. There is also truth in the fact that I have real memories and a love that is not erased by death. I am still married to Frans in my heart; our parting is different from a break-up. We did not want our life together to end, so we continued together day by day until our joint life was taken.

***

Colleen writes me this morning on Facebook messenger. Our conversation goes like this:

COLLEEN: Your daily Facebook posts are so good. I really am looking forward to reading the book whenever you finish it … I imagine it will take a while to read because it will likely be very emotional. I'm glad you are writing down happy memories, reading those will be very enjoyable I suspect.

ME: Thank you, my dear—feeling quite sad writing them, though I imagine others will be glad to read about our inspired relationship—intense and fruitful. Hard to imagine anything like it will ever be again but I keep hearing people say very positive things about my future, also relationship-wise.

COLLEEN: I imagine that it is difficult to reconcile the depth of "these times were so good; I will treasure them" and "these times were so good; yet he is gone therefore we cannot make more together." As an outsider to it, I can only find the memories heartwarming, still able to feel sad for your loss but not in the same conflicting way. Your emotions on this are very complex, naturally. I hope the writing today helps you feel peaceful this evening. Most of your writing about grief so far, even the really honest and more difficult posts, have still had a sense of hope intertwined throughout and beneath the surface of the message, at least when I read them, the knowledge that you have other things that fill your life with meaning helps the darker moments you write about have glimmers of light. I find that very inspiring.

ME: Thank you, Colleen. Another person wrote and said, "It is good to hear you have not lost your lust for life" and that is perhaps what you are also saying.

***

Yesterday, a student dealing with the aftermath of a divorce after a long marriage spoke of being in the winter of life. He also wrote to say he has been thinking of what I might be going through in my months on leave as I told my students why I would be away from work in November and December. This poem took shape one evening when I thought about how writing allows us to share in the grief.

They wrote in winter

about how what had nourished them
and filled their lives for so long would not return
a thousand poets had said it before, a million voices now
lost in history, had known it before,
but they lifted their pens anyway
and told the unsentimental truth about it,
in their separate rooms with their separate griefs
eventually, they read each other
there was someone, it turned out, who knew about such days

***

Just when I think I don't want to write another word that will cause me to feel more grief and sadness, an e-mail comes in from a student of mine who is sending me a bouquet of flowers to thank me and to send her condolences.

If you stay open, there is encouragement everywhere. At least that's how I am taking it.

***

Writing about the Day Frans Died

I have been putting off writing about the day and actual moment that Frans died.

First, of course, the topic is difficult, and the content is detailed and lengthy. Second, I may re-experience the feelings I had on the day of his death by writing it out and experience them as freshly painful. Deep breath.

His warm body was like a heavy, floppy doll in my arms after he stopped breathing; I stayed with him in those early hours so I could still feel this part of his aliveness before it faded. Soon he would really feel and look like a body and not the man I knew and who was my lover. Tears erupt as I write this now and it is only the first in a series of powerful memories of that final day.

I now also notice such internal images seem to be followed by memories of him alive: him eating an ice-cream cone with me on a street corner in New York City; him holding my hand while flying; his bright smile across the table in a quaint café in San Francisco where we had breakfast each morning.

There are two worlds—Frans alive and Frans dead. They continue to co-exist. They say relationships never fully end, even if they have been broken off or death parts us. I think loved ones never die; Frans is alive within me.

Someone recently wrote this line to me: "Your love is inseparable." Perhaps that is at the heart of what I am experiencing.

In the evenings the tears frequently come. That's when I'm tired and relaxed and out of workmode. It also happens when friends ask good questions.

In the silences after dinner or in writing in the evenings as I do now, thoughts like, "He is dead; he is no longer in this world; he will never be there again" enter my mind. I come apart willingly.

As I have written before, emotions come to pass and not to stay. I always feel better for having let sorrow wash through me. Sometimes my crying is pained; sometimes I weep quietly. It usually doesn't last for more than 5 minutes at a time.

If anyone asked me for advice on grieving so far, I would say, *Allow all the feelings to be there without inflating and inflaming these with additional thoughts.* For instance, I was sitting in my chair creating a back-up earlier this week on a USB stick. I came across a photograph of us that I hadn't seen in a while. I stopped to look closely at a picture of Frans, noticing his eyes, his hair, the expression on his face, and our joy. My eyes filled with tears and I just let that happen.

In such moments, a thought like, "Never again" or "He is gone" might also arise. I let those thoughts be just what they are and I pay close attention when I start hearing thoughts in my mind that project worry into the future or pain me from the past: "Why could I never solve the …" or "The next 30 years will be lonely …" Even thoughts like, "Being single is and will be hard" pass by, and I don't let them land where they can burn in.

These kinds of ruminations add gasoline to feelings when I invest in them; if I just notice them as thoughts and don't believe them, they simply ebb away. The discipline is simply to be aware of the danger of adding fuel to the fire of worry, terrible yearning, or arguing with reality as I write about earlier using the Byron Katie exercise.

At a 2-hour grieving workshop this past week, an expression I have read before and have repeated myself came along again: "In life, pain is a given, but suffering is optional." This is my experience with this pain of Frans's death, too. It causes me pain. The pain comes through me; all feelings visit; I notice and coax myself to allow them instead of clenching around any of them, inflaming, or resisting them.

A few days ago, I turned 49, and many people sent kind messages. Some said, "It must be a difficult birthday this year," or "It must be so strange," and I sense their kindness and care. Yet, I did not experience the day that way. Maybe it's because I had good company with Margot and Maya close by or because I usually invite friends in the week of my birthday and that is what I did this week too.

Frans usually took me out to a very nice dinner on or close to my birthday. Two years ago, he bought me the book *Consolations: The Solace, Nourishment and Underlying Meaning of Everyday Words*, by David Whyte (just as I was about to buy it for myself). He asked me, "Is it terrible that I did not think of a gift for you myself?" I smiled at him and said, "My dear, we are in San Francisco! What better gift?" This year, I remember those things and know that if he were here, we would have gone out to eat in a good restaurant.

There is no one and no thing to blame; there is no entitlement.

This birthday is an extension of my life as Frans and I lived it. I might even say that he's given me full permission to enjoy. We spoke about this while he was ill.

Over the years, he often quoted his mother. "Celebrate whenever you can, because the days for crying come of their own accord."

I might mint my own expression that is a variation on hers. "Celebrate whenever you can, even when the days include crying."

You said

the caravan
of life moves on
without me
I am only sad that I will
be left behind as all of you
go on to live

but live you must
it is the only thing that rests.

***

February 10, 2019

Yesterday was a good day. Maya and I had to be up early to get her to her volunteer work, so we saw the sunrise. The night before we'd been out to stand-up comedy with a group of friends and family, so we had to make the extra effort to get up.

While waiting for her, I wrote in a café; I worked on putting together the poems for my newest collection, with the working title *Fifty Poems While You Were Dying*. I wrote 40 poems while Frans was ill and many more after his death. Fifty is a symbolic number: Frans was born in 1950.

I believe Frans would smile from his chair with a thick book on his lap if he saw how this day has gone. His picture smiles at us warmly in the kitchen workspace.

***

Recipe for a Broken Heart

February 14, 2019.

Ingredients for Valentine bereavement pie

Three cups wisdom of patience
Two cups all-purpose feeling tolerance (try the organic brand, it's smoother and allows for deeper integration)
One 1/2 cup hydrotherapy
Five friends who love you dearly
Sleep (as much as you can get)
A daily walk—in the sunlight is preferable, so don't waste the sunny days
A pinch of past good memory
Sift ingredients to add lightness to future thoughts and hopes.

Then add the name of the beloved made from almond paste.

In addition, put in 55 grams of humor to laugh at the absurdity of life and six drops of unabashed courage and cheekiness.

Mix in intuitive order in a large bowl (nonstick brand "Holding Space" by Winnicott). Set oven to heartwarming. Wait until it smells done. Share with visitors. Best served with tea and stories.

PS: Apologies from the publisher as the ingredients for Joy Pie are the same.

***

Emotions Help Me Through Grief

March 9, 2019

I took a partial break from writing in February and March when my friend Margot came to stay with me. We walked daily, even when it was -25 C with a windchill. On our walks through the neighborhood, past the pines, spruces, naked black poplars, and the comforting mountain ashes, we spoke about our heartbreaks. She about a breakup, me about Frans. I can speak to her about my anger as well as my sorrow; she does not see the two as mutually exclusive, even when I wonder about this myself.

We speak about how Frans's death is changing my life, what I miss about being partnered, what I don't miss about Frans, ongoing sexual desire, and what I have written so far about all of it. I also spend time finishing the collection of poems about his illness and passing and I have been looking for additional research and writing on bereavement. Teaching commitments increased as the semester got into full swing as well: life goes on, those words keep coming back. I keep hearing Frans say them.

I spent this past week in Calgary for a nonviolent communication workshop that I took with my sister Elke. I went to the impressive new library downtown. There was a section, almost 3-ft long, on the loss of a loved one. I read several shorter books while there and found the work of George Bonanno, a Columbia University professor who has been researching grief for over 20 years, he recently published an accessible book called *The Other Side of Sadness* (2009).

His book debunks several widespread and longstanding myths on grieving; for instance, that if a person doesn't express a lot of emotion, they must be repressing grief and this means they will inevitably have to face a delayed grief reaction. Research does not bear this out. Some people may feel sad but not be very expressive about it while others are more overtly emotional.

In a book on how men might grieve differently than women, I later read that there is a continuum of grief responses: on the one side intuitive (i.e., more emotionally expressive) and on the other side instrumental (i.e., more apt to plan projects and do practical things). What one's aptitude is isn't necessarily tied to sex or gender, though as people age, they seem to get closer and closer to the middle of the continuum. In other words, they end up being emotionally expressive as well as planning activities (Doka & Martin, 2010).

Bonanno (2009) writes that it's a myth that a less overtly emotional response is an indication of a more superficial relationship, though this may be what some assume. The notion of "grief as work" (which was an idea Freud proposed without much research to support it in 1917) is countered too, with insights about how emotions are not merely reactions to overcome grief but adaptions to help us through.

For instance, sadness, which we generally see as a natural consequence of loss and therefore a symptom, actually helps us come to terms with the death of a loved one. This is because when we're sad, we slow down and turn inward, and assess things more truthfully than we otherwise might (Bonanno, 2009).

Reading this, I was reminded of Gordon Neufeld and Gabor Maté's (2013) book *Hold on to Your Kids,* where the authors speak of coaxing an angry child gently toward sadness, as "tears of futility" are what allow a child to accept the inevitability of limits and disappointments which they at first resist. This is the same with grieving adults: sadness is the physiological way we actually get in touch with the fact that that person we loved is really dead.

Emotions, as they occur, help us to get below the magical thinking that seems to be a feature of the mind. In more poetic language, I would say that the "soft animal of your body" (to borrow from poet Mary Oliver) can realize loss through visceral experience while the mind can speak or think of death, but does not fully comprehend it. In everyday language, we say, "It has to sink in," and it seems sadness helps that to happen.

Sadness, which is visible on our faces, Bonanno (2009) points out is also adaptive because it elicits social support. That doesn't mean, however, that more sadness is better. Reading Bonanno's research, I got the sense of living with as opposed to working through grief. In the nondoing and allowing, we are resilient, and resilience is not a fixed trait (though some may be more predisposed to it than others). It is rather an emergent trait, dependent too on our community and our ability to form and maintain bonds.

Sadness is not the only adaptive emotion, Bonanno points out. Laughter is also adaptive and it's common for grieving people to joke, smile, and laugh. I experienced this regularly with Frans (and his daughters) while he was ill, and many times afterward too. For instance, we joked about how his body was going to fit through the narrow hallway and out of the house after he died, and we came up with various scenarios that included lifting him out the window on to the market square. We riffed off of each other about how we might have to do this after shopping hours so that we wouldn't upset people walking by. We also joked about not wanting to do anything that looked illegal.

When I presented my autoethnographic work to a group of 80 colleagues at our annual research forum over a year after Frans's death, I told them about my conversation with Frans about cooking for me once I got my full-time tenure-track job, and they too had to laugh when I said, "He proved doubly that he was not into cooking; he conveniently died six weeks before he would have had to start …" There was also audible laughter when I told them he was an atheist, but that he'd assured me in a chipper voice that this didn't mean I couldn't call on him at any time after his death.

When a friend winced in pain from a muscle cramp not long after Frans's death, I joked, "That muscle, I hope, is on top of your ribs and not underneath! I can't have you dying on me; there's been enough dying for a while." Humor is good medicine: it lightens the load, and in this way, Bonanno says, grievers make it easier to bear their own pain and also make it easier for others to feel and remain connected with them.

We all know people who are hard to stay connected to because they seem to treat their lot in life as if it were a punishment. If one can laugh instead, a lot of space for living is created. Our friend Ellie, who has suffered serious long-term health issues, recently reminded me of this when I visited her in hospital and saw that her patient whiteboard had creative discharge plans. They went as follows: "Build time machine, transport myself to 'ye olden days' to time when I was healthy … Nah, how boring! Go back to roaring 20s and dance, drink champagne, and date Scott F. Fitzgerald."

Bonanno's grief research also shows that it is common for people who have lost loved ones to experience relief, first, because they see their beloved is out of pain, but also because caring for an ill spouse or family member can become taxing and can change the nature of a partnership. I didn't experience the latter as Frans wasn't ill for very long, nor did he need enormous amounts of physical care, but certainly there was a relief knowing his pain was not going to get worse. If a relationship has known recurring conflict, as ours did, a spouse may also be relieved not to have to deal with the strain of such patterns anymore.

The numbers on resilience are interesting and somewhat comforting: according to Maccallum et al. (2015), 68.2% of people have little or no depression after losing a loved one. They also report that those with pre-existing depression (7.4%) continue to have depression; 13.2% of people have chronic grief following a loss (this is more frequently associated with violent death); and 11.2% have pre-loss depression, which decreases following the loss (pp. 72–79).

***

March 13, 2019

I reflect back on the many dialogues I've been having with Frans. There is some consensus that maintaining a bond with the beloved in these types of dialogues is healthy (Klass et al., 2014; Neimeyer, 2016; Paxton, 2018). A day after writing another dialogue with Frans in my journal, I read further in Bonanno's (2009) book and he spends almost a chapter on this topic.

At first, it seems researchers were very positive about maintaining a bond, but Bonanno speaks about some caveats. People who keep all or most of a deceased's belongings or insist on keeping everything arranged the same way usually fare poorly as they maintain the bond, and are likely suffering from more complicated grief. Chronic grief is associated with "preloss dependency," which shows in these behaviors (Bonanno et al., 2002).

Those who were insecurely attached or who felt unsure about the quality of the relationship also suffer in their way of connecting to the beloved. Those who felt they had good and secure relationships either maintained a bond through dialogue (usually in a verbal form, while I do this through writing) or through strong pleasant memories. The research on this shows that it's also important that the conversation with the beloved happens at a time that the pain of the grief is a bit less fresh; otherwise, the conversation could stir up painful longings that might upset a person's equilibrium (Bonanno, 2009, pp. 138–144).

***

A week ago, I visited my oldest student who is turning 95 this month. Louise, who survived World War II in England, serves us tea with delicious lactose-free cream and honey from her grand daughter's bees. She laughs frequently. All my students are online, but occasionally I have the opportunity to meet one of them in the flesh, and for Louise I make a special effort. Doing all the work through the computer is not always straightforward, and I think it's only fair that she has met and seen the person who will be guiding her through the course.

Louise has been a widow for 44 years and writes poetry. When her husband Tom died, she wrote a poem that helped her right after he died, but also many years into the future. She still has it memorized. The last two lines became a kind of mantra for her throughout her life.

Yesterday, I e-mailed her to ask for a copy:

Dear Louise,

Are you willing to share the poem you wrote after Tom died, the one where the last lines are about "standing on your own two feet"? This really moved me and it's quite pertinent to my current life journey, as you know.

Of course, any other widow advice you might have for me would be most welcome. (No pressure, of course.)

I look forward to hearing from you,
Reinekke

Her reply came this morning:

Dear Reinekke,

Certainly, you can have a copy and I am glad I could help you a wee bit. I do not know if you felt like me as so many people say "I am sorry" until you want to scream. I also found comfort in the last two lines and, I am being absolutely honest when I say those lines have made a difference in me. I think I can say that I am standing on my own feet and am looking forward to the future instead of sitting feeling useless. I did, for a long time after Tom died, keep reciting that last verse and it worked like a talisman and I could go on. I think that holding on to some phrase you can believe, does act like a talisman when you think your life has stopped. I have made mine "keep your brain working and keep on laughing." It is working for me. Write to me or come whenever you want. The pain does get less and does fade away but keep the memories, they are precious.

I still can see him sitting there
Hear him speaking like a ghost
Your husband, he's got cancer

He has three months at the most.
He died his pain was ended
but mine had just begun
Because I was left in darkness without a gleam of sun.
I'd always been a clinging vine
and clung to him in the past
But God has given me two feet
Now He's made me stand on them at last.

Louise

***

Today was one of the first warmer days, though there is still snow everywhere. The winter has been long, but the walking is now more pleasant. I have just put the crockpot on with chili for later tonight. I will be alone for the evening. This always gives me time for reflection and sometimes for crying. My walk today revealed some interesting insights and the morning began with the first day in an online course called "Radical Acceptance," based on the book by Tara Brach (2012). We're a group of seven women who will meet online via video call every 2 weeks and speak about our relationship with ourselves.

Besides my studying grief and the internal dialogue, my meeting and corresponding with others sustain me too. Maintaining bonds with the living is, of course, as important as exploring bonds with the deceased! Or, said more simply, my connections with others do me good, while going inside continues to be a place of solace where I meet Frans, and where I nurture myself.

***

March 12, 2019:

Today, I wrote with inspiration from author Elizabeth Gilbert (2019). I listened to an interview she gave about losing her partner Rayya Elias to cancer. She speaks of sorrow, the ups and downs of taking care of Rayya, and the possibilities now that she is widowed. She doesn't treat grief like the negative aftermath of loving, or a tragedy, but rather as an integral part of living fully.

Like Elizabeth Gilbert, I am a willing student of grief. I make notes as I'm listening to the podcast interview: "Relaxing in the awesome power of it as it goes through you. Grief is a full-body experience. Something you bow to; you don't control it."

When I listen to the interview a second time, I clean the living room, on my hands and knees plucking lint off my huge Persian carpet and re-stacking my papers and books neatly on my rolling desk cart, the entire time concentrating on what she has to say.

Questions arise as I listen and I ask them using her language:

> How is this living life without Frans a path into somewhere I can't yet imagine?
>
> How can it be a path toward a fuller life even? How can I be "into me" when I have lost the person who was "into me" and I "into him"?

I make more notes:

> "Don't seek out dark nights of the soul, they will come to you … Beauty, resilience, grace … that's at least half the story of life." Gilbert's expression reminds me of Frans's mother's advice about enjoying the good times while you have them.

What Gilbert is expressing reminds me of the pieces I've been sharing in my Facebook posts.

"I will feel whatever I need to feel …. I am willing to be in all of it. Feeling is the absence of depression."

The attitude, "'I am willing … ' is useful. It allows us to pass by the gates of resistance without the usual suffering of not wanting to go there."

Then she says, "It's an honor to be in grief." I agree. It's an honor in two ways: you get to feel your love all over again, and grief breaks you open to see so much beauty if you'll let it.

As I listen, I also notice how she laughs fully as she speaks about grief, and even her partner's moment of death, which was not peaceful (and yet was completely true to how this woman had lived, although it was not what Gilbert had imagined). Even Gilbert's role in her girlfriend's illness process and death was not what she'd expected it to be.

There is so much illusion-busting potential in grief, I think to myself. My illusion—which was only brief before it blew up—was that I could grieve without being angry. Gilbert too encounters anger in the early months following her partner's death. She tells her audience how she bows to it all and lets the body express the hurt. Later, Dorothy Rosen, a widow I meet in an online course, tells me about her anger too: "I get mad when I think about all the things that Steve has left me to do" (personal communication, July 9, 2020). Krista, another widow, shares that she is angered by the lost intimacy after years of her husband's ill health, and how death ended any hope of experiencing such closeness again. Yet another widow finds her husband has left her with a mountain of debt. There are differing reasons for the anger, but it seems to be a common reaction in grief, and it turns out this emotion has a purpose.

Bonanno's (2009) research into the adaptive function of feelings shows up in Gilbert's story, and Bonanno also mentions that anger can be less taxing on the cardiovascular system and cortisol levels as it can give us a sense of empowerment.

Anger is an adaptive emotion that helps us protect ourselves from threatening situations. In the form of indignation, it gives us a feeling of temporary strength. Gabor Maté (2011), a Canadian doctor and author of *When the Body Says No,* calls anger part of the body's psychic immune system and necessary for boundary setting.

Of course, this is not the case if anger is chronic or obsessive or turns to bitterness. Anger can help prevent us from feeling entirely downtrodden or despairing, which is what I make of Bonanno's (2009) conclusions. He also writes that it "may help us negotiate shifting social relations in the wake of loss" and help people develop a sense that they "will be able to survive" on their own (pp. 35–36). It's closer to courage and resilience than feeling like a victim, either of the death or other matters associated with the illness, death, or relationship.

Gilbert (2019) also talks about how she can live life more fully as the filter of her beloved accompanies her and she sees the world through her partner Rayya's eyes as well as her own. I also see life more fully when I put on my Frans lens and imagine his perspective in various situations. What would he say to our PhD student? What would he say about my friend's problem and what she most needs right now? What would he say about the university's current politics?

Today I dialogued with Frans on paper again. He felt very present and reminded me, "My dear, please hear me when I say how much I wanted to stay with you, even though I couldn't! I would so much have liked to have been there for you! You're doing so well. You continue to go on with life. All will be well with you; also in love." Frans used words like *very*, *really*, *completely*, and *so much*, and also used a lot of exclamation marks!!! This sounds so like his exuberant voice.

Gilbert also speaks daringly of "bright futures ahead," about the life she "can live now that her great love has died." We have lost the life we could have had with our beloved, so instead, we get the life we have now. "This is incredibly exciting; now I get to get whatever's coming," she says.

Within what we can't control, this is the opportunity and it's freeing to embrace this, even though we generally don't allow ourselves to speak this way, as it somehow implies we are celebrating the loss. What we're doing, though, is celebrating life in the face of the loss.

Gilbert was due to deliver a novel to her publisher shortly after her partner died, and this forced her to get back to work. My new job also started 6 weeks after Frans's death, and I was determined to start. Gilbert realized while writing her book that her vitality came from doing her work, rather than grieving first and hoping vitality would return so she *could* work.

I too am glad to be working on my writing project and doing my teaching. Even when people think my intellectual endeavors are ways to avoid grief.

"Don't worry," Grief says. "I'll be keeping my appointments with you."

***

7
DEATH

It is April 3, 2019, and maybe I am ready to write about the day Frans died. As I say in my introduction, he died on November 16, 2018, and I have written more than 100 pages of our life, his illness, and how I am doing in the aftermath of his death, but I have yet to tell the story of the day and moment itself.

To some extent, it was a surprise to us both that we managed to sleep the night before Frans was to receive three injections that would end his life. It was to happen around 3:00 p.m. on a Friday afternoon.

In the last week of October, two physicians had visited him to see if he was of sound mind and could make the decision to receive euthanasia. He was afraid it was a kind of exam he had to take, but it turned out to be nothing of the kind. The checks and balances around ending one's life this way in The Netherlands require a private conversation with two doctors who want to make sure you know what it means to receive euthanasia, and that no one in your life is pressuring you to take this step. The family physician already has all the documents and medical records to confirm there is no physical hope of your recovery. Frans didn't want to "lose my mind, shit in my pants, or lie in bed for days or weeks"—and again, in his customary and determined fashion, he made the decision to die on November 16, which was some 3 weeks after the doctors had come to visit and given their okay.

On the night of November 15, I slept for about 6 hours, from midnight until 6:00 a.m. Frans took sleeping pills and I had sometimes been taking some melatonin which seemed to leave me feeling calm and relaxed, even in the hours when I would sometimes be half-awake (not kept up by conscious thoughts, but not sleeping deeply either).

Those last 2 weeks of Frans's life, his daughters came often. They would arrive around 9:00 or 10:00 in the morning and stay until dinnertime. They brought novels and laptops and sometimes they'd watch movies and a TV series with Frans. Ally McBeal was a favorite of his youngest daughter and Frans, and sometimes I'd watch parts of it with them.

I worked until November 1, and requested 2 months off; I wanted to rest, start writing my book, and start my new job on January 1. I told myself, "Well, you will have about six weeks to be ready to go back to work; he'll die, there will be a funeral, you'll pack, move your stuff to your sister's in Amsterdam, fly back to Canada, and try to feel normal enough to carry on."

Frans wanted me to be this pragmatic about it and he wanted it for his daughters too. Not only did he value work all his life, but he didn't want us to fall apart or have our lives be disrupted and complicated because of his death. His youngest had important meetings at the beginning of December, I had my new job starting, and Maya, 15, was on the other side of the world.

I asked Frans whether all of these things factored into his decision to die mid-November. He said yes, and that he didn't see the point of getting weaker and weaker and suffering more, for a few extra weeks. "Besides, I have said my good-byes. I have said everything I needed to say. There is no use dragging it out," he told us.

His sister-in-law, who had worked in palliative care for many years, estimated that Frans was about 3 weeks away from a natural death when he died, though we will never know.

***

The Day

On the morning of November 16, we spent time alone until about 9:30 or 10:00 a.m. Frans's daughters came mid-morning. My mother and my sister Charlene came at noon, as did Frans's ex-wife. I had invited her to be at his deathbed if she wanted to be, respecting their long relationship and acknowledging the importance of her role in supporting their daughters.

That morning, I sat beside Frans on our yellow couch, and his daughters and their mother and my mother and sister sat on the other larger couch. At one point, he held his adult daughters under each of his arms. I took a picture for them, but later when I looked at it, I wondered if I should have. There was a moment he looked so sad and lost, and they squeezed their eyes shut in pain. Later, around lunchtime, the mood lightened, and Frans joked and spoke of politics. Everyone engaged and his girls stayed physically close to him, while their mother sat with them.

I don't remember if we had lunch, but if we did, no doubt my mother and sister prepared it; I didn't move much from the couch, nor did Frans except to go to the bathroom. My mother took pictures of us that I treasure now; there was so much vulnerability in our faces as we looked at each other in those last hours. There was no more alone time.

At around 1:30 p.m., the paramedic came as planned and installed the IV port in Frans's left wrist; it would be used for the final injections. This ambulance man was tall, and dressed in official garb (orange and bright yellow reflective clothing). He asked Frans if he knew what the IV was for. This was like a kind of double-checking, maybe an extra protocol around the euthanasia. We'd expected the paramedic by about 1:00 p.m., but when he hadn't shown up quite yet, Frans started asking a bit anxiously whether there was a problem. He became agitated and had me phone the doctor's office to make sure everything was still going according to plan. In a way, this was a good sign, as it showed us he was still determined. There was no hesitation, no questioning his decision; true to his habit, once he'd made up his mind about something, he would see it through.

The family physician and his assistant (a doctor in training) arrived, as planned, at 3:00 p.m. I let them in. I remember being at the bottom of the stairs and feeling momentarily "complicit." They went up the stairs ahead of me, and once upstairs they went into the living room. I was about to offer them tea and ask them to sit down, when I saw from Frans's body language that he didn't want to have them sit down or have tea. Understandably so.

Frans said that he was ready, and he stood up from the couch.

He hugged my mother and my sister Charlene good-bye, and then he headed down the hallway. In fact, he did it so quickly that I nearly had to sprint a few steps to keep up. I wanted to stay close to him and not let him out of my sight. When he'd arrived at this death bed, he hugged his daughters and his ex-wife and laid down.

We had decided he would die in the guestroom. It was the room at the end of the hall that had a door that led to the roof terrace where we often sat outside when the weather was warm. In the guestroom, which had been my girls' bedroom when they were living in The Netherlands on my sabbatical in 2012–2013, there were two single, metal-framed beds that I'd fastened together with wire as we often had couples stay overnight with us. The bed formed a large double with one of the long ends against the wall.

I had Bach instrumental music playing in the hall and candles on the table in the room. Frans's friend Ellen had suggested the music and the ritual. It felt good to do it and to create some warmth in the room this way.

The day before, we'd practiced how to position ourselves, with his daughters close by sitting behind him. They didn't want to rehearse it, but Frans insisted. Frans and I lay belly to belly on the bed on the outside, with enough space for the doctors to stand beside us. Frans's youngest daughter and ex-wife sat behind his head and shoulders, respectively, and his oldest daughter and her husband sat behind his legs and feet. They all sat cross-legged, and he and I lay facing each other. Like lovers. Like we had done so many times in our years together.

He was still talking when the doctors began preparing the first injection: something to relax him. The doctors asked him if he could feel anything after the first needle; he said he felt a cooling sensation but that it didn't hurt.

I looked him in the eyes and he me. I didn't want to miss any part of what was about to happen. I felt his left arm lean on my right side—it was stretched out with the IV port. I couldn't see them doing any of the injections, I could just feel his arm and wrist lifting off and returning to my side as they worked. I could hear their voices, but I kept looking at Frans, and he kept looking at me.

Then he said, "Thank you" to everyone behind him, and to me he said, "I was so lucky with you."

I kept saying, "Have a good journey, beautiful man; have a good journey my beautiful man … beautiful man …" Tears were streaming down my face. I am sure my face was cracked in an awful look of sorrow. I remember someone reaching out to touch my leg to comfort me. I think it was Sanne, his oldest daughter.

I remember he stopped talking mid-sentence and that the sensation of him holding me as firmly as I was holding him started to loosen. His iris and pupils rolled back out of view. That was the last time I remember seeing that his eyes were a beautiful blue. Eyes I had looked into so many times and that had always been lit with life. My focus from his face shifted to his throat where I could see a slight pulse still, or maybe I only imagined it. The doctor leaned in with a stethoscope (it was only about 3:20 p.m.). He confirmed Frans's death. Within what seemed like 5 or 10 minutes, his daughters, son-in-law, and ex-wife left the room. I stayed holding Frans's body and crying. He was still so warm in the blue cardigan I had bought for him; it almost seemed that his back was perspiring still. My hand was on the small of his back and I could feel the moisture of sweat coming through the knitted material.

I stayed with him in the hours that followed. It felt like he was still there in spirit, even though I don't know if I believe in spirits. I didn't want to leave his side. I felt comfortable and content to be with him (even as I start crying writing this). After a while, the doctor came to ask me how I was doing.

I just remember saying, "We made so many beautiful things together."

We'd been so much in love.

***

Washing Him, Dressing Him

I don't know how many hours I stayed with him, I only know that it started to get dark outside. I was calm, deflated, and solemn all at once. I knew many more feelings would be on the other side of this day, and I took them as they came, not judging whatever appeared or didn't.

Once in a while, someone would bring me a glass of water, usually my mother or my sister. Jesse, Frans's son-in-law, also came to sit with me. He and I had developed a friendship over the years and I had helped him get work. He is also a writer with a penchant for the kind of reflection that I do. He said, "I realize it must be hardest for you, as he was your partner. I was thinking about how I would feel if I lost Sanne."

I appreciated this acknowledgment and his gentle kindness. I experienced that again when I re-entered the living room and Frans's oldest daughter, Sanne, stood up to hug me. I joked that I needed a drink (everyone knows I don't actually drink), so this evoked some laughter. I hadn't eaten since noon or earlier, but I wasn't hungry. I didn't end up drinking. I wanted to stay in the mind I knew and the way of being I could trust; I must have realized on some level that I had used up most of my energy stores for the day.

Shortly after Frans died, an additional doctor had come to confirm the death and call some judicial body to ensure that they knew it was euthanasia and that all the boxes had been checked and procedures followed. I don't remember when his family physician and the assistant doctor left. I do remember that Frans's ex-wife was loud and laughing from the living room, which I assume was her way of coping.

A bottle of whisky was being emptied and there was a lot of boisterous talking. No one in the group usually drank excessively, so I understood it was a form of dealing with the magnitude of what had just happened. I didn't like the noise in the house; I realized that this was a difference in emotional style.

I was, however, feeling the need to be at home quietly, and my mother and sister were noticing I was starting to become exhausted by all the different energies in the house.

The undertaker came in the evening, around 7:00 p.m., and she sat with us with a list of things we had to discuss, though most of the rest of the planning would happen in the next few days. We spoke about the invitation card, the men who would come in a few days to pick up Frans's body and take it down the narrow stairwell. How his body would be moved from the stretcher to his basket at the local funeral home, walking distance from our home. There was something comforting in knowing the steps.

My mother and sister served coffee and tea as we talked. The undertaker had already brought the freezing plate that would be put on the bed to keep his body cooled for the next several days.

But first, it was time to wash Frans.

The undertaker asked who wanted to help. We all knew the invitation was directed at me and his daughters, as Frans had always insisted the three of us were the ones who would be deciding things about the funeral. His ex-wife seemed poised to help as well, but I said that I wanted to do this and I motioned to the girls that they were welcome too. The oldest didn't want to see Frans dead anymore; his youngest was okay for me to do it alone with the undertaker. It felt right to me as well, and I appreciated the space to be able to do it this way.

The undertaker and I went back to the room at the end of the long hallway and began to undress Frans. I remember he had a hole in the black Smartwool socks that I'd given him. While he was ill, he'd worn these almost constantly, as his feet were frequently cold. It seemed a bit funny, and for a moment I felt awkward that I, his spouse, had let him walk in socks with holes. I simply hadn't noticed. He would have probably said, "Don't worry about it, I won't need them much longer anyway, and they're still warm!"

We removed his pajama pants, which he had been wearing for weeks now, as they were softest and most comfortable. I had cotton pants for him to wear to his grave, and a light blue, long-sleeved, thin linen shirt that he had worn several times, once especially for me when he'd come to the train station to pick me up when I returned from my August job interview in Canada. Thinking about it now, I remember how frail he was as he arrived there, a friend beside him to help him keep his balance.

His body was still floppy, and in some ways, it had not yet changed much. It was like when kids play dead on a soft couch and they lift and drop each other's arms. He was still warm, but cooling. I got the yellow bucket from the bathroom and filled it with warm water. I brought two washcloths from the shelf—turquoise ones I had bought when we moved in. The undertaker and I washed him, and while we did, we talked. She gave instructions on how to lift him this way and that way and move his arms so that we could remove his navy t-shirt effectively. As his body became more naked, I said, "We were great lovers." She smiled and nodded gently, with compassion. I looked at his penis for the last time: resting there, it still looked like he might be alive; it was as if he was just sleeping on his back without covers on.

She explained about not removing the IV port as there would be bleeding. We left it and the gauze wrapped around his left wrist. That plastic port would be the one bit of nonorganic material that would go to his eco-grave. That, and his two heart stents that had been there since 2003.

We slid a diaper over his thin legs. It was the first diaper that I'd ever seen him wear, and he would have been happy about that. It seemed a bit ironic in that moment that he'd have to wear one at all, but she explained that sometimes body fluids leaked. I could see nothing leaking and this seemed congruent with his choice to go in a dignified way. Frans had been determined not to leak, and he'd spared himself that.

We put on the khaki pants I'd bought for him months earlier, that at first had been too tight (but I had kept them, knowing that they would fit, eventually). Above that, a clean white t-shirt and the linen shirt . We rolled him this way and that way. He only weighed about 140 pounds now, but it still took both of us to move him. We completed dressing him with socks (without holes)—regular cotton ones that he liked to wear in summer.

She asked about shoes. It was optional. "For some people, it's really important," she said. I said it wasn't necessary. He took his shoes off when he got home, though it was not custom to do so in the Netherlands. He'd proudly taken on the Canadian habit and he had moccasins from Edmonton. We left just the socks. Jesse had the same foot size and liked everything Western; the moccasins, as well as the thicker Ugg winter slippers, would be passed on to him. They still had lots of wear left in them. These were happy gifts. Frans and I had already spoken about the destination of the slippers.

The undertaker put a rubber-covered wire brace under Frans's jaw and against his neck to hold his mouth closed so it wouldn't begin to droop. The brace would be taken off later, she said, but for now, it left him looking restful and dignified. Under his eyelids, she put small pieces of paper used for rolling cigarettes, as that created just enough friction to keep his eyelids closed.

His beautiful full head of grey hair was already brushed; he had done it himself that morning. He'd had his last haircut about 2 or 3 weeks before. I had gone with him one morning and watched. He was so thin already; he walked slowly; the walk was 5 minutes, but he'd been tired coming home. We both knew then that it was his last time at the hairdresser.

His body lay there peacefully. The undertaker and I both stood back to look and check if anything else was needed. We'd slid the cooling element under him: its motor hummed in the background, and she explained how to watch that it was still working. Every day she or her colleague from the village would come to check on the body; it was law for a body to be checked daily, she explained. She asked that I turn all the room's radiators off completely.

***

Six Months On

May 16, 2019

The beautiful ironies: I am not unhappy about being sad. Perhaps the gold that repairs the broken pottery in Kinsugi is metaphorically made of the tears we shed for love.

It's been 6 months since Frans died. Does the timeframe matter? Six months is a period measured in human- (or moon-) made chunks. Is it not arbitrary to want to keep track this way? No. What I am doing by reflecting on this is marking the distance between his death and the present moment.

In the context of losing a partner, 6 months is both incredibly short and a length of time that begs the question, how am I doing now that a half year has passed? What is alive in my heart, body, mind?

Sadness has deepened this past month as I went to all our old places in The Netherlands, visited his twin brother, spent time with our friends, went to his grave twice, and flew home very much without him. His gone-ness is palpable and feels more final this time.

Getting sadder a half year in may sound a bit worrisome, but it isn't. Before my sorrow wasn't as consistently present; maybe it was the brain's way of protecting me from the hugeness of the loss and life shift.

In December and without crying, I remember telling someone about how Frans died and how I'd held him. Now I'm not able to speak of those specific moments without sorrow filling me to the point where I sometimes have to pause before I can complete the sentence.

A lot of feelings have come and gone these past months. What is especially present now is *droevenis* (the Dutch word is so much better than anything I can say in English). Underneath this is a missing, a remembering of our connection and intimacy, and an appreciation of the attentiveness we provided each other on a daily basis.

We humans are made for loving, this is the positive conclusion. As my friend Ellie wrote to me recently, "Sadness is an affirmation of our love and deep-set feelings."

On Tuesday evening this past week, I had about an hour where I was so bereft that I actually understood what it means when someone says, "I wanted to crawl into a hole." My friend Margot reached out (poignantly on time, as she is apt to), and I typed a short reply to her text, "Did the work I needed to do—doing it well and with attention. And sad. But don't feel like talking about it." Fortunately, she knew how to take such a message without feeling rejected. "I hear your heart," was her reply.

I sat in my writing chair, a recliner with lap desk, and wrote about what I was missing. Not only Frans as the man and lover of my life, but the absence of physical touch and being partnered. I admitted to a longing, both to be held and to be affirmed as a loving spouse. After expressing the rawness of my longing, I realized there was nowhere to go; no comfort that would be ultimate; no other who would make living daily without Frans feel fully okay again.

After feeling what I'd written, I faced a fundamental loss of hope. I bowed to the hopeless present. The paradox: without the hope for anything, I was free again. In my mind, I said good-bye to the idea of partnership. I broke up with my longing to fill the void left by Frans.

I put the computer away, and within half an hour of writing, my inner sky cleared.

Any tendency to clench or resist or bargain or insist or wonder or wish seemed to let me go.

It was as if I had rejoined the world or experienced what grief counsellor and author Julia Samuel (2017) describes: "We may no longer be innocently hopeful, and we may always have times when we feel the pain of loss, but the deeper understanding of ourselves that we have gained will, in time, feel like growth" (p. xvi).

***

Sighed.
Surrendered.
Slept.

The morning was new. I got up and showered. I made a grilled cheese sandwich for Maya, took her to catch her train. Came home. Got to work.

Again, the beautiful ironies: I am not unhappy about being sad. It's quite possible to live well and work productively while sad, for one thing. Sad is just another word for being with loss; no love is actually lost.

What felt insights are taking shape just now?

1. Affirmation: I'm not afraid to love (again).
2. Discovery: I'm less afraid of dying.
3. Curiosity: I think I might be good at being single.

When will I be done with this? In a year? When I finish the book? Never? Some readers may be wondering.

Multiple choice:

A. When I stop writing about it?
B. When grief is done with me?
C. When life gets bigger and bigger around it?
D. All of the above.

It seems I'm on a need-to-know basis. For foreign-language readers, this English expression means I surrender to only having the information that is on hand right now and I'll assume it is truly all I need to know. No "know how" is ever provided before its time and one must be satisfied with that.

***

The Funeral

Frans's body was moved out of the house on the morning of November 21, 2018, the day of his funeral. Two men in identical dark blue coats came to load him on a stretcher and wrapped him in a kind of vinyl cover. Underneath that, he was already in a woolly cream-colored shroud that now covered his face and head. His body had to be strapped in so he could make it down our narrow stairs, be stood upright, and then turned a quarter turn out the door. Right outside the door, he was loaded into a van that drove his body less than a block to the funeral home.

Though the Dutch seem to be quite sober about death and dying, they didn't carry him openly down the back road to the funeral home where his willow basket was waiting. There he was switched to the basket, a coffin made out of rattan and rounded at both the head and foot end. The immediate family met there and he was loaded into a dark grey Mercedes hearse. On the funeral invitation, we had asked everyone to dress in bright colors, true to Frans's style and *joie de vivre*. He liked to wear bright blue, red, purple, and sometimes green. The hearse of slate metallic grey looked solemn, but also respectful.

My friend Alex came to drive me and my mother and sister, Charlene, to the funeral. I had the old blue Volvo, but I had chosen not to drive. I'd been asked if I wanted to ride in the hearse, but it didn't feel right. It felt cold, too stately or removed; it was not our style, though I was happy to see such a nice car transporting him. We traveled to the funeral directly behind the hearse, in Alex's green Volkswagen hatchback. On the way there, I noticed a sundog, which was a very unusual sight in The Netherlands. Frans hadn't even known what a sundog was until I'd shown him one in Edmonton in the bright, cold winter. It looks like a sliver of a vague rainbow, lit from behind by the sun, in the shape of a dog, sitting straight and tall, as if on its haunches. It seemed symbolic—a moment we'd shared in Edmonton. Yes, the bereaved look for signs, even the agnostics among us. I pointed it out and the others were surprised to see it too. Behind us were the other cars, Frans's daughter and son-in-law, then his ex-wife and his youngest daughter, and behind that Frans's twin brother and his family.

The site, near the town where Frans was raised, was beautiful and natural. All the graves were marked by tree trunk slices with names that eventually fade. People visit their beloveds there, but also walk there and bike through on the paths. There is room for picnics.

The funeral home was like a chalet lodge with a large glass wall looking out into a field beyond. The service was nonreligious, but very meaningful. His girls, a close friend named Barbara, the funeral director, and I had arranged it together. My girls weren't there as Sophia was doing final exams for her third year at university, and Keath and I had decided not to fly Maya over by herself during such an emotional time. In order to have her there and rested for the funeral, she would have had to arrive just when he was to die, and that felt like too raw a transition. Maya had bonded with Frans as a younger child and it made her deeply sad that he was dying.

There was a slideshow of pictures from his whole life that showed on large screens. Beautiful and fitting songs were played between each of the five 5-minutes talks. I still hear his voice, "Don't let it take longer than an hour!" He didn't want to force people into sitting there endlessly, though he otherwise kept himself out of the planning—that is, besides insisting that no one else but his daughters and I had a say.

Frans had suggested two of his colleagues speak as well as his twin brother. His youngest daughter, Eva, wanted to speak, and I was the last to speak. I had chosen Mary Black's song, "Only a Woman's Heart," to play before I got up so that I could cry before I would stand up to read my two pages. There was solemn silence, but also laughter during each of the speeches. In all of those short presentations, it was clear that Frans had been deeply appreciated and that everyone had recognized his feisty and at times aggressive approach. I felt gratitude and relief knowing I had not been the only one to experience and see it all: his incredible warmth, impressive academic achievements, tireless helping spirit, and his short fuse.

The service ended with Louis Armstrong's "Sunny Side of the Street," one of Frans's life mottos. Everyone seemed buoyed by this and stood up to walk with us to the grave. Frans's basket was lifted on to a hand-drawn carriage and taken down the path, with Sophia's shroud on top fluttering gently in the wind. It was a cool November day that oscillated between clear and cloudy. My mother had sewn rocks into the corners of the silk shroud to keep it in place.

Frans's basket was lowered into the sandy grave with three large ropes, and close family members stepped forward to lower him down, including me and his twin Jan on one of the middle ropes. Jan said to me, "I've been halved ..." He and I both were, each in our own way.

His daughters and ex-wife had generously brought fresh flowers for everyone. It was an eco-burial, so the flowers stood unwrapped in buckets near the gravesite. Frans would have approved and appreciated the naturalness of that. I kneeled down to gently let the first rose fall on the basket. There is a picture of me doing that, as his daughters had suggested we document the service and burial, and I agreed. I have a book of photos from that day; I am glad I have it, though I rarely look at it. Sometimes I show it to a friend and then get to look at it myself that way. It is beautiful and painful and sometimes I prefer to feel how it was then, instead of seeing it from another's visual angle. I have it in the bedside table on his side of the bed, along with our rings, notes he wrote to me, his shaving cream, and an album of pictures.

My girls could not be at the funeral and they have not asked to see the pictures or the recording. We may watch it together at some point; I will ask them if they would like to. I kept in close touch with them the day before and the day after, and told them how it was. I also talked to their dad, Keath, about how it was all unfolding. He and Frans had become close over the years—they'd shed tears together about the diagnosis. For Frans, Keath was one of the rare people who could make him cry just by the sound of his voice.

At the gravesite, everyone took a turn to put a flower on the basket until the whole thing was full of myriad different kinds. I don't remember what kinds of flowers as I'm not great with flower names, but I remember it was lush and colorful. People hugged and came to stand with me.

They said that it was a beautiful spot; they said they were so sorry; they acknowledged how hard the loss must be for all of us; there was a great friendliness that abounded. I thanked and hugged each person who approached me. I was calm and quiet inside. It was as if my feelings were partly on hold. I was very present and even social. I remember the warmth of Frans's Afghani friends; Charlene constantly at my side; and walking back with Jesse's family, feeling supported, and even cheered.

After the burial, we returned to the chalet-like funeral home building and spent the afternoon and early evening eating and drinking together. Fittingly, there was a bit of whisky for those who wanted it; it was Frans's drink. One small whisky each evening until he got sick.

We had all agreed not to be cheap; I liked how his daughters said, "None of this boring, cold cheese and ham sandwiches and crappy coffee." They chose the menu items and there was plenty. The food was savory: cooked vegetables and meat on toast, and there were endless cups of coffee and herbal teas.

There were 150 people at the funeral. We kept it purposely small and the space would not allow more either. Over the next hours, I had a constant stream of visitors. I eventually had to sit down as I ran out of energy to stand, and I started to feel faint. One of Frans's friends brought me tea. Someone else brought me gluten-free food; I couldn't eat much.

One of Frans's nieces, a young woman I'd never met before from his ex-wife's family, came toward me and gushed in her sorrow and exuberance, "You were so in love!!" She grabbed my hands as she said it. I was touched to think she had seen our passion in the photos that were shown on the screens or perhaps she had heard parts of our story. I thanked her. I smile as I remember it now. I was also grateful for a host of my family members being there, as most of my siblings were in Canada and weren't able to come, nor did I expect them to travel so far at great expense to their families. Many of our colleagues were there too, and almost everyone who had visited us in the previous months.

Besides blended family realities—a kind of clinical-sounding term that I've used before—and some of the tensions that created over the years, the funeral was beautiful and most of the credit for this goes to Frans's daughters. Some said later that it was the most beautiful funeral they had ever been to.

***

It took me until August 7, 2019, to write this recollection of the funeral. I wrote it in a café in Edmonton, where I'd chosen a quaint window spot with a yellow table and blue chairs. Before I sat down, a thought crossed my mind: "Should I really pick the best spot in the place?" A table just a few feet away near a bookshelf also looked pretty cozy. Interestingly, a young man came up soon after to ask me if I'd be willing to move so he could propose to his girlfriend at their "first-date table." It was to be a surprise; she was just outside and about to come sit down. He was very polite and didn't want to insist, in his Canadian way, but of course, I was happy to move. I told him what I was writing, "A memoir of my husband and his death." He was about to say, "I'm sorry," when I smiled and said, "No, it's beautiful, beautiful! It's the cycle of life! Now it's your turn and I bless you. See it all as very precious."

I congratulated them afterward; she was holding back her tears and said so. "Tears are good," I said to her.

Such is life.

Tears of joy.

Tears of sorrow.

Love pain and the whole damn thing, as the Amy Sky song goes.

***

In the days after the funeral, I packed what was left for me to take from the house. My friends Kashvi and Alex came to stay with me so I wouldn't be alone. We went out for dinner at the restaurant on the square the night of the funeral, but it was hard for me to eat. About 15 minutes into the meal, I suddenly felt like I was going to break down crying. Alex and I were sitting across from each other and I mustered a joke as I started to feel the emotions rising: "They are going to think we're a couple and that you said something that upset me and now we have to go." He helped me with my coat. I was worn out. It was only 30 steps to the house across the square. I was grateful to sit down on the couch. We made tea right away.

There was not a single day or night anyone left me alone in the house and for that, I'm still grateful. I remember sitting in the living room with Kashvi and Alex that evening after the funeral and leaning into Kashvi. She was wearing a soft and fuzzy sweater the color of Tweety Bird. Remembering it now, more than a year later, I think, "Yes, those two, the friends that lead with the heart."

As I would be going back to Canada and giving up our rented apartment in Wijchen, I left behind the couches, bookshelves, the TV, almost all Frans's books, garden chairs, guest beds, the dining-room table and chairs, the bed we had bought together, and the oak table in the corner where I had written most of my PhD.

Alex had borrowed a cargo van from his boss at the pump repair company where he worked, almost 200 km away. I was grateful and happy to pay for the fuel. We loaded everything ourselves in the morning. All my books, several lamps, my office chair, sheets, my favorite dishes from the kitchen, the beautiful sand-colored curtains, and several paintings. Most of it would go to Charlene's place in Amstelveen which would become my new "home" when I traveled back to the Netherlands. I gave a large box of food and spices to Alex and a painting to Kashvi.

I left the kettle, thermos, ground coffee, an assortment of teas, and some snacks behind for Frans's girls, who would be clearing and organizing the rest.

The afternoon we drove away from the house, Frans's daughters Sanne and Eva, his son-in-law Jesse, and grandchild Flynn came to say good-bye. I gave them the keys, and some papers they needed that the funeral director had given me. We hugged. They were gracious and kind.

Ironically, leaving the comfort of our Dutch home would signal the beginning of active grieving. Maybe it happened in this order because the active parts of caring, accompanying, burying, and moving were over. Maybe it was because I was going home to everyone who felt safe to me and there were no more complex dynamics to navigate.

Slowly over the next months, I started to unwind and feel.

***

8

SEXUAL DESIRE AND ASKING TO BE HELD

Lover's body

I try to describe to
a friend how you are
leaving my body
How the images of you
as my lover are mercifully fading
without me ever losing you or the memories
My cells, the ebb and flow of hormones,
the once synchronized heartbeat
are uncoupling while love watches unshaken and wise
The body doesn't give it up without keening
some of the cells die along with the grief - even glad to
Fine synapses are laid down on the blue prints of whatever will take
shape on the ground
of the present I call "my life" (though it lives me)
Other dreams sometimes appear
a touch that helped me heal is an imprint
and there is a breath of trust like a hand between my
shoulder blades, a slow unwinding of the belly,
- a spaciousness
they don't write about this in any of the books

May 29, 2019 (6 months after Frans's death)

***

Around the time I wrote this poem, I also came across a quote by writer and Dutch theologian Henri Nouwen. His words immediately speak to my longing for physical connection, "Your body needs to be held and to hold, to be touched and to touch. None of these needs is to be despised, denied, or repressed. But you have to keep searching for your body's deeper need, the need for genuine love. Every time you are able to go beyond the body's superficial desires for love, you are bringing your body home and moving toward integration and unity."[1] I feel some relief at the lack of judgment in what he writes.

Earlier in this book, I wrote about missing physical closeness and that sexual desire does not end with the end of one's partner's life. This may be different for older people; I can't speak to that. I can only imagine most everyone misses the affection and warmth of their partner in death.

I am a widow at mid-life (pre-menopause), and my sex life with Frans was vibrant, warm, and active. This all stopped in June 2018, several months after his diagnosis, and was the result of his illness, especially the increased opioid-based medication that killed both his appetite for food and his sex drive.

I was aware of missing touch and physical intimacy in the early months of grief, though some of that yearning has settled now. I have always been a partner-oriented person, so not being partnered took some getting used to. In August 2019, I felt the urge to have or consider seeking a partner subside entirely, and I began to plan my year of work and travel ahead with enthusiasm and a sense of freedom.

That said, what I have missed most in the daily exchange of partnership are the conversations and the simple pleasures of being hugged or held. One of the most treasured moments Frans and I had was going to bed in the evening and then curling up naked together. He told me he had usually slept with t-shirt and underwear (I used to as well), but that with me he had to be naked; I too felt that any bit of clothing between us was too much.

I often scratched his back and he would frequently lie close behind me, holding my belly with his right hand and kissing the back of my neck. I have a voice recording of a few weeks before his death where he is groaning happily at my scratching. We also played a "question game" each evening, where we asked each other all kinds of things, both work-related and personal.

FRANS: *Liefje* [sweetheart, beloved], do you have a question for me?

REINEKKE: Did you like your sexual freedom? Did you ever make agreements about it, or was it accepted at that time that people had multiple partners?

FRANS: I didn't think about it much. When I look back now, I see how superficial it was. How I was following my libido more than anything. I did fall in love once in those years.

Or

FRANS: What did you like most about that lover?

REINEKKE: He was warm. He picked up on my feelings. He liked my jokes.

Or

FRANS: Liefje, you must have another question for me tonight …
REINEKKE: When did you know you liked me in a more serious way?
FRANS: I already knew in 1993–1994. Remember I used to walk hand in hand with you in Leiden? Colleagues of mine could have seen me, but I didn't care.

Each morning Frans and I would wake up still holding each other and begin kissing again, always starting the day with another conversation. He would sometimes wake up before me and if I asked him what he was thinking about, he would frequently tell me he was piecing together an argument for an article.

In the early months of my grief, I corresponded actively with a number of supportive and inspiring friends and colleagues. Some of that contact was about bridging the gap between all the conversations Frans and I had and the emptiness that ensued after his death. Now I do that less frequently, as the need has become less intense, though I'm glad for several very steady people.

Many of those who supported me were women and several were men, each person supportive in their own way. I noted a desire to have males to correspond with; I missed the male energy in my life. For instance, I got in touch with a colleague at the university whom I had met through a mutual friend several years before. He works in a related field and is a good writer and an empathetic human being.

He had a basic understanding of grief as he'd been through divorce and lost his brother to cancer when his brother was in his prime. A friend of mine had dated him several years before and Frans and I had met them for a double date. I'd also met him one other time when he was gracious enough to pick me up from the airport when plans to fly with my friend at the same time had fallen through. He had reached out to me when he and my friend's dating had come to an end, and I told him Frans was ill when we received the diagnosis.

I asked for my friend's blessing to connect with this man and she gave it. Our correspondence began, and I wrote to him about Frans and my grief; he wrote back patiently and in detail. We also spoke over the phone about my new job, and he gave his advice about working toward tenure. In spring we had brunch and enjoyed 2 pleasant hours together; our conversation flowed easily and was warm. We hugged before and after the delicious meal in a breakfast place that he told me had good reviews, and where he'd made a reservation. It almost felt like a date, but we didn't express romantic energy toward each other.

Another man who made a difference in my life early on was the friend I mentioned earlier who lives in Calgary. The evening in December when he came to Ellie's party, we hugged at the door and he said, "I'm so sorry to hear about what happened." He was already a Facebook friend and would have been able to follow the progress of Frans's diagnosis to death there. On Facebook, I have been posting blogs about my widow's journey, and several people told me they had been reading the poems and personal reflections there, even those who didn't comment on or "like" the posts.

I noticed it was easier meeting this friend knowing he has been reading the posts, and I didn't have to tell him what happened devoid of the fuller context. In his presence, I noted feeling a bit shy; he seemed to be warmly comfortable around me, but also reserved and careful. This was in contrast to the last time I had seen him more than a year before, and months before Frans's unexpected diagnosis.

While Frans was still alive and well, a year before, I had spoken of this friend to Frans and told him that there had been an unexpected spark of attraction one evening at one of Ellie's parties. It had made an impression on me, so I thought best to clear the air immediately and I told the man in question in a text message that I was happily partnered, just in case the eye contact he initiated was a sign of interest in more. He acknowledged the energy of attraction and said he found the honesty refreshing.

When I phoned Frans from Edmonton a day later to tell him about the party and the spark, he lovingly teased me, and I admitted to being a bit surprised as I was rarely attracted to anyone outside my relationship with Frans. We recognized it as the normal "outside attractions" that anyone can experience within a committed relationship without feeling any need to act on it.

On Christmas Eve, 6 weeks after Frans's death, I thought to reach out to my Calgary friend and wish him a Merry Christmas, but I refrained. It seemed too proactive and even inappropriate somehow; it was as if the attraction I'd felt for this man, made what I shared with Frans seem replaceable and therefore less valuable.

I put the thought of reaching out aside as I was driving to my Mom's house for dinner. She and I were both alone and made a simple supper (and ate a few too many bonbons). At her table, after toasting and starting our meal, I noticed I had a message from the man in question wishing me a good Christmas. I told him that a half-hour earlier, I'd been on the verge of doing the same thing. The coincidence was fun and delightful. He sent me a flirtatious reply, "I was just napping, and I had an erotic dream about you." He later told me that saying this to me was rather out of character for him. It was bold and it brought some laughter and cheer; it reminded me I could feel the energy of romance even under the dismal circumstances.

We had several phone conversations in the months that followed, and what I most appreciated was that he said little but what was said came from the heart. He did not try to fix my grief. His few words of comfort meant a great deal to me. I remember a moment when it almost felt as if he had put his arms around me through the phone and when I said, "It almost feels like you're holding me," he replied, "I am; I am holding you."

He told me about his dog who had died the previous spring. He said, "I'm not trying to compare my dog's death to Frans's, but ..." He too felt the depth of the sadness of loss. He could relate, even as a long-time bachelor who had never been married and had never lost a parent.

In early March, on a visit to Calgary, I asked him if he would hold me. He said yes, and we spent an afternoon at his apartment. He held me. His hand on my heart, his eyes looking into mine. I cried.

We undressed bit by bit and kissed as we took each article of clothing off, starting from the top. I noticed that I could see a new (younger) body and enjoy how it looked. There were moments where I stopped to notice it deliberately; there were moments when he kissed me and I noted how different a new person's kiss can be. Some of the arousal seemed familiar and comfortable, some of it brought tears and pauses as I would tell him about a memory I had of Frans. He was receptive and loving to me and my body. We stayed on top of the covers; hours went by and we enjoyed all the caresses. We pleasured each other to orgasm.

Later that day we went for dinner and I remember how his hands reached across the table. He looked up at me and asked, "Did that really happen?" Yes, we had spent the afternoon naked in bed, both aroused, and both at ease, which in hindsight was a grateful surprise. He was both bold and reserved, and I was in the middle of raw grief. We had navigated it and in the months that followed, we were able to stay in touch, though the texts and sporadic phone calls did not have the makings of an enduring intimate connection.

When I think back to that day, I remember the poignancy of the view from where we laid in his bed: there were two mountain ashes outside his window in full view. I wanted to take that as a sign, perhaps of permission, or of a kind of rightness.

REINEKKE: Frans, I spent a whole afternoon in bed with a loving man. [Showing him a mental picture …] This man. The painter. The one I told you about before. He had very young and smooth skin. He was sensual, not shy to touch me. You would have approved. There was no roughness, or coldness, or weirdness. I asked for what I wanted. I was a bit shy, but also relaxed.

FRANS: Yes, that's you, liefje. Naturally you; just the way I know you. (Smiling with a look of sexy flirtation and warmth in his eyes.) What you're telling me is that it was a wonderful afternoon.

Had I read Joan Price's (2019) book *Sex After Grief* at that time, I would have been a bit more prepared to navigate the renewed feelings of attachment I experienced, while not wondering about the actual potential of a new relationship. In Price's book she quotes Tina Tissina, a psychotherapist who writes on finding new love and romance after loss:

> Don't be surprised to experience any of these things when you're starting to date again: massive panic, fear of rejection, renewed grief and guilt over moving on, exasperation when your date doesn't measure up to your

> deceased partner. These are common reactions. You'll feel both giddy and scared, elated and disappointed. Expect an emotional roller coaster.
>
> *(as cited in Price, 2019, p. 47)*

After that special afternoon and dinner, my painter friend brought me back to the apartment where I was staying with my friend Margot. The next morning, walking along the river's edge, the water still full of snow-covered ice chunks in the full sunlight of a Calgary blue-sky morning, I phoned him. While we talked, I also heard my own internal conversation, "It was lovely, it was what it was; he is not interested in a relationship and you're not ready anyway … Take it for what it was." His words were, "You're wonderful. I can't have a relationship; I don't have the resources to hold up my end; we don't live in the same city. I love your heart, Rein …"

No doubt he could hear the raw, howling grief that was under my breaking voice and my gaping heart. I was still awash in Frans; Frans filled me; and he was still part of my body. What felt like a rejection from this man wasn't; this gentle person who had held me, accepted me just as I was in the moment, and my wisdom about meeting him where he was, was also present.

We left each other warmer, and I think a bit braver, and eventually, I would commission a painting from him with the theme "renewal," about my old life dying and the new life emerging. He spent months on it and a year and a half after Frans's death, it would hang in my home and become the cover of this book.

***

Onward

I've heard several times now that the second year of widowhood is harder than the first. This is not encouraging, and I remember Frans telling me that his mother told him this as well. She said to him that people expect you to be "over it"; they don't ask about your grief anymore, while it remains a consistent uncurrent. Frans's mother was in her late 50s when his Dad died at 60.

That things might get harder or people less inclined to hear about one's sorrow is not a comforting thought, but I have decided to take it as it comes, and I feel a sense of faith in the basic goodness of living. One day at a time still seems the best advice.

These last days there are peaceful moments and then there are weird, surreal, wrenching moments. There is discombobulation and balance. Then there is a great workflow. Then there is the practicality of replacing a toilet and getting Keath's help with that, and subsequently feeling grateful. Then there is a half-empty nest and evenings of solitude when both kids are away. Then there are feelings that seem embarrassing, yet genuine and vulnerable, like remembering how I can feel attracted to someone again.

Then there is the realization that my feelings only shift when I accept them fully as they are. That my body is ultimately most at ease when I'm not arguing with what is moving through it; that I freeze things in place uncomfortably by denying. It seems I keep coming back to noticing that everything is subject to change. My anger arises and dissipates, my joy ebbs and flows, my arousal is familiar, weird, and welcome when I don't think of it in terms of what should and shouldn't be. If ever I have felt that it's crucial to be with all that is, it's now. This is one of the truths of grief.

A friend reaches out this morning and shares a link on bereavement. The evening I spend doing a scholarly peer-review, utterly satisfying (not that it always is). Before that, in the middle of the afternoon, I forced myself to walk along the new sound barrier that smells of cedar. I'm glad I did it and notice my gait slowing as I settle into my body.

In July there are visitors coming from the Netherlands, our friends Janus and Els. I'm grateful to these friends of Frans and mine who are taking the trouble to come all the way to Edmonton.

In the evening, there is smoke in the air from a distant fire, and later a clear evening sky and windows open in the bedroom. On Mondays, there is the Zoom group of loving women studying nonviolent communication and radical acceptance that I've been a part of for more than a year now.

There seems to be a learning here about being in the body, where all the happy memories are, and the sad ones too. To practice benevolent tolerance in response to all that arises. Writing all of this, I wish Frans could see the work I'm doing now. Just as I type that, the phone beeps mysteriously.

> A poem follows ...
>
> There was a man
> with your hair
> standing in line
> at the Timmies
> I imagined
> what it would be like
> to touch that hair
> I go there in imagination
> my heart drips warm anguish
> some lesson
> this opening to the other
> half of life

As I consider my pain, there is simultaneously the realization that so many people are struggling in this world and that my problems are (still) first-world problems. Then there is a worry about the future of the environment for the generations to come; whether the planet can even sustain them. Then there is grocery shopping and the antique mall on the weekend. Then there are dishes. Then there is a good night of sleep, followed by a bad one.

Then there is remembering my friends who lost a son to suicide and our shared tears and gratitude for the harsh and soft broken-heartedness of it all.

Then there is a friend who says the perfect words, then there is the friend who doesn't and jolts the fragile balance and reminds me of what matters and how to take care of myself better.

Then there is a text that flashes on the phone in the middle of writing this: "sending you love and hugs."

***

Note

1 Source: https://www.quotetab.com/quotes/by-henri-nouwen (Retrieved, 2019).

9

SECONDARY LOSSES AND COLLATERAL BEAUTY

Secondary losses

A hole opened in the universe
and you went into it
along with anything you and I were done with
after that, in the still pulsing gap,
things that resembled our fight went down heavy and quick
and your wisdom also infused my determinations
At first it seemed weird
like I was so fine with more abandonment
"Well, if it has to be death, let all the other things that want to die go as well!"
It felt like an incantation, recited wisdom
that had written itself into the background of my life in the years of daring
Some of it I even dropped into the hole myself
and I said aloud
someone else's raging inner child is not my problem
if there is one to listen to, it will have to be my own
eventually as I walked with these further loses
they began to resemble rooms I'd once felt nurtured in
but with wallpaper I'd never loved
and windows now too small and facing the wrong direction
You have left me with much through both love and trespass
including discernment
I can bow to this too and see I have had a clear hand in things
that fall down with life's gravity.

***

As I reread this poem, the lines that stand out for me are:

> *A hole opened in the universe*
> *and you went into it*
> *along with anything you and I were done with.*

What am I done with? The question is important if I am to give an honest account of how I feel and why there have been secondary losses in this first year of bereavement.

What the fierceness of these lines brings to my attention is the memory of the fights Frans and I had. I do not miss his habit of using words like "you always, you never, you completely." These exaggerations were dismissive and blocked the opportunity for a fair appraisal of a situation. I will not miss his pseudo-rational tactics, for instance when he would say, "research shows" to push a point but not be able to tell me which research and by whom. Or his outright denial that he was angry when later he admitted he was fuming but didn't want to give me "the pleasure of being right."

While my sorrow is often soft and loving, filled with all the good we shared, there are times when I have seethed and spoken through a pinched mouth after his death and said, "Good riddance to the ways you were unfair and mean. I do not miss it."

On filling in Holland, Klingspon et al.'s (2020) Unfinished Business in Bereavement Scale (UBBS) more than a year after Frans's death, I was strongly distressed on 4 of the 28 items and scored a 2.3 on the "Unresolved Conflict" scale. A 3.4 would have been "indicative of problematic unfinished business" (p. 77). It puts the severity of my unfinished business in perspective, though it does not erase the distress.

When I took off my wedding ring, I remember trying to put it back on for comfort, but it was the memories of our unfinished business that kept me from being able to wear it again.

Frans would say that we should learn from every situation and I will take his advice on this now. What I am learning from our relationship is that I didn't care for his short fuse and that I am now on a "low-bad diet" (Tierney & Baumeister, 2019), which means I limit my contact with people who cause me stress. Anything that Frans (you) and I are "done with," I am done with in general. I sum this up bluntly: I don't want to be close to anyone who is volatile, who makes accusatory judgments, is undisciplined and harsh with words, drains my energy, or doesn't respect boundaries (e.g., stays on the phone longer when I have indicated clearly that I have a need to get back to my writing).

In the process of going through grief, I've come across several places in the readings where the griever or researcher speaks about losing friends or that even family members drift away. Although my network still feels diverse and generous and has not been decimated by 75%, as widow Christine Frangou (2016) warns is a possibility, I have lost touch with several important people during this grief process in ways I had not expected.

For the most part, the secondary losses feel benign. People get busy with their own lives, not all colleagues that I met through Frans will stay in touch regularly, and no doubt some of his family members need a break as they process their own feelings around his death. If I am to sum up my secondary losses, I would say 90% of them are innocent and 10% are painful, but necessary.

In each of these cases, I have had a clear part to play. In most grief literature, there is a sense of these losses happening to the bereaved, but I don't think that is an accurate picture. At least it is not accurate in my situation. I am not a victim here. Again, I have been making some deliberate choices about who I want close to me (right now), and it truly feels as if some people don't fit into the new landscape of my life.

That said, it has not been easy to admit and surrender to this reordering of my world. I've felt heavy-hearted at times and a hint of useful doubt accompanies my ongoing reflections. I am also open to reconnecting with friends and family who are more distant now, but I am not actively seeking out some of these connections, and I believe others are making those same choices about me.

Speaking to my friend Tom about this recently, he explained this phenomenon using the Perceptual Control Theory (Powers, 1973/2005), which explains that when a big life change happens, other things also need reordering. This reordering, however, doesn't happen as a result of thinking logically: "It can neither be executed nor controlled by the thinking I, but it can be stimulated by directing awareness" (Luken, 2020, p. 140). Tom explains why rational thought is overrated in decision-making and I read his article, intuitively understanding that this "reordering" is unfolding without me having any sense that I must "decide what to do." I am aware of some discomfort and I make space in myself for the ambiguity of my feelings. Eventually, useful and healthy actions seem to unfold from there as if I'm watching myself enact things or sitting back, and in both cases, there is a rightness to the process.

I welcome the reordering and while describing it here, I happen upon a useful analogy: Maya recently moved down to the basement suite in the house, which left her room upstairs half empty, dusty, and without purpose. That lead me to move my own bedroom into the (largest) room, which she left behind. That in turn leads to a need for re-shuffling closet contents and me doing a thorough shifting of all the closets and dressers on the main floor of the house. I did not have to "decide" in any deliberate way what ended up where, but somehow my hands knew what to do. It seemed my only intentional act was to make things clean and aesthetically pleasing.

One room change affected the whole house; one significant death affects my whole life.

Tom also writes about additional healthy growth that occurs after difficulty as we "slowly become more independent of what others think and dare to choose our own perspectives" (T. Luken, personal correspondence, November 2019). In a small book on relationships, I read, "Until you are loyal to yourself, you can't be loyal to another person" (Katie, 2006, p. 52). I see my commitment to be good to myself growing, which includes stopping to acknowledge and reflect on the impact and reality of secondary losses.

I became partly estranged from one of my siblings shortly after Frans's death, though fortunately, that turned out to be temporary. When I arrived back in Canada, I left a voice message to say that I needed time and space to grieve and to write and that I didn't want to talk at length on the phone about topics that we often spoke about. I set a boundary on my time and upon reflection, I could have delivered the message in person, though likely with the same result: hurt feelings. I have learned from this that I should speak up sooner about what I have the energy for. I remember that "A dishonest yes is a no to yourself" (Katie, 2006, p. 17). I know that saying "no" to others may mean that some will feel rejected or unwelcome, while the reality is that there are other needs in me that I want to meet. The same goes for others who say "no" to me.

In each shifting relationship where I have become distant from someone important to me, things happened or were said that I didn't have the energy or willingness to engage with (anymore), and so I stopped engaging. That does not negate the things enjoyed and shared in the past and the gratitude I feel for many things that were offered in these friendships. To once again paraphrase Byron Katie, one of my favorite teachers, "You can love someone totally and still leave them" because something important is not working or is missing. This wisdom feels applicable here.

In the wake of Frans's death, as I allude to earlier, I have lost a willingness to engage with people who can become verbally aggressive. I accepted this as part of my relationship with Frans, as much good compensated for it, but now I see I have a choice to make: I can allow loving but temperamental people close to me again or I can be clear on how I want to be treated, and this may well mean building in some pauses.

One discovery I made in my therapeutic dialogue based on Neimeyer and Konopka's (2019) prompt shared earlier, was that different (family) cultures have different styles of relating and dealing with conflict, and thus individuals do as well. In some families, shouting or storming off to slam doors and being insulting may not signal a serious breach of trust, but that's not how I grew up.

To me, it is understandable to want to shout (or even fire off insulting or passive-aggressive comments), but it's important to refrain and pause as damage can be done. Tierney and Baumeister (2019) confirm this in their online article on negative bias:

> First, do no harm. We pride ourselves on the many good things we do for our family and friends, or for going the extra mile in pleasing customers and clients, but what really matters is what we don't do. Avoiding bad is far

> more important than doing good. You get relatively little credit for doing more than you promised, but you pay a big price for falling short. (2019, p. 5)

Marriage research shows that there should be a 5-to-1 ratio of good interactions to compensate for the bad (Gottman & Silver, 1995), so the bad interactions clearly have a big impact. I am 50 now, and I don't think my views or preferences will change on this point, not because I'm too old for change, but because I see what I value. Though clear and difficult-to-hear words need to be said in close relationships, it's important to me to leave someone's dignity intact and to be accountable and express accountability without further insinuations of blame.

Frans and I differed in this; he at times shouted insults that he later said he did not mean. I considered this undisciplined and disrespectful. He found it hard to apologize, and though he attempted to set things right, the behavior was a repeating pattern. These exchanges left scratches on me and I told him that I experienced his lashing out as destructive, intended or not.

Two friendships have changed, and in hindsight, I see that one of them had started to shift while Frans was ill. One friend, probably out of her desire to be helpful and caring, made statements about how I was coping with his inevitable death that I felt pathologized my feelings. I didn't want or need her help in the way that she wanted to be needed (at least that is my version of the story). Another friend, passionate and fiery, had the same penchant for volatility that Frans could have; my decision to not engage when a conversation escalated over a small matter felt like the rightful outcome of my learning with Frans. I experience a strong love for this friend and an abiding connection, just as I do for him, but I am glad I respected my well-being and chose to reduce our engagement for a time.

My recent choices about who I spend time with have been informed by Frans's darker sides, but also by his wisdom around following one's own track, which I allude to in the poem above. Our varied and engaged dialogues trained me to reflect like this, and if I spoke to him today, I would likely say, "These dynamics did not sit right with me and now I'm heeding my own wisdom. I've learned from what didn't work for me with you and now I'm applying it here. This is my track and you helped me to see it."

An old Chinese proverb says we learn tolerance from the intolerant, and I feel I have learned to honor my feelings in the face of having my feelings, at times, treated dishonorably.

What I contributed to the difficulty in our communication has, perhaps fittingly, now also become a point of reflection for me. Now that my focus is less on the "problems out there," I can become even more diligent with my own speech. For example, I realized that, in the past, I might have written to one of my estranged friends and pointed out what I needed for resolution, but now if I send a message, I write in the spirit of gratitude for the many years we shared as friends. What she wishes to express in the way of accountability is outside my responsibility; if it happens, I am grateful; if it does not, I can surrender to that. I also realize that volatility creates fear in me, and therefore I should not engage until I am calm and clear-minded again.

What I want to say to anyone who has lost someone very important: it's a turning point in your life. It's okay to reassess who belongs in your life. It's okay to set boundaries and to take care of yourself. Maybe grief is just the crack that opens us up, allowing the clearing that we were due for anyway.

And you will lose people. You will also be responsible for that; people will say things that you can't bear; some of it will be unfair; some of it will be insightful and you can work with that later. You will trigger each other despite your best intentions; you will feel misunderstood; others may have a need to be needed or appreciated and not see what you actually need (and vice versa).

Trust yourself in this change.

I think what I'm saying can be summed up this way: don't burn bridges but raise the bridges for a while and allow yourself to re-evaluate. Let the ships and sailboats (i.e., thoughts and opinions) move between you, without inflicting (more) harm.

Simply pause.

Those who will fit with the person you are becoming will be there; old friends may eventually return; it's okay if they don't. You will also meet new people whose conversations will be fresh and engaging. Some who you thought would be there aren't, and relative strangers may offer exactly the heartfelt understanding you need most deeply.

Know that death also unveils things you already knew and didn't want to look at before.

Ultimately, no one is to blame.
People die.
Friendships end.
Family members grow quiet or we become quiet toward them.
We don't always know why it has to happen.
You're still in the middle of the story.
(Of course, this was the advice I needed today.)

***

The Things I Would Have Told You if You Were Still Alive

June 23, 2019

It's Sunday after a full weekend. I am counting my blessings in the midst of a heart that is in touch with the reverence of sadness, joy, and contentment. It seems all of it comes and goes by the hour like changing weather.

The girls hosted a solstice party on Friday night. Ten kids were here until 1:00 a.m. They decorated the sunroom with lights and streamers and table cloths. They cooked and cleaned and their being here brought cheer and a bit of good chaos.

I went for a gourmet brunch this morning at my friend Andrea's place and she and I and her husband Adrian had conversations on life, loss, intuition, and the aesthetic satisfactions of home life. She made me frittata and the most wonderful fresh coffee.

Then I came home alone to books worth reading. I am finding that the things I'm learning about grief often apply to life in general.

Paradoxically, Frans dying means I can learn to live better

Moments of tender sadness continue to erupt, and I am learning to surrender to that again and again.

Frans, I wrote a conversation to you and felt your presence, which is still a comfort.

Remember Milton Erickson's (1991) book, *My Voice Will Go with You*? Here I go; the conversation comes out in a poem.

> You're here love
> and not,
> the quiet of the afternoon
> is filled with beautiful music
> the sound of wind and summer rain
> outside the open patio door,
> I hear bird songs
> sitting in our favorite spot
> of course, I look over at your chair and
> (still) ask, where are you?

***

Collateral Beauty[1]

> Cloudscapes
>
> Everything is more beautiful and painful now
> and that's the deal no one escapes
> you showed me light and shadow
> enacted and reflected
> Enriched by love's long apprenticeship
> I thought today about how you dove toward death[2]
> I had never seen someone do it like that
> that shows me the way forward
> to bow to the unfixability of nearly everything
> May what doesn't belong
> shed away

you made me less afraid of losing
what isn't meant for me:
things that don't come freely
all that requires tired striving
words that are only honest sideways
I am seeing it all better now
even our damning imperfections
and I want to tell you
how the old friends aren't the same.
They say illusions are like clouds passing the sun
dangerous and beautiful
You would smile,
I am learning to include it all

June 25, 2019

***

Visits and Good Memories

July 1, 2019

Today it seems you visited
in my coffee cup
I looked into the foam swirl
(usually it's a heart) and
found a swan and an oak tree instead

Both images in the poem (and coffee cup) had meaning for Frans and me: the swan reminded me of the swan pair we always used to see near the pond we walked around in our town (Wijchen, The Netherlands), a symbol of couplehood and loyalty. The oak tree Frans associated with his growing up in the province of Noord Brabant and walking with his father in the woods; I associate it with Frans and the old world.

The barista was at the counter, some distance away, and suddenly asked me, "Are you okay"? She must have seen something cross my face as I looked into the cup. I nodded, "Yes, I'm okay." I could have told her what I saw but wouldn't have been able to get it out.

I sat next to a blind man there who touched my shoulder and, because he couldn't see me, I felt heard but not looked at. It was easier to talk. He asked me direct questions because he explained that's what you have to do when you're blind. Side by side, we found out we are both writers. He a retired journalist, me poet and academic. Ha, of course, he was already good at asking direct questions; this is his occupational deformity[3].

Later I learn his name is Lyle. Lyle and I talk each time I work in that particular café and he always asks me what I've been up to when I haven't been there for a while. When I tell him in early February 2020 that a publisher is interested in the manuscript, he asks me if we might celebrate with champagne once the book is out. On my initiative, we hug for the first time and I tell him that our conversations have brought me comfort.

***

A few things that feel true for me at the moment—things that come more clearly into view by writing them down:

1. If you listen carefully and observe what and who is around you and what is asking for attention within you, everything you need to be well and supported is there. Every day. No exceptions.
2. In my writing, I meet Frans. He feels immediately present which he said he would be, even though he was an atheist. His responses seem to consistently be about love, acceptance, unconditional support, and the importance of working on things that matter. He emphasized being on one's own track in something that offers others value. I think writing to our dead beloveds can be useful and meaningful, whether a person believes in a spiritual life or does so from a more psychological perspective. You don't need to make up your mind about spirituality or psychology to be and feel connected.
3. Sorrow doesn't end, not only because the death of a loved one is devastating, but because love does not end and it includes everything. Sorrow is not depressing or awful, it feels like warmth and tender vulnerability mostly. That said, sometimes it's painful yearning and it's best to bow to that when it arises as resistance seems to make it heavy and at times almost unbearable. Letting the feelings be what they are opens my heart. There is more empathy and kindness accessible in me than before. Also toward myself.
4. Everyone is grieving someone or something. I read this week that there is no becoming fully human without pain.
5. Blessings are countless and ongoing. And as I wrote before, there are secondary losses too. If these can be seen without the victim narrative, they are blessings too.
6. This big life change seems to reveal things that no longer fit: several relationships are shifting and I have little energy for things that I experience as negative or draining; it can be hard to read the news. New people arrive regularly as well and frequently bring fresh perspectives. A recent conversation with another widow was validating as she talked about those who interpreted her grief in benighted ways.
7. Even in lonely moments, I only want connections that feel uplifting and true, not just company.

Sitting at home now, in my chair, blanket on my lap, I realize I write for a few different reasons: to cultivate my own awareness of what is happening (a kind of active grieving), to offer some of my lived experience as a possible comfort to others, to retain a connection to Frans and our vibrant life.

Working from home, with an increasingly empty nest, I am in Yoda mode now: stirring my little pot of beans, living in my comfy cave, and being there for students while in not too distant worlds there is a lot of strife and bullshit.

Many great teachers have said that to change the world we need to cultivate self-awareness and compassion; it's foundational so as not to add more strife and suffering through our projected shadows and fears. This is what I hope to contribute and am called to work on in myself.

***

This morning I found your black shoes in the downstairs closet when I was looking for the old hiking boots that I needed to haul firewood. Those black shoes looked so ordinary and comforting and they also reminded me of your absence. I am not quite ready to part with them. I remember all the walks we took around the pond and the beauty of big trees. We bought those shoes together. I remember your quick gait, your short steps, determined always to get somewhere efficiently. You told me your mother had admonished you for waking inelegantly as a young man, so you had changed your stride. Only after your diagnosis in the lushness of the spring did you slow down.

***

Good, and Sad

As the writing of this book progressed, I noticed that I went from daily writings to weekly writings, with more and more gaps in between. I sense this signifies that grief has become less acute.

When Tim, a colleague from another university who has been following my posts on Facebook, invites me for coffee in early June and asks me, "How are you today?" …

I say, "Good, and sad."

As I reflect on my own words, "Good, and sad," I notice that I've gone from unresolved anger and frustration to growing acceptance and appreciation over the last few months. A liberating sense of independence is also taking root, almost imperceptibly, which in a few months' time turns into overt joy. I am happy to be able to choose my own projects and plan all my travel without mutual deliberation.

Though completing the first draft of the book by late fall, almost a year after Frans's death, doesn't signify the end of sadness, it does feel like a new chapter of grief is about to begin. This may even involve research with other widows. I make notes for such research, and in late August I add a small video to my website about the key questions that have come up for me during bereavement: Does our identity change when we lose a partner? What do we do about unfinished business and some less than flattering things we want to say about our partner? How does writing help?

As I get closer to completing the book, I feel intuitively that doing so signifies the start of another leg of the journey. A lonelier leg, perhaps, or a quieter one, or one marked by more reinvention.

I do not know, actually, and I do not need to know.

In writing everything while it was fresh, I stayed close to what happened and how I felt about it. I stayed close to Frans and the life we lived.

Many of my work habits and rituals have not changed from the time that Frans and I worked long hours together, but I'm listening more closely to my own intuition and rhythms. It feels as if, in grief, I have been at sea on a large sailing ship, working hard to navigate the first big waves. Now it feels like I am entering the harbor. I am arriving back from my mission of going with him through illness and death and facing the first months of life without him.

I am arriving at what will be a different life and this time no one is waiting for me. Frans is truly gone and my daughters are growing up.

It feels like uncertainty and opportunity. It means there is a void but also a space for new adventures and learning. There is sadness and courage and openness will be needed.

***

Frans's Garden

Today I did some more reading on bereavement, this time from a book by grief counsellor Joanne Cacciatore (2017). In one of the final chapters, she lists all the things people say to the bereaved that ignore the process and the lack of finality grief actually entails.

As I read down the list, "Everything happens for a reason," and "It's not normal to hurt for this long," and "Remember the good times," I came across one that made me laugh out loud in the café where I have spent the morning working, "God needed an angel to tend His garden" (Cacciatore, 2017, p. 130).

What the …!?!?

Writing this now makes me laugh again. I know it's meant as a metaphor and as a comfort, but come on!

Frans disliked cooking, as I have said before. He also did not care for gardening, and I don't know if God is interested in career theories. If there is an "up there," mind you, I'm sure Frans is at work.

It's good to catch myself laughing. I acknowledge it as an integral part of healing, along with a good night's sleep and community.

Tonight, I will meet with the widow and widower's group in North Edmonton. They like to have a drink together, the meet-up ad says. I rarely drink. They say they understand each other in half a glance. That, I can believe.

They say they laugh a lot, too, which sounds like a damn good idea.

On my Facebook post about Cacciatore's (2017) list of things said to the bereaved, I add, "PS: next time you see me, please ask how Frans is doing with Heaven's garden." My Dutch friends Janus and Els take great pleasure in the absurdity of this. They cannot imagine Frans as a gardening angel either.

> All of us are on the way to disappearance
> make the most of it now
> paddle with the living
> and along the way, remember death
> that will bring you back to now
> where all your second chances live.

***

Intense Presence and Contentment

I thought the line "where your second chances live" was a good way to end this book. But then it was August. Harvest time, literally and symbolically, and my spirits seemed buoyed and there was more to say. Perhaps it was because of the many good visits I had with people during the summer. I spent several days in Athabasca with friends, 10 days with Janus and Els traveling through the mountains, and then a trip to Ontario to learn more about marketing and communications from Kat, my PhD student, who specializes in this area and was offering a course.

While there, I noticed I was completely content, but this state of being did not seem dependent on any outside circumstances. I felt like I appreciated everything vividly. Mist over the Bruce Peninsula landscape was stunning and like sheer grace as I made my way to the composting toilet at Kat's *Writing Farm* in the early hours of dawn. The sound of bird calls and cars going through the town were equally welcome, and the walk into town for coffee in the mornings had me stopping to look into old storefronts and admiring the way well-built brick houses weather the years.

One of my other graduate students, Susanna, an artist, poet, and social worker, drove down to where I was with her husband Jeff to meet me in person. We walked a portion of the Bruce Trail and in the cooling air of late afternoon enjoyed the views over huge lakes and islands.

They tell me proudly about the "escarpment" of this region. I understand, as they are speaking, that there is something profoundly stabilizing about familiar ground under one's feet; this is their holy ground and I am feeling mine everywhere now.

This being feels like a deep reacquaintance with the basic goodness of my own company.

I have intense dreams while there and they seem to point toward hope. Again, I am not less sad, but I feel more open and present. My sorrow has a benevolent quality to it. It keeps me company as much as my joy; sometimes there is a grumble that I still express as I remember past hurts with Frans. I notice when I am nursing them or when they are just present and when the latter is the case, I feel like the pain needs to be visited just as it is. I consider this part of gleaning everything I can from what I learned with Frans.

I'm also finding it surprisingly okay to be single, while I have been partnered for the majority of my adult life. There is still yearning, but there is no edge to it and no sense that things should be other than they are at the moment.

In the night

I wake up with desire
and grief
I dream I am in a large square room
something bare, with unlacquered boards and
white vintage sills,
beyond I see a wide horizon
and the kind of wild grass that everyone secretly loves
the place is for rent
and the agent
smiles knowingly
it suits me perfectly
(and I know how to decorate, again)
I lie awake in this benevolent night
and cry
you seem farther away each day
In moments, I walk with fresh grace
younger even,
mourning offers up her blackened peel
the first layer splits and the dead skin pulls away
ripened for a cycle of renewal
while my smiling face shows what I have lost
and ages me, marks me, our dance interrupted.
Where now,
in this good dark?
Someone has sent me a Yiddish poem
(gratefully friends make sure the effect
of your disappearance
doesn't go unnoticed)
the other widow writes
"the house under the tall pines

Where no one waits for me anymore" -
mine are spruces,
but you get the picture.

August 25, 2019

In the morning I read the news on my phone. I see what is going on in the world and it feels heavy. Later in the day, I go with Kat and her family to her father Phil's farm in a place called Hopeness. Once we get there, it's as if I've entered another time.

He serves us food from his garden. I sit at the table in his ramshackle kitchen while the meal is being prepared. That evening tucked in Kat's cozy studio apartment at her *Writing Farm*, I can't sleep right away. I feel I've been infused with the most profound beauty of presence by having lived the day just as it was offered.

The morning begins with a poem after a dream and the night ends with another poem before the next vivid dream.

Don't miss all the beauty

Tonight, I eat baked pumpkin and purple beans
grown by a father and granddad
in the soil of Hopeness,
We eat off "grandmother's plates"
all generations represented at the table,
the butter is passed crisscross and
semi-circle and
there is time for stories;
there is time.
Afterward, we wash up by hand
the west light is so sublime
that we are drawn outside,
meandering through dampening grass
raising our eyes to
maples, willows, cedars,
and the buildings of those who are now gone
(their brushstrokes, the names of their animals loved
and lost scratched in pencil into cupboards,
their dream gardens, once immaculate,
still show the old pathways.)
Below and around us
there is so much growing
I don't even know the names,
but no matter
wordless, I drink in

a hundred shades of green.
I know the news is bad
the burning forests
all the bills of human greed coming in,
already long overdue.
the old hatreds banal and terrifying.
And still,
some inner voice clearly
reminds me,
don't miss all the beauty.
I know no single poem can save the earth
or change the heart of a fearful man
or unclench the beliefs
that make strangers of us all,
but I wish I knew why people wait
for apocalypse.
Why the old, tried refrains,
we know they don't work.
Death is already all around us
why hasten it?
Are we so bored
so traumatized
so king-of-the-hill?
Did you know each apple tree is unique?
You can graft here and there to work out a special
blend of tart, sweet, grainy, crisp
and still they will astonish you
if you really look,
it all will.
Tonight, I tasted seedless raspberry concentrate
and stirred part of it into vinaigrette
my small contribution to dinner
as a new guest at the table,
everything was perfectly lush
do you see?
Our smashed hopes can be tinged by bile
or be remade slower and sharply alive
and hearts actually do speak,
they say,
don't miss all the beauty.

August 25, 2019

I later send the poem to Phil via regular mail and he writes back to tell me that he adores it.

***

Almost Normal

September 2, 2019

It is a peaceful Labor Day morning and the sun is shining in. I've prepared the house for a busy fall semester by cleaning thoroughly and sorting through stacks of papers and printed articles. The more my environment is clean and clear, the easier I find it to work.

Sophia is in town and has been making canned apple sauce from our own apples that are in various buckets and baskets in the coolness of the basement hallway. While she is doing that, I have piled up a bag of documents for shredding.

The upstairs closet full of art and office supplies takes us 4 hours to clean out; now I know I have six pairs of scissors and three staplers.

The academic year is starting, though winter still feels far away. I associate September with my parents' birthdays and fresh productivity. Six years ago, my Dad also died this month on the day my Mom turned 72. Frans and I said our vows in September, and my sister and brother are coming to visit from Amsterdam later this month so we can visit and let our Dad's ashes fly free.

All the blessings, the fullness, and the sadness lives side by side and intermixed.

This past month, a few new developments have become part of my process of moving through life with grief. While most of my grieving has felt psychological and emotional, I have started a new food plan a month ago called The Metabolic Factor (a cheesy American-style advert caught my attention). It had the right arguments about the value of healthy fats and proteins, so I bought the program. I felt I had been carrying 10 extra pounds that don't suit me. After a few weeks on the program, I feel energetic and the pounds are coming off without a problem. It seems the good food is affecting my body but also my mind: I am more cheerful and serene without the highs and lows that sugar brings.

How is the old heart? Several friends are still graciously asking. I still sigh deeply five times a day and weep. How could it be otherwise?

Music helps me grieve and stay in touch with feelings. Especially classical music and a few songs from the recent remake of *A Star is Born*.

When your partner dies, one of the most important witnesses of your life dies. I have said this before. When Frans died, a part of my dialogical world died off like a room full of life that had to be closed.

This is not something you just get over.

In his last letter to me, he said he had no regrets except not being able to continue our life together. That I could call on him whenever I needed to. I still do that, but less on the page and more in the quiet moments.

I do feel his presence still, but it is more subtle now.

***

October 2, 2019

I remember the mornings in the early weeks after Frans's death when I used to wake up and write something about Frans first thing every morning. Then every few days, then once a week, and now I see it's been a month. It reminds me of the way we mark the age of our babies. When they are new, we mark days: "She is 10 days old"; and then we say, "He is 6 weeks"; and then we say, "18 months old"; and then we speak in years. Having them never gets ordinary, however, and in the same way the death of a loved one is unforgettable.

***

One Year Since Frans's Death (November 16, 2019)

Today

I build a small altar in the house
on it
your photo
the invitation to the funeral
your glasses (which soon I will donate)
candles to burn for most of the day
and cups from our Dutch home.
I want to bring up your shoes
but then I don't
I don't want to be a crazy lady,
how long does one grieve is the question
in an article a colleague sends, perfectly timed
The reply: how long will your beloved be dead?

Notes

1 This term was inspired by a movie by the same name about a father, played by Will Smith, who grieves the death of his young daughter.
2 The inspiration for the line "dove toward death" came from my friend Margot, who pointed out the painting *La Tomba del Tuffatore* [Tomb of the Diver]," c. 480 BCE, an image of a figure diving that has been interpreted as symbolic of going from death to the afterlife. A copy hung at the home of Janus and Els in Batenburg, the Netherlands. We visited Frans's grave all together on that visit. It seemed extra poignant because of the way that Frans chose to die.
3 Occupational deformity is a translation from Dutch [beroepsafwijking] which means quirks that creep into one's way of acting and being as a result of one's career skills and knowledge.

10

SHARING THE WORK

A colleague who works in the field of English composition and emotional disclosure sends me a number of questions to consider. These questions bring up the niggling concerns that have played in my own mind throughout the writing of this book.

1. How do the author's children (and parents, aunts, uncles, etc.) feel about the spousal loss memoir? How can an author be self-disclosing without violating the privacy of other family members?

This is a question that has been very much alive for me as I write. I will be discussing it with the series editor as well as another colleague of mine who has more experience publishing personal stories.

What I think is that if I had written a book only singing Frans's praises, I might still have offended someone (e.g., Why didn't you mention more about his kids who were so important to him? Why did you not talk more about his amazing work accomplishments? Why was it all about your relationship?) Something Carolyn Ellis (2018) says brings me some solace: "The goal should not be to get readers to like you but rather for them to believe, trust, and learn from you" (p. 335).

It remains tricky what to disclose and what not to, and it's important to be respectful in addition to being honest. I am also cognizant that what I am sharing is my own experience of my relationship with Frans and not everyone will agree with my version. Nor will everyone close to us even be interested in reading it.

It may be uncomfortable for others to read things about Frans and me, even if they already knew these things, but didn't expect they would be published. I have left various things out of this manuscript with this in mind. I did write about the tensions with his first wife, as they directly affected me, and the lack of resolution about this with Frans complicated my grieving. I thought about how to name the problem and put myself in her shoes as well; I hope it has come through in my writing that I acknowledge(d) their bond, her enduring care for him, and his continued regard and care for her.

There is no easy solution here and perhaps no solution at all. There will be those who read and say, "Wow, I didn't know this about Uncle Frans, what an adventurer he was!" And someone else will say, "Frans is not entirely the man I thought he was; that's disappointing." Or simply, "Such private matters should not be shared." Ultimately, the book is not about presenting a perfect picture of Frans (or me), or about presenting grief as some lofty journey of love and forgiveness, but about "writing the self" in order to make meaning of an imperfect love that was lived and lost.

As Ellis (2018) says in her autoethnography of losing her life partner, whose influence on her writing and research had been great, just as Frans's was on mine,

> I understand now that I have to tell my own story in my own voice, as partial and incomplete as it may be… . I already know that when one writes an evocative text, she relinquishes control over what it evokes in readers. (p. 325)

I will not please everyone, nor is it my job to, but this remains difficult for someone like me who has cultivated a "thin skin" in order to do the work of writing the self sensitively with others. The nature of the autoethnographic beast is that we must be honest and divulge difficult truths while still respecting the community we are a part of. As I say, I have shared very personal things and I have left quite a number of things deliberately unsaid. I do not believe it is possible to strike a perfect balance.

What is more important is to be intentional and to prune parts where I felt the urge to speak without nuance about perceived injustices, or where I hid behind an undue need for identity maintenance. It is important to practice "permanent vigilance" (Zylinska's term, as cited in Ellis, 2018, p. 345), which "means we must continue to ask endless questions about our responsibilities to others and our narrative privilege, question our premises, and ask others to think with us" (Ellis, 2018, p. 345).

In considering what I've told about Frans in this book and what I would ultimately include, I sent two colleagues of mine a file of several pages labeled "dicey bits" and asked them if they thought it was respectful to include these. Both responded that they found these sections a vital part of the text and a respectful telling of our relational history and our issues. One of my colleagues, novelist and nonfiction writer Angie Abdou—who has taken far greater risks than I am taking here—says, "If we were only telling the easy parts, anyone could write. Taking on the hard parts of life, saying the things people don't normally say, and putting ourselves in such a risky and vulnerable position—these challenging tasks add up to the true job of being a writer." She considered my efforts "measured and thoughtful." She herself regretted publishing one passage that was fueled by a "foul mood," which was later posted out of context on social media by someone in her community. She also told me, "I am always nervous before a book comes out" (personal communication, May 27, 2020).

2. How does a spousal loss memoirist avoid the almost inevitable idealization that occurs when we remember and write about the dead?

Indeed, another risk of writing about someone we loved so dearly. I have not idealized Frans! This has at times been a struggle for me, as I wanted to tell a truthful story but also wanted to emphasize how dear Frans was (and is) to me. I'm true to two ethics at once, (1) the writer's ethic to tell things accurately and truthfully—as much as that is possible within one's subjectivity—but also (2) the ethic of partnership. Frans was a good man who inspired countless others; he was a beloved and devoted father; he was a loving spouse to me in most ways; I want to honor all of that, without making him into a saint.

I have wished at times that I could have felt the bliss and contentment that telling an idealized version might evoke. That said, I trust from my research that not naming the more difficult things might actually get me stuck (Miller & Loring, 2016). My writing, I concede, as autoethnographer Ellis (2018) does, "must tell the truths of my experience as I know them" (p. 344).

3. What's the impact of reading a spousal loss memoir on a future romantic partner?

This is another good question and now, a year and a half after Frans's death, I am in the position to ask it. (I will say more about re-partnering at the end of the book, as it is a story in and of itself.) Interestingly, my new partner was attracted to me in part because of reading my Facebook posts about Frans's illness and my grief. He said reading the posts that "they may have scared certain men off, as you're so open and vulnerable, but not me. I saw your tenderness and honesty and thought, that is the kind of woman for me."

I have been sharing much of the manuscript with him and he asks good questions about it. I have asked him if it was too much to hear or if he perceives me to be overly involved with Frans. He says that he sees that I am very involved with Frans and the book, but that this is to be expected and he does not feel diminished by it. He is interested in what I am learning about grief, which he believes has implications for other forms of loss as well (e.g., divorce). My being able to share the story with him has brought us closer, but I cannot know if that will always be the case.

If a (new) partner includes the grief about the loss and stories of the dead spouse as an unalterable part of the griever's life, truly embracing this with care and gentleness, the new partner stands to reap some very rich rewards. I'll touch on this in the final chapter.

4. What's the effect of the memoirist rereading a spousal loss memoir years after it was written?

This would be interesting research to do. I suppose we are always changing our viewpoints and that if we updated our story, we would want to alter a number of things or write a whole new foreword. Carolyn Ellis (1995, 2018) tells me that she decided "not to change anything significant" when she revised her story in *Final Negotiations* (personal communication, June 2020).

5. How important is it for a spousal loss memoirist to believe that his or her deceased spouse would approve of the memoir?

I have asked Frans for his approval in my imagination. However, the simple reality is that I have to make the decision alone. He once told me that living more honestly and transparently made his life lighter. His mission in life and work was to have true dialogues about the experience, and that is the intention of this book too. He said things that frequently shocked and offended people because he wanted to end the monological culture of education and the prison of his own youth where "vital things were not talked about." He speaks about this in his short biography as well (Van Engelen, 2015).

6. How might the spousal loss memoir help the author to recognize the bereavement changes that occur over time?

What I see from my own experiences—conceding here that I am but one grieving spouse—is that I already see this book changing in the span of the year and a half that I have been writing. I am reminded of Japanese bridge painters: once they have completed a very long bridge, they must start all over again because the side of the bridge they began on is already in need of the maintenance.

In this way, I have returned again and again to the first 100 pages of the book and see that my feelings are changing. Though I have left the rawness of what I have written intact, I see that I am indeed less raw and certainly less sad and angry.

***

Kindred Scholars

January 6, 2020

At the autoethnography conference in Florida this past week, I spoke about unfinished business in grief. This thread of discontent has echoed through my grieving process and colors my memories. Frans and my relationship, in my mind's eye, was a beautiful sky with various curves, flowing patterns and colors, and also a dark line running across all of it.

It remains tricky to talk about my discontent because we live in a culture where it's taboo to speak ill of the dead. Somehow, we intuit, it's not good for us and not good for them. But what do we do then? To share this dialogical process in front of an audience of 40 of my academic peers this past week felt like a capstone to the grief research and embodied learning I have been doing.

It was as if I had to say, "This is the truth of my experience and I'm 'coming out' to tell you; perhaps it will free you as well in some way."

On the flight home from the conference on January 5, 2020, an additional compelling thought arrived unbidden: "It's time to live forwards, and to let go." Of course, the moment I think it, I concede that letting go is not do-able unless you're on the brink of doing just that anyway. It's a result of a learning process, not the action itself.

In the literature, there are two kinds of unfinished business in grief: "Unfulfilled Wishes" and "Unresolved Conflict" (Holland, Klingspon et al., 2020, p. 73). Mine was in the latter category. The more I accept that it was so and the more resolute I feel about not accepting certain treatment again, the more the tension releases and the more gratitude I can feel about what was positive.

My writing has also led me to reflect on my human failings. This helps to balance the story and allows me to see the futility of some of my ways. A colleague asked me, "What were your failings in the interactions with Frans?" I responded as follows:

I thought my basic weakness was expecting people to be better than they were or could be, but upon reflection, I see that this is not really it. What I am pointedly insistent about is that a partner be accountable to himself and to me when he is not being entirely honest, or loses his temper, or is unfair in the way he argues. I see that I was enraged at times at the lack of accountability, but not the humanness behind it, which I can understand.

It's not enough to say, "I'm a hothead," and continue to lash out. In fact, Frans never would have accepted such an argument from me or anyone else. When someone in his life would say, "But this is just how I feel, I can't help it," he was entirely unconvinced and would say, "That's learned helplessness! You can't just say, *I'm like this and I can't help it!*"

I would have been a lot more forgiving of Frans's trespasses had he had the humility to admit them more readily. Losing one's temper and going ballistic should, I feel, have been accompanied by a "Sorry, I realize how hurtful my behavior can be. While I love you, I am not always able to stay respectful in the moments that I am triggered." Some might call me intolerant in this regard and ask, "Who makes you the judge of what good or bad behavior is?" Reflecting on how I could love Frans dearly and trust him in so many ways and still experience such aggravation confused me for a long time.

When I listened to a talk on the elements of trust, by vulnerability and shame researcher Brené Brown, more than a year after Frans's death, pieces of this puzzle began to fall into place. Brown (2018) breaks down the components of trust into seven elements with the acronym B.R.A.V.I.N.G: boundaries, reliability, accountability, vault (keep each other's confidence around private matters), integrity, nonjudgment, and a generous interpretation of the other's behavior. Frans and I trusted each other in almost all of those ways, but Frans's accountability for his temper was a weak spot in our trust. His integrity about personal relationships had been wobbly and his boundaries with a number of his exes unclear. My interpretation of his behavior was not generous; I judged him.

I could see his fervent goal was to please us all, yet, to me, this did not justify half-truths and aggressive deflections. I wanted to keep respecting Frans, so I did not lower my standards or ignore his temperamental moments. I could have said, "He has poor impulse control," or, "He was used to doing it this way for so many years, I can't expect him to change now," but to me, those sentiments sound like excuses. He chose me, so that means he chose the challenge.

R: I was unrelenting, my love. I know that.

F: I needed you to be unrelenting. But what I also needed was for you to trust me anyway.

R: I did, and I didn't.

F: I know, my love. It's okay now. (Embraces me.) You know, liefje, it's okay that we failed at something.

R: (Crying). I will trust you on that now. I see there isn't another way to turn it.

F: Even when I was alive, there wasn't, liefje. Rest in this insight for a moment. You can let it be now.

Grievous

Our bitter seed swallowed
the wash of astringency that was ours
has grown into humility
even *failure* isn't a tainted word anymore

***

What am I learning? That human failings are par for the course and not everyone will feel compelled to own them. That's reality. Insisting that they do makes people less likely to do so and probably made me come across as if I were on some moral high ground.

The poem below expresses the intention to "let go," and acknowledges ownership of issues that linger; whatever still preoccupies us after a loved one's death must be part of our own psychic healing.

Now

that you are gone
our old gripes picked over
I see how they stand in the way of what you tried to give
and what I wanted to receive
On the wind I'll put them
so I can see the trust
that love keeps offering
I will undo where they stung
with the wisdom and laughter of the day
I should put them where they belong
in a chest labelled past, in the basement,
where a spider uses the box
as a platform for its home, no more, no less,
but better yet, I will put them with the laundry
to be washed into fresh poems
and made into pluck, pinned and flapping on the line
It will look like I finally heeded my mother's advice
"let bygones be bygones"
(though she couldn't do it either)
You are dead,

all the hard things died with you
and whatever echoes still
must be mine.

May 2020

***

New Beginnings

I had dared to make my decision that I would find happiness again one day. I realised that my decision back then had set my renewal in motion, more than that, made it possible
Katrin Den Elzen (2018, p. 187)

In late January 2020, author and autoethnographer Carolyn Ellis expressed interest in this manuscript. After I submitted it to her and Art Bochner for the Routledge's *Writing Lives* series, she gave extensive feedback on the first draft. She advised me to slow down in the process of editing. Two weeks later, during a deliberate effort to follow her advice, my mother handed me a stack of papers from elementary and junior high school and on a report card one of my teachers writes, "Reinekke's assignments are always complete, but I think she could achieve a higher standard if she worked more slowly." I chuckle to myself and determine that I will slow down even more, not only to increase the quality of the work, but to savor the experience—and, as Carolyn advises, "Let the writing do its work."

I begin the process of revising in part by reading Ellis's (2018) updated edition of *Final Negotiations*. I correspond with her about a number of questions I have regarding autoethnographic writing. It seems fitting that I should read her book again now, after Frans's death: I am not the same person I was when I read it the first time. And frankly, Ellis is much braver than I am and thus reading her work gives me room to go back into my writing and flesh out various details, in particular about Frans and our unfinished business.

In her updated book, she reflects anew on her relationship with Gene Weinstein and her journey with him through chronic illness and death. The foreword to the new book is written by Art Bochner, Ellis's life, research, and writing partner of 30 years. I see the parallels between her life and mine and am grateful that of any editor I could have ended up with, I have the chance to work with her. I send her several questions, one about how to end the book and whether I should speak of new beginnings.

Dear Carolyn,

Frans did not like to cook, so I cooked for us despite our emancipated views and our both being equally busy academics. In the book, I speak about how some years ago, Frans said, "When you become a full-time professor, you can support us both financially." And how I had quipped back, "Then you can cook for us." Although he was a very verbal person and a great debater, he seemed stunned into silence when I said this. It was as if his emancipated hippy (and feminist-minded) side was battling internally with his dislike of cooking and traditional male values. He died 6 weeks before I became a full-time professor and I joked at his funeral that he obviously disliked cooking so much, that he made sure he wouldn't be around to do it when I started working full-time. When I tell this story during presentations, it always induces a chuckle in listeners and lightens the story of grief, both for myself and others.

Now, this story has an additional ending. At the end of last year, a man who has been following my grief and widow posts on Facebook asked me out. First in June, as colleagues, and again at the end of September. A new relationship has slowly been taking shape since September.

In the body of her return e-mail, Carolyn writes, "Wonderful."

REINEKKE: And this is the cosmic joke: the very first thing he wanted to do for me was to cook!

CAROLYN: Reading that made me chuckle.

R: He is a foodie it turns out and really loves to cook! This was not even on my wish-list for future partners; in fact, this was not even on my radar and I was quite fine being on my own since August 2019. That said, it was very meaningful to me that he (Tim) came to see me on November 16, 2019 and cooked for me on the anniversary of Frans's death. I had set up a kind of altar with many of Frans's pictures and our books and other objects of significance and Tim stood with me and asked about each picture and object.

C: Wonderful, sounds like Art, who read my whole 700-page manuscript and put up with all the memories and photos, only once asking me if I minded taking down a large photo of Gene that hung beside my bed! I of course removed it and put it into storage immediately.

R: Tim was coincidentally wearing a blue shirt that day, one identical to a shirt Frans used to wear, even though Tim rarely wears blue and Frans often did. I have been able to share my love and grief about Frans with Tim very openly and in some ways he has helped me to heal some of the scratches Frans left as Frans could misinterpret my intentions toward things like setting boundaries with his exes as "your insecurity" or as "some trauma left over from your childhood" (diagnosing, psychoanalyzing, and at times bull-dozing).

I want to say something about Tim at the end of this book, but I don't want to take away from the story of grief and loss (or potentially dilute it) by speaking about a new man in my life, as if I've simply replaced Frans. Tim's presence in my life is significant though, and I think this too is part of the story of life, that is, opening up to new love and possibility.

C: I agree and wonder if some hints would be okay. I'm thinking just to have a scene where this man wants to cook for you, to show that life goes on, and there is hope ahead. To me this doesn't take away from your love with Frans at all. You could even have a conversation with Frans about meeting this man and his wanting to cook for you. I like that story. Readers do want to be hopeful that not only have you survived this loss but that there are good times and adventures ahead. This is sometimes the negative bias that autoethnographic researchers are accused of, that it is all about death, dying, and tragedy, while the actual intent of this work is to show and reflect on how life actually happens.

Later, as I delve into the work of Jeffrey Berman in his book *Writing Widowhood* (2015), I see that my concerns about this are shared by other women. In fact, "The story of falling in love again after a spouse's death is a part of the story of widowhood that almost always remains untold" (Berman, 2015, pp. 55–56). I ultimately decide to break some of the silence around the topic and go beyond giving hints about my new love. I revisit this topic in an upcoming chapter and conclude, as Carolyn does, that "it doesn't take away from your love with Frans at all."

***

How Grief Keeps Showing Up

In early March 2020, I attend a grief workshop with Robert (Bob) Neimeyer. He arrives in the city just as the COVID-19 crisis begins to unfold and is presenting to a group of nearly 200 participants. In weirdly synchronistic fashion, I e-mail him about a journal issue we're co-editing on "Living with Loss" one morning, and he tells me he's at the Portland airport waiting to fly to Edmonton! He does not know that I live in Edmonton. He's coming to teach a 2-day workshop and I manage to convince the hosting organization to let me register last-minute. Bob invites me to dinner, and I take him to a local Japanese restaurant close to the conference center.

Over dinner, we find out we have at least four mutual connections around the world: the network of narrative research scholars is rich and tight-knit, it turns out. I tell him about my book and writing-the-self. We have close mutual friends who knew Frans and I read Bob the poem I wrote for Frans a few weeks before.

He asks if I might share it at the workshop the next day as an example of healthy continuing bonds. I read it to the group.

Let's keep meeting this way

Yesterday as I worked
I straightened someone's line of reasoning
I nod to how you sharpened my game.

Last night I told the story of you lecturing,
your flamboyant Catholic self at a Protestant school
using the Lord's name in vain
with gusto but never to offend,
they called you on it and you blurted out "oh, Jesus!"
The day before yesterday
your good advice was on offer
in my dialogical mind and
last week I stacked up our
impressive list of books,
we do not have biological babies
but we have these.
You still come with me everywhere
a bit quieter now than you were
but always large in my life.
Today I look at your photo and tear up
with gratitude.
Let's keep meeting this way.

February 14, 2020

After the workshop, Bob and I continued to correspond and exchange grief poems with a view to co-write an article. He writes about a painful shift in an important relationship and I write about Frans. I realize again how much grief can open us if we let it and that it makes closeness with others possible—that is, if we surrender to its ways.

***

My life has been touched by loss and grief. I thought it would be an experience with a beginning, middle, and ending, but now I see it does not end. Just like having children—whether they survive us or not—we have become parents and this love can never be undone. As a result of having had this experience, I also find myself relating to others who have experienced intense losses; it's as if I am training a muscle that now has memory and responds immediately in recognition of the terrain underfoot.

***

April 2020

In recent weeks, I've been taking a course on women's empowerment through exploring desire as well as sensual and sexual pleasure. It's called "Virtual Pleasure Bootcamp"; I first came across the idea that pleasure might be a useful compass in my life as a woman when I read the course leader's book years before (Thomashauer, 2002).

On one of the video calls, we were asked to name a favorite moment from that session. I said, "I was taken by Dorothy" (one of the women who had spoken earlier on the call). "She seems to have such a wonderful and natural sense of humor."

Dorothy later contacts me through Facebook and asks if I'll be her practice partner for some of the exercises in the book. I say yes. It turns out Dorothy Rosen lost her husband Steve exactly 6 months to the day after Frans's death. We are both widowed! We are both in a course to expand our joy. Steve died of cancer; Frans died of cancer. Of all the 120 women on that call, how is it that I connected with her? Perhaps these coincidences are really not as surprising as they seem, as all of us will lose loved ones throughout life—nonetheless, I am grateful for the synchronistic way our meeting unfolded.

Dorothy and I plan our weekly calls together and continue them after the course is done.

Then a new editorial assistant, Aathira, joins our team at the *British Journal of Guidance and Counselling*. She has studied the therapeutic arts and has lost her boyfriend to cancer while working on her Master's degree. I e-mail to welcome her to the team and tell her about my book project and Frans. I write her a poem, as if to say, we don't do grief alone. It is our common fate; I'm reminded of this again and again as I go through the days. Aathira responds warmly and sends me poems of her own.

Across the world

a young woman grieves for her mate
just as I do,
she finds solace in words,
just as I do,
she knows the word cancer
as I do
she knows the look of illness and death
as I do
and this reminds me how we are at once whole
and part of one whole
that the separations and aloneness of our losses
are never true
that which brought us joy will keep flowering
even when the beloved dies,
There is but one condition: open to the howling heart of sorrow
and all the beauty
that keeps offering itself to us
will have more color than we ever saw before.

***

11

WRITING THE SELF IN BEREAVEMENT

While writing this book, I said to the recently widowed Bonnie, who has practiced meditation for many years (both before and after her husband's death), "I recognize in you a griever who lives as both bereaved spouse and one who reflects upon the experience. Always on these two tracks simultaneously." My colleague Katrin Den Elzen describes a similar principle of getting close to our visceral experience but also developing a wider lens on it using the writing process,

> Writing means to oscillate between the focus on the specifics, the sensuous detail, listening to the story of the body, and the broadening of the picture which puts these fragments in relationship with the larger world - the remembered past, the present and the imagined future - and in relationship with others, present and absent. Exploring these relational dynamics from the initial vantage point of the focused detail makes reflection and alternative discoveries possible. It is this interplay between delving into the close-up of experience and then to include, bit by bit, the rest of existence that allows the fragmented picture to become whole again. (2018, p. 184)

Indeed, writing and meditation have this in common: they allow us to engage with the realities of the human condition while at the same time training our capacity for observation. We make space for pain, and we are also aware of the dangers of drowning in it in unproductive ways. While loss is inherent in living and pain a given, suffering can be ameliorated and even made fruitful by the act of heartfelt engagement and benevolent detachment.

In the context of healing, both meditators and authors can share the peace of their mind; the meditator radiates and embodies the gifts of their internal process, while the author aims to articulate effectively a piece of their mind. And I believe the writer enjoys an additional benefit: we have the chance to make of our losses art and beauty.

Writing is a companion for life. It has brought me both comfort and insight in the wake of Frans's death. It also steadied me and expanded my capacity for equanimity and receptive caring when he got his diagnosis and become increasingly ill. In the last 2 years, since we first got the news of his terminal cancer and in the year and a half since his death, sorrow has washed through me many times, and continues to do so—but less frequently. Anger has erupted regularly, though that is rare nowadays. My thoughts have at times been distressing and tension-filled, and I have found collateral beauty in the experience of loss. By writing, I could welcome all of my thoughts and feelings and meet them with understanding, even if some of what I felt was first accompanied by fear or resistance.

As I reflect on the act and process of committing words to paper in the middle of grief, I notice too that I have rarely been lonely. In this dance of poetic creativity, in the process of composing this autoethnographic work, I feel connected to myself and to others. I have been and remain fully alive in the midst of this impactful and heartbreaking life change. I continue to feel Frans's absence, in particular his warmth and exuberance, and our dialogical world, while I also feel his presence, remember his vibrancy, and continue my/our work in an extended dialogical space that includes his voice.

Inner equilibrium, which I cultivate, allows me to reach out for the comfort of others in healthy ways and has resulted in rich conversations. There is no edge of desperation or panic in my need for human connection. Writing allowed me to go back time and again to connect to a sense of abiding relatedness: with myself, with Frans, and with the inevitable course of life, including death. As an agnostic, without culturally obligatory rituals around dying and grieving, and with the "freedom" (and rather the necessity!) to make meaning of my loss, writing helps me to create my own symbolic acts of reverence, reflection, and restoration.

Berman's (2015) book *Writing Widowhood* analyzes the lives of authors who are widowed and refers to writing as both ritual and re-creation:

> The widows' stories reveal courage amid adversity, unexpected resilience, and the crucial role of writing and reading in recovery. Oates, Gilbert, Godwin, Didion, and Jamison have different attitudes towards religion and spirituality, but they would all agree that writing about their deceased spouses became a sacred death ritual for them, one that was necessary for their own survival. Spousal loss may have shattered their assumptions about life and themselves, but writing helped them re-create their worlds. (p. 7)

Indeed, writing offers a number of specific and essential benefits that I will discuss in this chapter, which should make clear why it might be meaningful for those who don't identify as writers, are unfamiliar with writing-the-self processes, and/or are in any way cut off from rituals and practices for dealing with grief meaningfully.

The process of writing-the-self in bereavement invites us to stay present to our feelings and to notice them with an open, compassionate, and inquiring mind. I use the notion of "invitation" deliberately because there are other choices we might make that seem equally valid or useful; for instance, we may power through, or get very busy soon after loss, or we may remain mired in a victim narrative. The dual-track of being attuned to our emotions and observing ourselves that I consider the "winning combination" in responding to loss is but one creative and inspiring possibility. In my experience, it represents self-care and offers a "how to" for resilience without necessarily being prescriptive.

The key discoveries I have made about why writing may serve us in bereavement can be summed up as follows: (1) writing can help promote a (healthy) continuing bond with the deceased; (2) writing is a companion for life, supporting me in having a healthy relationship with myself through microscopic noticing. Writing has also helped me to (3) actively process unfinished business, (4) make meaning while noticing that the need for meaning-making subsides over time, and (5) uncover and articulate taboo subjects and release a need for "identity maintenance" in the context of sexual desire, repartnering, and ambivalent feelings.

Writing also made it possible to share my story with others with the possibility of inspiring hope for other grievers; I was heartened by the many responses I got along the way as I shared poems and insights in regular Facebook posts.

***

The Benefits of Writing

1. Continuing Bonds and the Dialogical Self

> *Living with death allows us to acknowledge the continuing presence of absent people, the ways in which they remain alive to us. They have left us, but we have not left them.*
>
> *(Berman, 2007, p. 6)*

Frans's death meant the literal end of our conversation, which for many years provided us with warmth, inspiration, companionship, and a place where we could sharpen our minds. His sudden absence created a visceral echo in my being. When I returned home to Canada 9 days after his funeral and woke to the chirping of birds on the giant blue spruce outside my window, the first words that filled the pages of this book warmed that space, entered the painful gap, and allowed me to continue to inhabit parts of our relationship. Our conversation had ended, but our dialogical world remained accessible, especially through writing.

As I write, I keep Frans close to me, just as author, academic, and widow Kay Redfield Jamison (2011) kept her connection with her deceased spouse as she wrote about her grief in her book *Nothing was the Same*. "She remains close to her deceased husband, who guides her in death as he did in life," writes Berman (2015, p. 177) in his analysis of her memoir. Frans feels close to me when I am writing, and he would have encouraged me to keep working. Jamison, who also shared an intellectual partnership with her spouse, repeats words her husband wrote to her on a Valentine's card. I relate strongly to these words, which could have been said by Frans, "Your work is important. It will help you when you are missing me. It will draw us close" (Jamison, 2011, p. 164).

However, in sharing the dialogues I write with Frans and the poems I write to him in this book, I don't explain how writing sustains our bond, I only claim that I feel it to be so. Someone reading this might say, "Well, she's talking to herself and imagining it's him and that brings her comfort." Someone else, with a more esoteric take, might say, "Of course you can speak to the dead and they keep looking out for you."

I prefer to describe it as a phenomenon that can be explained using the theory of the dialogical self (Dialogical Self Theory, or DST, as advanced by Hermans & Konopka, 2010). Here the idea is that we are multi-voiced and our identity is made up of a dynamic and complex collection of voices or "I-positions" that are in conversation with one another (Hermans & Konopka, 2010). I-positions are all felt as "me" (e.g., me-as-mother, me-as-widow, me-as-bereaved) and seem to come from "inside," but these "selves" can also originate from outside the self and be experienced as internalized voices—for example, advice we hear echoing from a book we've read, or our mother, or from beliefs we have about identity, such as "this is what a woman should be" (Hermans & Konopka, 2010). Our partner can be a strong internalized voice or I-position in the repertoire of our dialogical self (e.g., I-as-Frans). The life-giving narrative we tell about ourselves creates a semblance of order and unity in those otherwise disparate or cacophonous voices and our identity is made up of internal I-positions that we consider "our own" as well as externally originating I-positions based on those who have influenced us greatly (Lengelle, 2016).

An example of the latter: most of us have had the experience of having an imagined conversation with our partner or spouse while we are physically apart, like:

> "I am still busy finishing my report for work."
> "Yes, but I would like dinner when I get home. You know I don't like to wait past 7 o'clock to eat."
> "Yes, I know that about you, but today I didn't get to grocery shopping on time."

> "Well, fair enough, when I get back, let's just go to dinner at the new place with the outdoor tables."

(At this point, you may phone or text your spouse and suggest the eating-out option before they do and avoid any friction that you anticipate by having had this practice dialogue).

Such internalized dialogues can happen while our partner is alive, and they can also happen quite easily when they are no longer alive. It is perhaps even fair to say that every relationship we have with a person, alive or dead, is happening inside us; the other may not even have much of a say in the matter! This could explain why two people can have a completely different marriage while married to each other.

Frans is an "internalized I-position" in my self-repertoire now, just as he was in life, only when he was alive he could contribute to the conversation in a literal way and now he only does so figuratively. Of course, his imagined responses are based on what I believe he likely would have said. I do not have complete liberty to have anything I wish come out of his dialogical mouth, post death, just as novelists may tell you they don't control their story's characters and thus cannot randomly determine what these fictional personalities will say (King, 2002).

The dialogue we have with a deceased spouse can (and does) happen in our heads, but writing that conversation has several advantages. Writing gives a sense of permanence and solidity and becomes a physical object on the page, making it more tangible. Even seeing Frans's name on the page seems to conjure him, in the same way, a photo might bring him closer. The activity of writing also slows the thought process, is deliberate, and requires focus, while having a conversation in one's mind can be ruminative or appear in random snippets. It requires a strongly disciplined mind to keep a conversation going in one's head, while on paper we can easily have a more sustained dialogue.

My experience too is that what I write down can surprise me; an insight might stare back at me and, as contemporary poet David Whyte says, can become "impossible to retreat from" (D. Whyte, personal communication [lecture], 2016). Writing also allows me to remember, not only in the moment but also later, when I might otherwise have forgotten a particular detail. For example, I wrote down Frans's last words to me; they are specific and I want to remember them exactly as he spoke them. In 10 or 20 years' time, I might not recall them as clearly. Paradoxically, "remembering is the best way to forget the pain of loss and go on living" (Freud, as cited in Berman, 2015, p. 94), and writing is specific and intentional remembering. It is a form of grief work and, as Toni Morrison advises, "do all the mourning things" (as cited in Berman, 2015, p. 94).

Besides my journaling and the writing of this book, I also re-member (i.e., assemble a sense of) Frans when I share e-mails with other widows, friends, and fellow researchers. There too I am in conversation, and if they knew Frans, this enhances my sense of his ongoing presence and allows me to honor him. It's as if

I'm saying, "My love, in writing this, I am visiting you. I am writing for you and about you. You are so important that I am writing a whole book about our love and my grief. One of your mottos was 'a day not learned is a day not lived,' so you would be happy to see me learning so much."

In summary, writing allows me to experience the continued bond that the bereavement literature speaks about (Klass, 2006). That doesn't mean, however, that writing to maintain a bond with the deceased is a healthy strategy for everyone. Grief researcher Klass (2006) maintains that a continuing bond with the deceased does not necessarily mean that we adjust well to grief and in some cases, it's better to leave the deceased behind.

In my case, I continue to connect with Frans and sometimes I hear his words of advice or exclamations echoing in my mind, though our conversations are less frequent now (a year and a half after his death). It's also true that I am happy to leave behind some aspects of our relationship: to discontinue my arguments with him, to not allow belligerence in my life, to unhook from the way he dealt with the residue of his previous relationships.

As I wrote this book, I spoke to various widows about their experiences of continuing bonds, and all of them—without exception—said they still "talked to" their partners and felt an abiding connection, whether it was after a year, 7 years, or 40 years since the death. It seems it's often a spontaneous act and reduces a sense of loneliness. That said, in cases where the relationship was fraught with difficulty or abuse, a continued bond might be unwelcome and detrimental. Also, if the relationship in life was co-dependent or marked by insecurity and feelings of worthlessness or feeling lost and empty without the partner, striving for a continued bond is not salubrious (Bonanno, 2009).

The written dialogues I had with Frans in my journal, the poems I wrote where I address him specifically, and my attempts at designing my own resolutions to the loss and our issues (e.g., Lengelle, 2020) bring a sense of connection and relief. It's as if he can still take care of me in ways I believe he would have wanted to had he lived. My poems are often loving odes; they represent ways I can express the love that otherwise has no place to land.

The words that seem to come "from him" now are unconditionally loving. The latter fact can perhaps be explained by a simple superstition. In my family's "folk wisdom" and in the near-death experience YouTube videos that I watched in early summer 2019, 7 months after Frans's death, a common belief seems to repeat: when people die they go to a place where only love is real. They no longer speak to be right or in a way that would be hurtful. I smile as I write this, as it seems childlike to believe it, yet it also feels congruent. In my continued bond with Frans, I imagine that he views the mortals he left behind as beautifully imperfect and worthy of love—much like he would have in life, but his consciousness is now enhanced by greater patience, understanding, and mercy.

A continued bond is not only an echo of the past. It also represents a connection that is alive in the present and if relationships change over time, this means that my perception of our relationship can develop, even post death. For instance, in the continued bond with Frans, I am doing some identity healing: I imagine that Frans can now see that I am more lighthearted, playful, and funny than I believed he knew me to be. I smile and laugh a great deal with those around me now; for instance, I share a sense of humor with Tim and I am not weighed down by the stressors I had with Frans. I imagine that Frans would be able to see inside my heart now and know that I was not determined to create barriers between him and his previous partners, but that I wanted him to be more transparent about them and set respectful boundaries.

I can also borrow this heavenly dialogical I-position when I view him and update my opinion of him: dear Frans, you were generous, and you wanted the best for us all.

***

2. Writing as a Companion: the Observer, the Internal Dialogue, and the Art of Microscopic Listening

In grief

there were slow afternoons
and swampy mid-day mornings of discombobulation
there was waking with a leaden, burning heart
and wondering why nature invented whimpering
I watched myself as griever, as walker, as the woman who
put brie on crackers and re-boiled water in the kettle five times
If there is a "she" to observe in grief,
it must mean not every part of me was her!
Who was the watcher of that griever?
The writer,
the steely-eyed notetaker of life,
the warm poet of hard mornings
the humming scribe of candlelight hours
the shower singer, composer of lines good and sad
The writer never left me alone or exiled in grief
if there was a weeping HER
and a writing SHE
that had to mean, I had company.

May 7, 2020

I frequently tell my students, "Writing is a companion for life." But what do I actually mean when I say this?

Writing brings me a deep, contented aloneness. It allows me to be a comforting witness of my own experience. "I am accompanied" through writing: I accompany myself and am accompanied by others in sharing my words. Writing trains me in articulating more precisely so my communication with others feel more precise, and therefore salient. As I said in the introduction: writing is a companion for life because it does exactly the two things that the best companions do: it holds me close enough to be vulnerable (and thus comforted) and far enough to be honest (and therefore clear-minded).

The academic term Frans and I used to describe having a "companion in the self" is referred to as the "internal dialogue" (while the "external dialogue" refers to conversations with others or inspiration from outside ourselves) (Lengelle & Meijers, 2009). Cultivating an internal dialogue means learning to pay microscopic attention to the thoughts, feelings, and bodily sensations that may point to places in myself that are asking to be heard. The internal dialogue also involves a conversation within. It may, for instance, help me hear signals of hunger or sleepiness, and I can offer myself comforting words. Writing also serves, as Ellis (2018) experienced it, to "put all the 'little incidents' into a bigger picture of recognizable patterns that contradicts to some extent the sense of 'disorientation and disintegration' that threatened me when I lived the story" (p. 320).

We can do microscopic listening with or without writing, of course, but what writing adds is a way of making clearer what we notice, and it helps us not to forget as quickly. Also, the act of writing trains our inner observer, so even when we're not writing—but we have cultivated a writing practice—the observer is at work and paying attention. In that sense, writing is training for knowing one's own mind, in the same way, that meditation is. The ability to observe ourselves with some detachment has the potential to help us separate what is happening from the tragic stories we're telling ourselves about the events as I've mentioned before (e.g., "He died and today I wish he would be here to support me, but this doesn't mean that he abandoned me." Or, "We grieve alone … But wait, is that really true?").

In writing, we may also notice our patterns or things we want to change more readily. For example, we may find ourselves writing, "The photo I have of him in the bedroom brings me peace, but the one in the living room reminds me of a time when he was already sick." Once I have written something like this down, it is less nebulous; the discomfort is articulated, and I am more likely to act (e.g., take down the photo I associate with his suffering during illness).

In more poetic language, writing as companion means we use words to notice and be a loving friend to ourselves; we spend time and pay attention to the murmurs, movements, and machinations of our internal world. It doesn't mean we always believe that internal conversation (it's sometimes not very positive or sane), but we learn to tune into the different parts of us and identify our needs.

Being aware of and cultivating a healthy internal dialogue is necessary if we are to integrate any difficult experience into the fabric of our lives and doing so makes our conversations with others more fruitful too. It does this because we gain a reference point for our learning that is alive with the senses and is open to reflection and revision. We can take usefully from others, but we can also leave any advice or interpretations they provide if they have no resonance for us.

Ideally, we do not only oscillate between loss orientation and restoration orientation as Stroebe and Schut (2010) describe, but we also oscillate between the internal and external dialogue, accessing our inner worlds by noticing and inquiring, and being in dialogue with others (and other sources) to expand the possibilities of our perspectives. We may, for instance, read a book on grief, or cry with a friend over the phone about our loss and benefit from their experiences, but we do so in the measure that we can go within and integrate what they have shared in salient and resonant ways.

Fostering this relationship with self (i.e., the internal dialogue) is frequently under-encouraged in our educational systems; it may even be equated with navel-gazing. Going within to feel for and articulate our healing, challenges the monological paradigm of the knowledgeable expert.

***

3. Writing as a Way of Dealing with Unfinished Business

> *Later, I shall say too, that we were not perfect, that we each drew a mightier word …* (excerpt from my poem "Later," which appears in full at the end of this book).

I joke that our problems died when Frans did and that he shouldn't be allowed to aggravate me from the grave. Of course, I realize that when I repeat the story of his temper and our disagreements, I sometimes aggravate myself and use my memory to do so. While such a large portion of my grief was (and is) healthy, I intuited that a small but salient portion of my pain represented a struggle that threatened to complicate my healing. Doing Holland, Klingspon et al.'s (2020) Unfinished Business in Bereavement Inventory confirmed this for me. Four items on the scale show up as distressing, and one, in particular, was very distressing; in my case, item four on the 28-item list, "I never got closure on some important issue or conflict in our relationship" (Holland, Klingspon et al., 2020, p. 77).

I can appreciate this aspect of my grief now as it humbles me, showing me the potential complexity of healing from loss, along with the complexity of human relationships in general. It has forced me to look for ways to address my own hurt and assumptions about "how life was supposed to be."

In paying attention to this aspect of my bereavement through writing and sharing with others, I am delightfully surprised when I talk about our issues that no reader has hitherto (to my knowledge) batted an eyelash or seemed shocked or appalled by my admissions. It seems the joke is on me; most people experience various forms of marital difficulty or "perpetual problems" (Gottman & Silver, 1995), and aren't hung up on perfection the way I have been.

While I experienced the majority of my engagement with grief as a form of allowing and creating space for the feelings that moved through—in that sense surrendering—there was one aspect of the process that required an act of working through grief. Though the term "griefwork" from Freud's era is now considered outmoded, the contemporary term "meaning construction" (Neimeyer, 2016) may still be considered a form of work. I propose that writing-the-self processes around unfinished business represent one area of grieving where people can benefit from using specific writing tools to get to work.

Unfinished business in grief is generally defined as "unexpressed or unresolved issues between the griever and the deceased" (Holland, Klingspon et al., 2020, p. 65) and it is an important topic because, as Holland, Plant et al. (2020), explain,

> several investigations have found bereavement-related regrets to be a robust predictor of intensified grieving and other mental health outcomes, highlighting the possibility that regret may represent a unique construct in its own right (p. 42).

In the recent development of the Unfinished Business in Bereavement Scale (UBBS), researchers describe two main types of stress-inducing unfinished business: Unfulfilled Wishes and Unresolved Conflict (Holland, Klingspon et al., 2020, p. 73). In my case, I feel that many of my wishes with Frans were fulfilled (e.g., we had taken many trips, created work together, had been welcomed into each other's families, were sexually fulfilled, and loved being at home together. We would likely have done more of the same.) What will be clear from the previous chapters, however, is that the unfinished business that preoccupied me fell into the category of unresolved conflict.

There are three important ways in which writing helped me to come to peace with what felt unresolved between us. First, it allowed me to name the pain. Second, it allowed me to bring more understanding to our issues, with the potential of reframing some of the pain. Third, once naming and reframing had been done and I felt calmer on account of hearing and honoring myself, I could go a step further and see that what Frans had stirred in me was related to my life themes: things that had troubled me since earlier in my life. That does not excuse his behavior, but it does reveal why my reaction to it was often intense and why it was excessively difficult for me to live with or resolve without an emotional charge.

There were four writing approaches that helped me most with processing unfinished business.

1. Naming the problem: telling the truth and being specific enough to feel satisfied the story was told and the pain was named (while respecting the deceased).

It took me several drafts of this book before I could go back and explain what our unfinished business was actually about. At first, I had been a bit vague about it out of a reticence to disclose our issues, but an editor's feedback let me know this would unlikely bring sufficient understanding to satisfy the reader. It turned out that I too was more satisfied naming our issues in concrete terms, first for myself and then for readers. We did not have money issues, we did not disagree on religion or politics, we rarely argued about work; in my perception, our particular struggle was about boundaries in relationships and kind speech.

The challenge of wanting to respect the deceased while expressing ambivalence about our loved ones is challenging, but it is also liberating (Miller & Loring, 2016). It frees us to have a more realistic picture of how life was. Naming is a form of surrendering to the reality that life was imperfect and doing so after a beloved's death is also surrendering to the unchangeability of that. Though in a certain way our relationship continues, as I've explained before, in another way writing down the problem is also saying: our chances at resolving this are over. Fortunately, such an exercise in "naming" the problem does not have to be the end of it. We can go on to ask the question, "If these are the facts as I see them, what might I learn from this?"

2. Inquiring about the problem: The work of Byron Katie

I showed how a belief like "Frans shouldn't have got sick and died at 68" could be worked through with the four-question inquiry process and turnaround that was developed by Byron Katie (2002). I found by going through each step methodically—"Is it true?", "Can I absolutely know that it's true?", "How do I react when I believe the thought?", and "Who would I be without the thought?"—that the insistence on my stressful thought loosened and let go of me. The final step of this exercise, where one turns the stressful statement around to try on different "truths" led me to explore thoughts like, "He should have died at 68, because he simply did," and "If he had been but a day or year older, he would have suffered more, so 68 was the oldest he should have been."

This exercise is one I also applied to Frans and my unfinished business. I did this privately in journals and two of the most stressful thoughts I encountered there were, "Frans shouldn't have raised his voice at me" and "Frans should have set healthier boundaries with his exes."

Inquiring about the validity of these written statements allowed me to be less convinced by my own perspectives. I could see that he'd told me he had a short fuse and a temper and so I could readily have expected he wouldn't always be able to refrain from raising his voice. This allowed me to view it in a way that felt less personal. I also noted places where I had raised my voice to him. I acknowledged too that he did set some healthy boundaries with his exes and that it was a learning process for him to do this. He admitted that he had set poor boundaries around the time of his divorce and that this had affected the trust between us; something which was never wholly repaired.

Byron Katie's (2002) "The Work" was a powerful and useful exercise that helped me see the relativity of my insistence on particular perspectives.

3. Talking about the problem: Dialogues of healing

In an earlier section entitled "Deep dialogues of healing," I share the work I did, inspired by Neimeyer and Konopka (2019), where I revisited my unfinished business with Frans in written form but with the assistance of additional "characters" or "I-positions." This latter part was vital in feeling like I was being heard and that there would be no repeat of feeling bullied. It can be likened to a couple going to therapy, where the counsellor doesn't choose sides and serves as a kind of referee. What I saw reflected in the dialogue writing about our unfinished business was that the voice of Frans expressed tremendous kindness (like Frans in life) and that this was the part of him I saw and experienced most of the time. If marriage researcher John Gottman is correct that we should have a 5:1 ratio of good to difficult interactions with our spouse (Gottman & Silver, 1995), this dialogue showed this good ratio, despite my having set out to consciously deal with our "shit." The fact that the dialogue was on paper meant I could revisit it and meet Frans's kindness there repeatedly.

4. Letting the problem be: writing poetry and thus accepting life as it is

In reflecting on all the different writing approaches in dealing with unfinished business, I think it is fair to say that an academic wants to understand, a storyteller wants to tell the tale and bring it to some kind of conclusion, and a poet needs none of these certainties.

Poetry is often good at naming a problem without needing to resolve it. The writer gets the satisfaction of "getting a hearing" and also surrendering "to the unsolvability of nearly everything" (as I write in the poem "Cloudscapes"). A poem can offer liberating or unusual perspectives, but it can just as easily remain content with the is-ness of things.

A poem often reflects a moment in time; a fragment of experience, bringing forth its pain and its beauty.

The poem

is the rose
a friend gives us

when our heart is stricken by death
it does not explain why our beloved is gone
it does not need an ultimate understanding
it is satisfied in bleeding the receiver with its thorn
it is satisfied with its scent and grace that even then is already drooping
it is the gesture of love that a poem gives us
we know that the rose is already gone
and we don't argue with that
and that is a poem's wisdom too.

***

4. To Make Meaning and Beyond a Need for Meaning

In most contemporary grief resources, bereavement scholars speak about the need for meaning-making in the face of a loss (Bonanno, 2009; Neimeyer, 2016; Strobe & Schut, 2001; Thompson & Neimeyer, 2014). Also referred to as meaning reconstruction, the idea is that loss represents a situation where the stories we use to make sense of our world are no longer sufficient to explain the reality and this creates distress and a yearning to regain meaning.

In helping my students make-meaning, I too emphasize the need for a more life-giving story (for the model and a full explanation of the theory, see Lengelle & Meijers, 2009), which often involves a shift in perspective (McClocklin & Lengelle, 2016) and sometimes even benefit finding (Hall, 2014). However, in the model of writing and healing that Frans and I developed (Lengelle & Meijers, 2009), a "new narrative" may be characterized by acceptance without answers or without a sense that meaning can be made in any definitive way. This "acceptance" can represent meaning or may represent a lack of perceived meaning (e.g., Frans's death was inherently meaningless; I am thwarted in my explanation for this happening, and I acknowledge it as a fact.)

Something I've discovered through my many years of working with writing the self in my courses and in writing about Frans's dying is that there is a place "beyond story" that gives me great peace. I allude to this in the poem about the rose, above. This idea may be interpreted differently or not sanctioned by other narrative theorists and grief scholars, but I feel strongly that a "lack of meaning," when accepted as such, can also be a useful attitude toward loss.

There is a place beyond meaning

First, of course, I wrestled to understand
(why you got sick, why we hadn't known, why it had to be)
but no answer rang true
second, of course, I wrestled with identity

was I loving?
had I taken good enough care of you?
Third, I read the literature
because that's what proper academics do
they advise us to "make meaning" and I tell my students this too
but like a friend once said when her young husband drowned,
is there meaning in death and loss?
I was quick to offer her an answer, but she shook her head soberly, more accepting than I,
"there was a river; it had a hole in it; and he went into the hole with his kayak"
You got cancer, your body could not recover, you died in November,
I grieve and I live on
That hand full of facts satisfies me now
I am beyond needing to know or understand
The is-ness of your death and our imperfect life descends on me in memory
Now when someone says, "I'm sorry … he was too young …"
I say, "yes, there are many ways to tell that story …"
and beyond story there is
the way of it.
The
Way
of
It.

After writing this poem and reading it aloud, I thought, "Maybe this reflection represents the emergence of what we hope to achieve in cognitive behavioral therapy: there is no longer an emotional charge on the facts. Frans got cancer, he died, we loved each other, and I am still alive." Bereavement researcher Hall (2014) speaks of a reduced need for meaning-making as a sign of healthy grieving, and perhaps that is where I now find myself. I sometimes even find myself writing about grieving in the past tense (see recent poem "In grief," earlier in this chapter).

There is no inherent meaning in anything. I did not find some answers I had longed to find; yet the wrestling and discovering, at times the futility of meaning-making, had meaning. And, of course, part of what offers a sense of meaning is in writing a book. Frans's death is the impetus for research and writing and the commitment to this book project has kept me connected with him, myself, and a community of (potential) readers.

In talking about this, one evening while Tim was cooking, I asked him what he would say he could see someone learning from my book. He replied, "What had meaning for me around the death of my father is visiting with him in the meditation landscape I go to before sleep. There is no dialogue, no verbal exchange, but I feel him there, his presence, and that has meaning for me. Before reading your book, I don't think I could have articulated that."

This is perhaps the paradox, put in my own words: we make meaning because we are compelled to, and if successful, we either create a new story that works for us or we conclude that our questions around death and the deceased will remain unanswered. Usually, it's a bit of both. And there is a place in us that can be deeply okay with the unanswered. We may even find humor in our striving for some ultimate understanding.

Where religious people may find peace in the idea of "God's will," the more secular folks among us say, "That's the way of it." It takes a while before we embody that though.

***

5. *Dealing with Taboos and Identity Maintenance*

"It is important to free ourselves of our assumptions about what 'a good widow' is and understand our tendency to engage in 'identity maintenance' (i.e., keeping up appearances to solidify preferred identities) when there are truer things we think, express, and live out." (Lengelle, personal communication [Facebook post], April 2020)

It has been useful to me to explore a handful of taboo subjects around grief and ask questions about my life, my thoughts, and my self-image. Writing has been a way for me to admit things to myself first. By putting it on the page, I acknowledge inconvenient or uncomfortable truths and they stare back at me asking for attention. I liken this type of writing to exposure therapy, which is a way to process and habituate more stressful emotions as is done in treating complicated grief (Foa et al., 2007, as cited in Neimeyer, 2016, p. 27).

In layperson's terms, I scare myself on purpose, in small steps, so I get used to something that doesn't correspond with the notions I carry around about "what a good person should be." Writing differs from merely thinking or telling a friend these things; writing means I've committed it to the page and the word committed is no accident. I may be able to edit later, but what I admit about myself is now in black and white.

The discovery I made is that the difficulty in talking about these aspects of my grief is that I have to give up—at least in part—my desire to engage in "identity maintenance," which I define as "our tendency to uphold a desired image of ourselves and/or try to influence the perceptions others have about who we are." In theories of the related psychological construct "self-verification," researchers write that,

> People's self-views represent the lens through which they perceive reality, lending meaning to all experience … . [O]nce developed, self-views provide people with a strong sense of coherence. To maintain this sense of

coherence, people work to stabilize and maintain their self-views.

(Swann & Burhmester, 2003, p. 406)

The issue, however, is that too fixed an idea of who we are or should be can complicate our ability to grieve. In order to come to peace with taboo subjects in grief, we need the courage and willingness to give up acceptable notions of self when they conflict with what actually feels true for us. Although we risk being judged and misunderstood, the alternative is that we remain trapped in guilt, shame, or a reticence to express a wider range of our aliveness.

Three Taboos

It was difficult to be honest about longing for physical touch months after Frans's death, first to own my sexual desire, then to ask someone to meet my need for affection and sexual touch, and then to write about it for publication. It was also difficult to talk about having a new partner; I went out on a first date before the 1-year anniversary of Frans's death, and no doubt some would find that early and fast. The other topic that feels taboo is that I am glad that Frans's death meant that some of our problems died with him.

1. Sexual Desire

Several months after Frans's death, I wanted to be held by a man and once I was in a man's arms, I wanted more. I have the good fortune and habit of choosing kind men, so my sexual experiences in life have been good and pleasurable. But engaging sexually within the first year of Frans's death was something I kept quiet about. I minimized it, especially to myself. I talked with several close friends about it but didn't write about it much at all. The reason was clear: I didn't want to be considered fickle, disloyal, or superficial. I didn't want others to question my love for Frans. It wasn't something I posted about on Facebook when I told the otherwise raw and honest story of my loss and longing and how I was taking care of myself. Yet, acknowledging this human need was as important as the other ways in which I was being good to myself. I can only imagine it must be important to others who have lost a spouse too.

I have written about my ongoing sexual desire for Frans after his death. He was still the lover I fantasized about; thoughts of him could still easily arouse me. Even a year after his death, at the beginning of my new relationship, Frans would flash into my mind during lovemaking. Speaking about him still being my lover was only hard to write about because it seemed tragic and maybe even a bit weird; would someone perceive me as being in denial about his death? The upside was that this fact seemed to prove that I was loyal and loving, an aspect of my identity that I experienced as positive and hoped to cherish.

I also wrote about missing male connection, asking to be held by a man, and corresponding with several male colleagues. Once I wrote about it, I started to feel more relaxed, though it took me about five attempts at editing before I could say "pleasured each other to orgasm" instead of leaving the reader with the impression that I had shared an extended, sentimental hug.

Some ease with the topic grew over time, but it was not until I read the book *Sex after Grief* by Joan Price (2019), and heard about other widows' experiences and their frequent reticence to talk about sex and new love, that my guilt dissipated. This tells me that writing about taboo subjects and exposing myself to my own fears was not enough; only when I learned of others' experiences and how they had liberated themselves did I start to feel like I was "normal."

I can laugh about it now, but I had, until recently, resolved to leave the reader with the impression that, by the end of my story, I had received a home-cooked meal and a bouquet of flowers from a lovely man, and nothing more. But what kept me from chickening out was a nagging belief that, in failing to figure out what was holding me back from speaking about sexual desire, I would leave something important unaddressed and shortchange my reader, too, and in particular other grieving women.

The source of my troubles was of course not literally my social world, but the social world I imagined I was part of and the image I wanted to portray of myself. I realized that I was (and am) carrying around several ideas about what it means to be "a good widow" or "a good woman"; these seem to be my unwritten rules of acceptability.

The first idea is that a grieving widow who truly loved her spouse wouldn't want to share sexual touch and orgasm with someone else within a year of her partner's death. The marker of a year seems significant, like something in the fine print of an important contract.

The second notion was that when you're genuinely sad you can't be horny. I laugh at this now; the body will have none of these moral thoughts. The truth of grief is that we are not sad 24 hours a day, so when we are bereft, we might not be aroused, but sometime between the waves of grief, we feel a host of other things: hungry, amused, contented, hopeful, and aroused.

Third, sexual activity with someone would be reneging on my "grief work" and end up burying my real feelings if focused on someone other than Frans; this turned out to be entirely false, as I ended up grieving more fully in the arms of both men who have held me since Frans's death.

Fourth, I would not really be able to care for someone new. This was also untrue; the man in Calgary is a sweet and loving friend, and Tim has become my new and cherished partner. This in no way undermines my ongoing love and esteem for Frans.

Fifth, a respectable academic doesn't speak of such things. Here again, the issue of "identity maintenance" applies. After all, aren't academics people who research by reading books and sending out surveys and then process the anonymized data of their research subjects? If they study sex, they certainly don't speak about their own experiences! That is, unless they are one of those weird autoethnographers!

It is notable that the words I used to qualify my potential desired or failed identity in the paragraphs above are "truly, genuinely, real, really, and respectable." I would not have been able to fish those words out of the mix without having written them down first. What these words tell me is that my fear around my widowed identity as a grieving spouse is that I will lose respect by being considered a fraud in some way.

Humorously, Frans would not have been surprised by my desire for sex and physical connection; he would likely have smiled and teased me about it.

I might as well write to tell him about this again:

R: You would have known this about me.
F: Of course, my love, this was one of the best parts of our dance.
R: Yes, it was (with a smile).
F: I guess I'm right about you being too moralistic for your own good. Enjoy, my love. And let the love grow; love takes time to grow. Sex is instant, but to become full partners takes time.

Writing in this context did indeed involve a kind of self-administered exposure therapy, but it also required an "external dialogue" (Lengelle & Meijers, 2009); that is, a conversation with others and their resources. Our identities are formed through social interactions and our willingness to give up our narrow, fearful attempts at "identity maintenance" correspondingly happen within a social context.

2. Repartnering

> *Falling in love again is one of the most complicated parts of widowhood, raising vexing psychological, existential, familial, and legal questions .... Love regained following spousal loss is a greater taboo than the subject of how the dead are betrayed by the living. Indeed, often it is the same taboo!*
>
> *(Berman, 2015, pp. 53–55)*

As Berman (2015) explains, Joyce Carol Oates published her long, heart-wrenching memoir 3 years after her husband's death, leaving out the fact that she remarried 13 months after he died. The omission was severely critiqued in a review of her work, but at the same time her lack of disclosure was so understandable. Oates's omission might be explained by the fact she separated her personal self from her author self to the extreme (see Berman for a full analysis). The other reason why Oates may have done this—a reason I think many widows would be able to relate to—is that in sharing the story of one's grief, the author doesn't want to give the impression that the loss was not significant or that the spouse was simply replaced. In a culture where monogamy is the norm and the "singular-love fantasy" is held so dearly (DiGiulio, as cited in Berman, 2015, p. 103), "love regained … is a fascinating and instructive story, one that is much more challenging to write than the story of love lost" (Berman, 2015, p. 55).

Just as with sexual desire after spousal loss, there are a number of reasons why I hesitated to talk about this vital topic. First, I feared that others would indeed think I had "replaced" Frans easily or that my love for him did not hold the meaning that it did. Socially, I believed this meant that I would no longer be viewed as his partner and that I would lose more people from our family and work circle than I already had. This, of course, may have happened regardless of my being partnered or not, and I remind myself that I have no control over the way that others perceive my love or loyalty. Second, that being in love with someone else meant I would skip over some parts of my grief. That has not been the case; in fact, the opposite has been the truth. Not only have I been able to grieve more expressively in the arms of my new partner, but when we met, I immediately spoke about Frans. Because Tim embraced that part of my life and asked me more about it, I felt immediately close to him. There was no part of me I had to hide, minimize, or cut off. That didn't mean opening up was without adjustment, however. I noted the emotional and physiological impact of developing these new feelings while the grief was also omnipresent in my body.

After my first "date" with Tim, where I knew "something important had happened," I remember going home and sleeping poorly for several nights as my nervous system processed this new fire on very watery, grieving circuits. I said to Tim, "Fire and water are creating some sizzling in my body and I have to take it slow." It was fortunate that I was in Europe for a month just after that first meet-up so I could communicate with him at a distance by e-mail and video call as my body adjusted to the new feelings. Because I was able to "keep my connection with Frans and my grief" in Tim's presence, it was as if my body allowed him to connect to the neural networks of love that I had established so deeply with Frans over the span of a decade. Some of those wires had been frayed as a result of his death and our unfinished business, and it felt as if some of them were being repaired and reconnected.

A new partner does not mean diluting one's love for the dead spouse; we love both simultaneously and writing about new love is important as it is relevant to a widow's life and speaks of new hope. As Frans would say, "life goes on, my love," and as Berman (2015) suggests, a good marriage ending in death is grounds for another fulfilling relationship. Widow and writer Sandra M. Gilbert describes her new partner's perspective: "He understands quite well, I think, that one can love and grieve for the dead person who shaped the past even while loving and living with a new person who's central in the present" (as cited in Berman, 2015, p. 100).

Here again, reading widow narratives helped me to feel more comfortable about having a new partner. The writing that served to help me understand that my beginning love for Tim was not a betrayal of my love for Frans happened mostly in my poetry: in particular, two poems I wrote in the spring of 2020, one for each of them. The Valentine's poem for Frans was about our continuing bond (see "Let's keep meeting this way," which appears earlier in this narrative), and the poem for Tim (see below) showed how both the love and the pain in remembering Frans could be shared and brought Tim and me closer.

How we fell asleep

after bedtime
the energy of our wild kisses lingering
when the streets had become quiet
like our embrace
I told you how my other lover had died
how he had held me until
he couldn't and for a while
his warm body was still familiar in my arms
until, of course, death stiffened it
and they laid a cooling element under
what we still called him, but wasn't.
You said, that must have been so hard
and I felt the pulsing warmth of your
head against my sorrow-filled heart
my face cracking the way it does
to break me in the good ways love does
and we drifted to sleep tender and emptied
of our cares
a tear printed and still wet between my cheek
and your jaw.

In studying the rates of repartnering for widowed women, I made several interesting discoveries. The first is that it's rare (Wu et al., 2015). The second is that women tend to repartner less frequently than men, and for a number of clear reasons: they don't always relish household or caregiving tasks and they are more resilient on their own than men, though they sometimes struggle more than men financially (Statistics Canada, 2009). Women speak about "being selfish" and wanting their "freedom" after a loss of a spouse, while widowers rarely mention either (Davidson, 2001). Another important reason for not repartnering among (heterosexual) widows is that there are fewer potential partners (i.e., men die younger on average, are widowed much less frequently than women, and women don't tend to choose younger partners).

The literature on the topic of repartnering after widowhood is quite sparse, but what I did find shows a stark picture for women who desire to repartner: if it doesn't happen within the first 10 years of widowhood, it's unlikely to happen at all, which seems all the more reason to celebrate it when a woman wants to repartner and finds a suitable mate. Here are the results of a Canadian study by Wu et al. (2015) describing the rates of repartnering for those who lose a partner over age 45:

> Three years after widowhood, under 3% of widows have formed a new union, compared with 17% of widowers. Five years after widowhood, about 4% of widows and 21% of widowers are remarried or cohabiting. Ten years after spousal loss, about 7% of widows and 29% of widowers have formed a new union. There is little change in the cumulative proportion of repartnering after this, which suggests that most repartnering occurs within 10 years of widowhood. Most widows and widowers who have not repartnered during this timeframe are single 15 and 20 years after widowhood as well. (p. 501)

There are about 13.6 million widows in the USA, and each year 700,000 more become widows there (Kenan, 2018). There are 1.9 million widowed people in Canada, the gross majority of whom are women, as we outnumber men four to one when it comes to losing a spouse (LaRochelle-Côté et al., 2012). Most women will remain alone after losing a spouse.

In the grief literature, Kenneth J. Doka (1999) speaks about "disenfranchised grief," which refers to grieving a loss that others don't recognize but is undeniably felt by the griever (e.g., a woman grieving her married lover; a remarried man grieving his first wife's death). It no doubt applied to Frans's first wife: not everyone might think to recognize her loss upon his death in the context of their divorce.

In the case of repartnering, the risk of disenfranchisement is twofold for a widow (or widower). First, a death that was socially recognized might become less so when a woman repartners (e.g., she's okay now, she's over her husband's death; she has a new guy), and on the other hand, she may feel compelled to keep quiet about her choice to repartner so that her joy doesn't become disenfranchised in addition to her grief.

3. Ambivalence in Grief

> *Though you loved Ray, very much, and could not imagine living without him, you will begin to discover that you are doing things that Ray would not have been interested in doing, and you are meeting people you would not have met when Ray was alive, and all this will change your life for the better, though you might not think so now. – Eleanor Bergstein writing to her friend Joyce Carol Oates*
>
> *(as cited in Berman, 2015, p. 54)*

In the grief literature I've studied in the last year and a half since Frans's death, little is said about the disappearance of certain stressors upon a partner's death and the accompanying relief that provides, and/or the way one's life may change for the better in noticeable ways. It seems that, only when a relationship is considered abusive or a spouse has been severely ill, requiring protracted and/or demanding caregiving, is there mention of alleviation of negative feelings after a spouse's passing. That said, in her 1988 book on grief, Therese Rando sets this provocative and daring challenge to the griever:

> Identify the gain that has come from your loss. In every loss there is a gain. This is not to dismiss the intensity of your grief, not to minimize the tragedy. However, whenever a loss takes place, there is a gain that comes about. (pp. 250)

I've talked earlier about things I can do more easily now that Frans is gone (e.g., listen to loud 80s music in the car; change my diet; decide my own timing regarding trips and projects), but these things are not cause for relief. I've also spoken about our unfinished business and expressed gratitude that we don't have to have our familiar disagreements anymore. I miss Frans and sorrow still fills my heart regularly; I am also sad that we were not able to come to a full, compassionate understanding of the pain we each had that triggered the other's resistance. About all of this I am ambivalent. About telling others, I feel trepidation. While the term "unfinished business" refers to my perceived (external) struggle between Frans and me, ambivalence is the mix of feelings and tensions that I experience internally.

In reading over twenty books on grief, and many articles, I note that ambivalence around the death of a loved one is mentioned sparingly in the literature. That said, it is recognized by grief scholars as a normal part of bereavement (e.g., Neimeyer, 2016) and can stem from relational patterns in life, from traumatic death, and/or from unfinished business. The bereaved, however, frequently feel inhibited about speaking about this aspect of their mourning: "Resolution or integration of ambivalence is difficult and sometimes frightening work. It means acknowledging positive and negative aspects of a lost lifestyle, the relationship with the deceased, or the mourner's sense of him- or herself" (Miller & Loring, 2016, p. 165). Those grieving often feel guilty and ashamed about their struggles with the deceased, as I have. Sharing less than perfect attributes about the loved one feels like disloyalty, and who wants to be disloyal, especially about someone to whom we were (and are) so deeply attached and committed?

The clearest passage I found on ambivalence in grief was a four-page chapter in Neimeyer's (2016) edited volume, *Techniques in Grief Therapy,* by Miller and Loring. The authors, who provide grief support through a San Antonio mortuary, explain that we are indeed hesitant to speak "ill of the dead," but that not doing so can leave us feeling stuck. What they write and the way they run their grief workshops offers the griever permission to visit the shadow side safely:

> The bereaved discover that negative aspects of the relationship can be as productive as the positive, because these aspects have contributed to the tapestry of who they have become … . Ironically, ambivalence can be a powerful healer and enable the bereaved to grow into a new life.
>
> *(Miller & Loring, 2016, p. 166)*

In my life with Frans, I learned that kind speech and being able to communicate transparently about relational boundaries are key for my well-being. Our conflicts taught me what is of paramount importance to me in the kinds of relationships that I want now and in the future. Writing helped me name the problem and clarify my values; below I will touch on what kind of writing helped me to gain this insight and why I believe it did so.

Miller and Loring (2016) describe a grief workshop they held for older women where they took the participants through a meditation prompting them to remember what was less than ideal about their departed spouses:

> … and remember some less desirable aspects of your loved one … those characteristics or mistakes that were difficult to live with, or somehow impeded his or her or your ability to live life fully. This may be painful, but these things are just as much a part of who he or she was and they can also become, in a mysterious way, precious. And again, allow an image, color, or texture to emerge. This is a symbol of the darker side of your loved one …. Imagine the comfort and compassion you might need to bear this, for just a few moments. (p. 166)

It took a first brave participant in this non-judgmental gathering to come forward and say, "I sure don't miss the cussin'" to get the other participants to come forward with what they didn't miss about their spouses (p. 167). The process was often accompanied by humor. The facilitators were careful to "keep responses nonjudgmental and supportive of whatever awareness each member has" (p. 167), and conceded that some people remained quiet regardless of the invitation. However, even those who chose not to discuss the less admirable qualities of their deceased spouses could benefit from knowing they were "allowed" to (e.g., in the case of a spouse's suicide).

Speaking about my discontent with others and striving to accept what I considered a painful flaw in my trust with Frans was not enough to bring me peace of mind. Writing played a crucial role in living with and accepting ambivalence.

In the therapeutic dialogue I wrote with Goop, Grudge, and other players, writing helped to formulate two lasting insights. The first was that I have a strong need for fair communication and that I identified the lack of this fairness and my anger about it. Noticing and admitting to my anger later helped me to set healthier boundaries with others. The other insight was that Frans and I had indeed had a very rich, nourishing, and fruitful life together. We had, at times, even "made shit into fertilizer," as he liked to say.

The writing I am doing now in this more reflective portion of the book is helping me to do what autoethnography does best: combine the knowledge of others, research, and my own experience to weave a new narrative of understanding. Readings on the topic (i.e., the external dialogue) of ambivalence give me permission to say it applies to me too.

Writing serves as a confessional of sorts: as I divulge things that my internal (and cultural) censor says I should keep to myself, I experience relief and a sense of completion. Writing serves me well too as a deflator of my desire for "identity maintenance," a tendency I want to keep in check as I know it can compromise the aliveness of my story and myself.

In more humorous terms, writing what is taboo but true for me trips up my ego. I can free myself of illusions, and, I hope what I write may free my reader too.

Later

I shall say too
that we were not perfect
that we each drew a mightier word
me insisting on precise,
sometimes, in that situation, it seems
you on big,
completely, always, never.
Later I shall say too
that we had our misunderstandings
that you struggled with feelings
covering doubt with harsh voice and bravado
and that I pressed too perfectly for clarity
I will say with some humility
that our dignity
was shaken
though our devotion bound us
and lights the way even now
Despite our fervent intentions,
our thousand tries at it
the profound blossoming of joy and inspiration,
we never escaped the inevitable trespasses
of being human

December 2018

EPILOGUE

Grief, my teacher

A year has come and gone
and I still carry you in all I do and write
grief is not a harsh teacher as at first I feared
I have followed her ways and she has opened my life
The best teachers don't tell you
You can do this ... But, *you are doing this*
Not, you have to be strong
But, *your strength is in your being with it all*
Not, this was meant to be a lesson,
But, *how will you let this shape you?*
Not, there is a right answer
But, *keep telling yourself what is true*
Not, this is a big test
But, *this is your unique integration,*

Everything that happens
is flowering you into being.

I have, as autoethnographer Ellis (2018) did, constructed a story after my partner's death, "attempting to bring together social, narrative, and personal understanding and, in the process, construct a self with whom I can live" (p. 319).

One evening, when I am almost finished the book and Tim is preparing dinner for us, I tell him what I've accomplished on this writing day and how themes around loss continue to appear in my life. They appear in my correspondence with Bob, when I speak weekly with Dorothy, and recently in hearing about my new colleague Aathira's partner loss—which, at such a young age, seems doubly heartbreaking.

Some might say I am looking for everything to do with grief because of my own process, but it seems that grief is finding me too. My own sorrow continues to arrive unbidden as if to remind me that grief can be integrated into one's life in myriad different ways, but never gotten over.

Earlier in the day, Tim sits with me in the sunroom and brings me fresh coffee. He asks me how I am doing and suddenly tears flow.

Reinekke: In finishing this book, I realize I'm saying good-bye to him again, in a way. This book is like an extension of the dialogue we shared; a space we could be together. I'll be moving on to other projects, and when I do that, where will Frans be?

I cry.

Tim: But, is it true that you will be letting Frans go in finishing the book?

He smiles warmly and adds, "Frans has been too big a part of your life for that to be true. If he has been with you the whole way through writing the book, where you have been able to speak with him and have him stay part of your life, don't you think that will continue?"

Tim kisses me tenderly on top of my head before he leaves the sunroom. I close my eyes to take that in and feel the blessings in our sharing.

Then I think about the book coming out, sharing it with others in lectures or talks, and writing an article on the use of poetry in bereavement with Bob. The conversation is ongoing. Okay, Frans will not be gone, I tell myself.

In another moment, I am wistful.

A week later, I come across this quote by Jeffrey Berman (2007), who wrote a book about the loss of his first wife, Barbara, who also died of cancer:

> One of the paradoxes of writing a book about a spouse's recent death is that the writer must not only bring the deceased back to life, in the process re-experiencing the trauma associated with dying and death, but the writer must then rebury the dead at the end of the book, thus repeating the loss. (p. 7)

When Carolyn Ellis reviews my manuscript in June 2020, she writes in the margin next to my own admission of this sentiment, "I felt that too."

***

Frans, are you still there? I want to tell you how my life is unfolding without you. Sometimes I even think you have something to do with it. Dorothy tells me she also wonders if Steve is secretly orchestrating good things in her life. My Mom has told me she imagines my stepfather, Rudy, looking down from on high and blessing her.

I imagine you saying,

> Have her keep writing; make sure she's well-rested and doesn't have to worry about me anymore. And send her a man who will cook for her, she doesn't do it after a long day of writing and research. Also make sure she's attracted to him, so she doesn't have to remember me as *the* great lover of her life. Make sure he is kind and understands where I scratched her and missed the mark. Make him someone she can laugh with; I remember she said I didn't get her sense of humor and that made it nearly impossible to lighten the situation when it got tense between us. Also, another little wish of mine thrown in, be sure it's an academic publisher that takes the book, this will be much better for Reinekke! Her mind is too sharp now and too interested in learning and developing her field for her to write a mainstream self-help book on grief. That can always come later!

REINEKKE: Is this just wishful thinking, Frans?

FRANS: I always supported you, even now. Remember I promised that, liefje!

REINEKKE: Will I see you again?

FRANS: You still see me now. In that sense, I can never be lost.

APPENDIX

Identity in Grief, Dialogical Self Theory, and Composing a Life

"People in grief become more like themselves," is a quote by bereaved author Roger Rosenblatt, who lost his daughter to heart failure. His words appear in the inside cover as a singular quote, introducing Berman's (2015) book on widows writing grief. The idea sounds intriguing, and even intuitively correct; after all, would those grieving have the energy for anything else? Is this not a chance in life to drop all pretense? This idea about "the self," however, assumes a kind of individual knowable and consistent self that is somehow laid bare by bereavement.

Berman (2015) later uses the quote in a passage about widow writer Joyce Carol Oates and how her works of fiction prepared her for her husband's death, and that she grieved true to her character, "quietly grief-stricken but spiritually comforted" (p. 127). As I reflect more on this interesting phrase, which I find myself wanting to believe, I become increasingly doubtful about its veracity. I too grieve as I live (e.g., writing poetry, studying grief), but that does not mean I am more like myself.

Who is this self? Was I less myself before Frans's death? How might I conceptualize identity in a way that helps explain what is happening to the "me" in the wake of my spouse's death? In my experience, various aspects of my-self are engaged in grief and I see this variety of voices and perspectives as part of my resilience (e.g., the poet, the practical woman, the academic, the emotive griever). I am not a singular I. In fact, I am much more like the river Greek philosopher Heraclitus describes. I am at once that same river (feeling a familiar "sense of self") and never that same river, continually in flow and experiencing new and different things as I listen to the myriad thoughts and positions within the self.

We might say the words, "I am more like myself," but there is no singular self we can actually point to. After a loved one has died, our identity may change in a number of ways; for instance, we may feel acutely the loss of a role we had (e.g., spouse) and say that we "are no longer who we thought we were." The death of a spouse may also mean that parts of us also die off (e.g., the part of me that talked about career guidance theory daily; the woman who made love in Dutch). We may also experience a return to an old self we identify with that was less present in the relationship (e.g., in my case, the girl who likes 80s music).

Could it be just as true to say, "People in grief are less like themselves"? Or even, "People in grief are more extreme versions of themselves"? Or, "People in grief are a new combination of themselves"? There is evidence to argue for any of these statements and it is no coincidence that I write "themselves" as it seems there are many parts of us engaged in life's conversation, not just one "me."

When I turn Rosenblatt's idea around and play with it some more, I see it's just as fair to say, "I have become more like Frans." How does this apply? While before he supported me as a living spouse, he is now internalized, as a kind of I-as-Frans still speaking to me. It's as if I'm free to access and even take on some of his positive traits and strengths when I need them. For instance, I tend to worry less than I used to. He taught me by example the futility of worrying. Frans also asked himself every day, "What can I learn from this?" and I find this question is second nature to me now, while before it sounded preachy and overly rational and I resisted adopting his language.

Similarly, my colleague and friend Roberta, also widowed, writes,

> I also appreciated the part where you spoke of internalizing Frans, incorporating him into your very being—a counsellor shared that idea with me soon after Gerry died when I wasn't sure I could take on all of his various roles in our home and family. She told me that I'd served a long apprenticeship and could now use what I'd learned.
>
> *(R. Neault, personal communication, May 2020)*

Again, it seems we are not a singular, stable self, but a multi-voiced and somewhat integrated collection of selves, where we can even borrow from the selves of others. Some of our I-positions may become more dominant in grief and some may recede into the background. In the end, the new combination of selves we live out in response to loss may feel comfortingly familiar and wildly different at the same time.

To conceptualize identity changes in grief, I propose using the Dialogical Self Theory (DST; for a full overview, see Hermans & Gieser, 2012). This theory, developed by psychologist and scholar Hubert Hermans and others, conceptualizes the self as a dynamic collection of "I-positions" or voices that position and reposition themselves in the landscape of the mind (Hermans & Hermans-Konopka, 2010). This multi-voiced self is in conversation with itself and others, and others can be experienced as extensions of the self (e.g., my mother's wise advice to me). It suggests

> that the self might be better conceived not as a single entity with a true core but as a multifaceted structure, constituted by a diversity of positions that could be endowed with a voice and encouraged to narrate their own stories.
>
> *(Konopka et al., 2019, p. 2)*

DST can, for instance, help explain why in this book there are narratives, scholarly reflections, dialogues, and poetry written by the same person, each I-position emphasizing something different. The I-as-poet position stays close to feelings and creates salient vignettes of experience. The I-as-academic sheds light on how my grief is quite predictable and normal and allows me to compare myself with what is known about grief. The storyteller wants to remember and honor Frans and invites the reader to become a witness. The creator of dialogues builds a conversational bridge to the I-as-Frans position and allows the experience of a continuing bond.

In exploring questions of what is happening to my identity in widowhood and going back to Rosenblatt's idea, I again asked myself, how have I become more like myself? Or rather, which part of me has become more dominant or resonant since Frans's death? As I mentioned before, I have not raised my voice to anyone since Frans died, and I could say, "This sure feels more like me," as I don't like to raise my voice to anyone. That said, when I felt trespassed upon by Frans, the I-with-raised-voice was also "authentically me," as this voice represented a need for fairness and justice. Are there other "me"s (i.e., I-positions) that I would identify as "more like myself" or that I would like to bring forward more? As I have said before, I have returned to my own generation's music and now plan my own projects. However, I still listen to Frans's choir music with pleasure and do research in the way that Frans and I did. I have been permanently shaped by having had a spouse who was a social scientist, a researcher, a teacher, a writer, a singer, and a sociologist hippy.

I am not "more like myself in grief," but more interested in what selves are emerging and what selves I would like to enact more and which I-positions I don't need as much or prefer not to embody.

There are a number of I-positions that seem to be most necessary as I grieve and compose a new life; I seem naturally drawn to them. They provide both comfort and perspective.

In my journal, I draw a bird's-eye view of a table to see who is sitting around it. Which selves or I-positions are part of my healing? It is not a boardroom table, but rather a kind of high tea put on by the women's auxiliary. It seems these characters have been responsible for getting me through at least the first year of losing Frans.

At the foot of the table is the observer, which is what in DST is called the "meta-position" (it is able to observe all the other positions and make new combinations). At the head of the table is the wise woman, and close beside her is

"I-as-mourning." The wise woman is a combination of awareness, empowerment, and practicality—her influence is a kind of promoter position. In fact, she chairs the committee of my wellness and self-change. According to Konopka et al. (2019), promoter positions are

> Those positions that operate as innovators, imply a considerable openness towards the future, and have the capacity of organizing and producing a diverse range of more specialized positions. They give a sense of direction to the self and in this way provide a compass function. (pp. 12–13)

One of my wise woman's strengths is the ability to accept "shadow positions" that also sit at the table from time to time (I-as-angry; I-as-ashamed).

A bit further down the table is "I-as-poet" (and sometimes perched on a wide window ledge nearby), writing prolifically and paying careful attention. I-as-poet is like the documentary photographer of important moments. In the middle of the long rectangular table is the "academic/researcher of grief," alongside her twin sister "librarian," staring often into databases and looking absent, but keeping track of which grief resources I might need next. And then there is "health advisor," who says things like, "Today, she must walk again," and, "Please note that a person gets better rest in the hours before midnight"! I-as-correspondent is also taking notes and deciding with external dialogues (e.g., with grief scholar Bob, or DST theorist Hermans, or widow friend Dorothy) what will be required to learn more and to give I-as-writer a bit of help with the process of writing a book. There is also a kind of "housekeeper" who cleans around the table and serves fresh nourishment—she is the mental housekeeper of this party.

There are also "I-as-internalized-others" at the table. Very clearly, "I-as-Frans" is present. He sometimes gets up and leaves his chair, but the moment there is a need to speak with Frans, he sits down again and waits receptively. "Yes, my love, tell me what you need." There are also close friends who add their wise words or are silent, compassionate witnesses. My experience here is reflected in DST:

> Some I-positions are more central, others are more peripheral; some are more cognitive, others more emotional or somatic; some are hierarchically higher (and thus implicating a lot of different but related I-positions), others are more narrow in their impact.
>
> *(Konopka et al., 2019, p. 2)*

While editing my book, I shared individual sections with a handful of readers; in particular, Roberta Neault, Carolyn Ellis, Andrea Hankinson, and Bob Neimeyer. As I typed a section imagining one of them reading, I positioned myself for a moment as "I-as-Roberta" or "I-as-Bob," and this helped me shape the text, even on the rare occasion that they weren't able to read and respond. So, dialogically, they became extensions of myself and in conversation with "me."

In my reflections on this piece, and after sharing a small portion on Facebook, a friend came forward to tell me that her mother, who was recently widowed, had arranged all her finances and documents efficiently after her husband's death, even though this wasn't a reflection of this woman's personality. My friend notes this about her parents and her mother's identity:

> Dad handled all the business, and now for the first time in her life, her finances and bill payments, and the business of life is on her shoulders. She has aggressively modeled my dad in her approach to it. In some ways, she has become him in his death. She's perhaps the only widow I've ever known who completed all the "business" of death in less than a month after my dad passed. It was essential for her to have something productive to focus on, and she was relentless about it, the same way he would have been. I feel like if she was "more herself" it would have taken a lot longer to get done. (Weber, personal communication, 2020)

Again, here one might say that the bereaved are not more like themselves, but that there is more to their selves. If a grieving person can imagine themselves as a myriad of dialogical I-positions and allow these various parts to find their way into new configurations, a grieving person can, as widow and scholar Lisa Shulman writes, see that, "The aftermath of loss is a fertile time to see yourself with new eyes—to contemplate how you can compose a life that is fulfilling and realizes your potential." (2018, p. 108)

REFERENCES

Anderson, C. M., & MacCurdy, M. M. (Eds.). (2000). *Writing & healing: Toward an informed practice*. National Council of Teachers of English.

Barak, A., & Leichtentritt, R. D. (2017). Creative writing after traumatic loss: Towards a generative writing approach. *British Journal of Social Work*, *47*, 936–954.

Barthes, R. (2010). *Mourning diary*. Hill and Wang.

Berman, J. (2007). *Dying to teach: A memoir of love, loss, and learning*. State University of New York Press.

Berman, J. (2015). *Writing widowhood: The landscapes of the bereaved*. State University of New York Press.

Bochner, A. P. (2012). Bird on the wire: Freeing the father within me. *Qualitative Inquiry*, *18*(2), 168–173.

Bolton, G. (2008). *Dying, bereavement, and the healing arts*. Jessica Kingsley Publishers.

Bolton, G. (2011). *Write yourself: Creative writing and personal development*. Jessica Kingsley Publishers.

Bonanno, G. (2009). *The other side of sadness: What the new science of bereavement tells us about life after loss*. Basic Books.

Bonanno, G. A., Wortman, C. B., Lehman, D. R., Tweed, R. G., Haring, M., Sonnega, J., Carr, D., & Nesse, R. M. (2002). Resilience to loss and chronic grief: A prospective study from preloss to 18-months postloss. *Journal of Personality and Social Psychology*, *83*(5), 1150–1154.

Brach, T. (2012). *Radical acceptance: Awakening the love that heals fear and shame*. Random House.

Brown, B. (2018). *Braving the seven elements of trust*. Dare to Lead website. https://daretolead.brenebrown.com/wp-content/uploads/2018/10/BRAVING.pdf.

Cacciatore, J. (2017). *Bearing the unbearable: Love, loss, and the heartbreaking path of grief*. Wisdom Publications.

Chang, L. (2006). *Wisdom of the soul: Five millennia of prescriptions for spiritual healing*. Gnosophia Publishers.

Chavis, G. G. (2011). *Poetry and story therapy: The healing power of creative expression.* Jessica Kingsley Publishers.

Coenen, C. (2018). *Shattered by grief: Picking up the pieces to become whole again.* Jessica Kingsley Publishers.

Chodron, P. (2002). *When things fall apart: Heart advice for difficult times.* Shambhala Publications.

Davidson, K. (2001). Late life widowhood, selfishness and new partnership choices: A gendered perspective. *Ageing & Society, 21*(3), 297–317.

Den Elzen, K. (2018). "*My decision: A memoir" and "The young widow memoir: Grief and the rebuilding of fractured identity* [Doctoral thesis, Curtin University]. https://espace.curtin.edu.au/bitstream/handle/20.500.11937/70488/Den%20Elzen%20K%202018%20part.pdf?isAllowed=y&sequence=1.

DeSalvo, L. A. (2000). *Writing as a way of healing: How telling our stories transforms our lives.* Beacon Press.

Didion, J. (2005). *The year of magical thinking.* Vintage International.

Doka, K. J. (1999). Disenfranchised grief. *Bereavement Care, 18*(3), 37–39.

Doka, K. J., & Martin., T. L. (2010). *Grieving beyond gender: Understanding the ways men and women mourn.* Routledge.

Dreifuss-Kattan, E. (2016). *Art and mourning: The role of creativity in healing trauma and loss.* Routledge.

Elliott, I., & Coker, S. (2008). Independent self-construal, self-reflection, and self-rumination: A path model for predicting happiness. *Australian Journal of Psychology, 60,* 127–134.

Ellis, C. (1995). *Final negotiations: A story of love, loss and chronic illness.* Temple University Press.

Ellis, C. (2018). *Final negotiations: A story of love, loss and chronic illness* (Revised and expanded edition). Temple University Press.

Ellis, C. S., & Bochner, A. P. (2006). Analyzing analytic autoethnography: An autopsy. *Journal of Contemporary Ethnography, 35*(4), 429–449.

Ellis, C., Adams, T. E., & Bochner, A. P. (2011). Autoethnography: An overview. *Forum: Qualitative Social Research, 12*(1, Art. 10), 273–290.

Erickson, M. H. (1991). *My voice will go with you: The teaching tales of Milton H. Erickson.* W. W. Norton.

Fiddelaers-Jaspers, R. (2003). *Verhalen van rouw: De betekenis van steun op school voor jongeren met een verlieservaring* [Stories of grief: The meaning of support in schools for youths with a loss experience. Doctoral dissertation, Radboud Universiteit Nijmegen]. In de wolken. [In the Clouds]. https://hdl.handle.net/2066/19285.

Foxwell, J. (2020). Many writers say they can actually hear the voices of their characters – here's why. *The Conversation.* https://theconversation.com/many-writers-say-they-can-actually-hear-the-voices-of-their-characters-heres-why-139170.

Frangou, C. (2016, December 16). The widowhood effect: What it's like to lose a spouse in your 30s. *The Globe and Mail.* https://www.theglobeandmail.com/life/relationships/the-widowhood-effect/article33344335/.

Gibran, K. (1923). *The prophet.* Alfred Knopf.

Gilbert, E. (Diane Eros (2019). *I'm not a very private person.* [Audio podcast]. https://www.cbc.ca/radio/q/monday-june-10-2019-elizabeth-gilbert-swamp-dogg-and-more-1.5167026/i-m-not-a-very-private-person-elizabeth-gilbert-on-writing-through-grief-and-her-new-novel-city-of-girls-1.5167035.

Gottman, J. M., & Silver, N. (1995). *Why marriages succeed or fail: And how you can make yours last.* Simon and Schuster.
Hall, C. (2014). Bereavement theory: Recent developments in our understanding of grief and bereavement. *Bereavement Care, 33*(1), 7–12.
Hendrix, H. (2007). *Getting the love you want: A guide for couples*, 20th Anniversary Edition. St. Martin's Griffin.
Hermans, H. J. M., & Gieser, T. (Eds.). (2012). *Handbook of dialogical self theory.* Cambridge University Press.
Hermans, H. J. M., & Hermans-Konopka, A. (2010). *Dialogical self theory: Positioning and counter-positioning in a globalizing society.* Cambridge University Press.
Holland, J. M., Klingspon, K. L., Lichtenthal, W. G., & Neimeyer, R. A. (2020). The Unfinished Business in Bereavement Scale (UBBS): Development and psychometric evaluation. *Death Studies, 44*(2), 65–77.
Holland, J. M., Plant, C. P., Klingspon, K. L., & Neimeyer, R. A. (2020). Bereavement-related regrets and unfinished business with the deceased. *Death Studies, 44*(1), 42–47.
Jamison, K. R. (2011). *Nothing was the same: A memoir.* Vintage.
Katie, B. (2002). *Loving what is: Four questions that can change your life.* Harmony Books.
Katie, B. (2006). *Love, sex, and relationships.* Byron Katie International.
Kenan, R. (2018, July 5). *Suddenly single: A widow's challenge* [Blog post]. The Society Pages. https://thesocietypages.org/specials/suddenly-single-a-widows-challenge/.
King, S. (2002). *On writing: A memoir of the craft.* Simon and Schuster.
Klass, D. (2006). Continuing conversation about continuing bonds. *Death Studies, 30*(9), 843–858.
Klass, D., Silverman, P. R., & Nickman, S. (2014). *Continuing bonds: New understandings of grief.* Taylor & Francis.
Klingspon, K., Holland, L., Neimeyer, R., & Lichtenthal, W. (2015). Unfinished business in bereavement. *Death Studies, 39*, 387–398.
Konopka, A., Hermans, H. J. M., & Gonçalves, M. M. (2019). *Handbook of dialogical self theory and psychotherapy: Bridging psychotherapeutic and cultural traditions.* Routledge.
Lamott, A. (1994). *Bird by bird: Some instructions on writing and life.* Anchor Books.
LaRochelle-Côté, S., Myles, J., & Picot, G. (2012). *What are the impacts of late-life widowhood or divorce on income replacement rates?* Catalogue no. 11-626-X–No. 010. Statistics Canada. https://www150.statcan.gc.ca/n1/en/pub/11-626-x/11-626-x2012010-eng.pdf?st=iB2xcfLp.
Lebell, S. (1994). *The art of living: The classical manual on virtue, happiness, and effectiveness.* Harper One.
Lengelle, R. (2008). *Blossom & balsam: Poems that reveal and heal.* Black Tulip Press.
Lengelle, R. (2016). Narrative self-rescue: A poetic response to a precarious labour crisis. *New Horizons in Adult Education and Human Resource Development, 28*(1), 46–49.
Lengelle, R. (2018a). *Happy: Poems and reflections for writing and healing the self* [Syllabus]. Black Tulip Press.
Lengelle, R. (2018b). *Jezelf schrijven* [Writing yourself]. Gompel & Svacina.
Lengelle, R. (2020). Writing the self and bereavement: Dialogical means and markers of moving through grief. *Life Writing Journal, 17*(1), 103–122.
Lengelle, R., Luken, T., & Meijers, F. (2016). Is self reflection dangerous? Preventing rumination in career learning. *Australian Journal of Career Development, 25*(3), 99–109.
Lengelle, R., & Meijers, F. (2009). Mystery to mastery: An exploration of what happens in the black box of writing and healing. *Journal of Poetry Therapy, 22*, 59–77.

Lengelle, R., & Meijers, F. (2019). Poetic reflexivity and the birth of career writing: An autoethnographic love story. In K. Maree & C. Wilby (Eds.), *Innovating career counselling theory, research, and practice* (pp. 539–555). Springer.

Lepore, S. J., & Smyth, J. M. (2002). *The writing cure: How expressive writing promotes health and emotional well-being.* American Psychological Association.

Lewis, C. S. (1961). *A grief observed.* Seabury Press.

Luchterhand, C. (n.d.). *Whole health: Change the conversation. Grief reactions, duration and tasks of mourning clinical tool.* Office of Patient Centered Care and Cultural Transformation, Veterans Health Administration. (Retrieved March 21, 2020). http://projects.hsl.wisc.edu/SERVICE/modules/33/M33_CT_Grief_Reactions.pdf.

Luken, T. (2020). Easy does it: An innovative view on developing career identity and self-direction. *Career Development International, 25*(2), 130–145.

Maccallum, F., Galatzer-Levy, I. R., & Bonanno, G. A. (2015). Trajectories of depression following spousal and child bereavement: A comparison of the heterogeneity in outcomes. *Journal of Psychiatric Research, 69*, 72–79.

Maté, G. (2011). *When the body says no: The cost of hidden stress.* Vintage Canada.

McClocklin, P., & Lengelle, R. (2016). Cures for the heart: A poetic approach to healing after loss. *British Journal of Guidance and Counselling, 46*(3), 326–339.

Miller. C., & Loring, P. (2016). Ambivalence in grief. In R. A. Neimeyer (Ed.), *Techniques in grief therapy: Assessment and intervention* (pp. 165–169). Routledge.

Moon, J. (1999) *Reflection in learning and professional development.* Kogan Page.

Moran, M. H. (2004). Toward a writing and healing approach in the basic writing classroom: One professor's personal odyssey. *Journal of Basic Writing, 23*(2), 93–115.

Moss, J. (2014). The furniture game. In B. E. Thompson & R. A. Neimeyers (Eds.), *Grief and the expressive arts: Practices for creating meaning* (pp. 71–73). Routledge.

Neimeyer, R. A. (Ed.). (2016). *Techniques of grief therapy: Assessment and intervention.* Routledge.

Neimeyer, R. A., & Konopka, A. (2019). The dialogical self in grief therapy: Reconstructing identity in the wake of loss. In A. Konopka, H. J. M. Hermans, & M. M. Gonçalves (Eds.), *Dialogical self theory and psychotherapy: Bridging psychotherapeutic and cultural traditions* (pp. 105–119). Routledge.

Neufeld, G., & Maté, G. (2013). *Hold on to your kids: Why parents need to matter more than peers.* Vintage Books Canada.

Nye, E. F. (1997). Writing as healing. *Qualitative Inquiry, 3*(4), 439–452.

Nye, F. A. (2011). *The Work of Byron Katie: The effect of applying principles of Inquiry on the reduction of perceived stress.* [Doctoral dissertation, Institute of Transpersonal Psychology]. https://www.pendragon.ch/TW-Forschung/Nye_Dissertation_The%20Work%20of%20Byron%20Katie_2011.pdf.

Paxton, B. (2018). *At home with grief: Continued bonds with the deceased.* Routledge.

Pennebaker, J. (1990). *Opening up: The healing power of expressing emotions.* The Guilford Press.

Pennebaker, J. (2011). *The secret life of pronouns: What our words say about us.* Bloomsbury.

Powers, W. T. (2005). *Behavior: The control of perception* (2nd ed.). Benchmark Publications. (Original work published 1973).

Price, J. (2019). *Sex after grief: Navigating your sexuality after losing your beloved.* Mango Publishing.

Rando, T. A. (1988). *How to go on living when someone you love dies.* Bantam.

Rando, T. A. (2012). "Is it okay for you to be okay?" In R. A. Neimeyer (Ed.), *Techniques of grief therapy: Creative practices for counseling the bereaved* (pp. 149–151). Series in death, dying, and bereavement. Routledge/Taylor & Francis Group.

Richo, D. (2008). *The five things we cannot change: And the happiness we find by embracing them*. Shambhala Publications.

Samuel, J. (2017). *Grief works: Stories of life, death and surviving*. Penguin-Random House.

Scarfe, E. (2002). No time to die. In C. Edwards & K. Stewart (Eds.), *Wrestling with the angel: Women reclaiming their lives* (pp. 264–272). Canadian Issues, Suppl.

Shepard, S. (2017). *Two prospectors: The letters of Sam Shepard and Johnny Dark*. University of Texas Press.

Shulman, L. M. (2018). *Before and after loss: A neurologist's perspective on loss, grief, and our brain*. Johns Hopkins University Press.

Singer, M. (2007). *The untethered soul: The journey beyond yourself*. New Harbinger Publications.

Smernoff, E., Mitnik, I., Kolodner, K., & Lev-ari, S. (2015). The effects of "The Work" meditation (Byron Katie) on psychological symptoms and quality of life—A pilot clinical study. *Explore, 11*(1), 24–31.

Statistics Canada. (2009, November 12). Widowhood: Consequences on income for senior women. https://www150.statcan.gc.ca/n1/pub/11-621-m/11-621-m2004015-eng.htm.

Stroebe, M. S., & Schut, H. (2001). Meaning making in the dual process model of coping with bereavement. In R. A. Neimeyer (Ed.), Meaning reconstruction & the experience of loss (p. 55–73). American Psychological Association

Stroebe, M., & Schut, H. (2010). The dual process model of coping with bereavement: A decade on. *OMEGA—Journal of Death and Dying, 61*(4), 273–289.

Swann, W. B., Jr., & Buhrmester. (2003). Self-Verification: The Search for Coherence. In M. R. Leary & J. P. Tangney (Eds.), *Handbook of self and identity (Second Edition)* (pp. 405–424). The Guilford Press.

Thomashauer, R. (2002). *Mama Gena's school of womanly arts: Using the power of pleasure to have your way with the world*. Simon and Schuster.

Thompson, B., & Neimeyer, R. A. (Eds.)(2014). *Grief and the expressive arts: Practices for creating meaning*. Routledge.

Thompson, K. (2011). *Therapeutic journal writing: An introduction for professionals*. London, UK: Jessica Kingsley Publishers.

Tierney, J., & Baumeister, R. F. (2019). For the new year, say no to negativity. *Wall Street Journal*. https://www.wsj.com/articles/for-the-new-year-say-no-to-negativity-11577464413.

Ueland, B. (1938). *If you want to write: A book about art, independence and spirit*. Gray Wolf Press.

Utz, R. L., Caserta, M., & Lund, D. (2012). Grief, depressive symptoms, and physical health among recently bereaved spouses. *The Gerontologist, 52*(4), 460–471.

Van der Kolk, B. (2014). *The body keeps the score: Brain, mind, and body in the healing of trauma*. Viking.

Van Engelen, A. (2015). Een jongen uit het dorp: Levensportret van Frans Meijers [Boy from the village: A portrait of Frans Meijers].

Whyte, D. (2001). *Crossing the unknown sea: Work as a pilgrimage of identity*. Riverhead Books.

Whyte, D. (2003). *Everything is waiting for you*. Many Rivers Press.

Williamson, C., & Wright, J. K. (2018). How creative does writing have to be in order to be therapeutic? A dialogue on the practice and research of writing to recover and survive. *Journal of Poetry Therapy, 31*(2), 113–123.

World Health Organization. (2019, April). 6B42 Prolonged grief disorder. International Classification of Diseases, 11th revision (ICD-11) for mortality and morbidity statistics. https://icd.who.int/browse11/l-m/en#/http://id.who.int/icd/entity/1183832314.

Wu, Z., Schimmele, C. M., & Ouellet, N. (2015). Repartnering after widowhood. *Journal of Gerontology Series B: Psychological Sciences and Social Sciences, 70*(3), 496–507.

Yalom, I. D. (2012). *Love's executioner and other tales of psychotherapy*. Hachette UK.

INDEX

Printed in Great Britain
by Amazon

62589885R10136